*A*dventure Guide to
Utah

Madeleine Osberger & Steve Cohen

D1466803

HUNTER
PUBLISHING

Hunter Publishing, Inc.
300 Raritan Center Parkway
Edison NJ 08818, USA
Tel (908) 225 1900
Fax (908) 417 0482

ISBN 1-55650-726-7

Maps by Kim André

Cover photo by Michael H. Francis

Other titles in the **Adventure Guide Series** include:

NEW MEXICO (1-55650-727-5/$12.95/250pp)
ARIZONA (1-55650-725-9/$12.95/250pp)
COLORADO (1-55650-724-0/$12.95/220pp)
HIGH SOUTHWEST, 2nd Edition (1-55650-723-2/$15.95/400pp)
COSTA RICA, 3rd Edition (1-55650-722-4/$16.95/550pp)
GREAT SMOKY MOUNTAINS (1-55650-720-8/$13.95/340pp)
COASTAL ALASKA & THE INSIDE PASSAGE, 2nd Edition
(1-55650-731-3/$14.95/228pp)
BAHAMAS (1-55650-705-4/$12.95/176pp)
BERMUDA (1-55650-706-2/$12.95/176pp)
CATSKILLS & ADIRONDACKS (1-55650-681-3/$9.95/224pp)
OREGON & WASHINGTON (1-55650-709-7/$11.95/160pp)

*A*dventure Guide to

Utah

About The Authors

Steve Cohen

Steve Cohen is the author of more than a dozen books on travel, including the outdoors classic *Adventure Guide To Jamaica*, first published in 1988. As an adventure-seeking travel writer and photographer specializing in the unusual and off-beat, his self-illustrated articles appear regularly in dozens of domestic and international publications, including many of North America's newspapers and magazines. While reporting on life and cultures around the world, he has lived in the High Southwest for the last decade with his wife, Jodie, and his son, Sean. He is a member of the Society of American Travel Writers.

Madeleine Osberger

Madeleine Osberger is a regular contributor to *Snow Country, Ski Area Management, Travel Weekly* and *Sojourner* magazines. She is also an Aspen-based correspondent for the Associated Press and the *Snowmass Sun* newspaper. A co-author of the books *Hidden Southwest*, and *Ultimate Santa Fe and Beyond*, Madeleine is currently at work on *Country Roads of Colorado*.

We'd Love To Hear From You!

Hunter Publishing makes every effort to ensure that its travel guides are the most current sources of information available to travellers. If you have any information that you feel should be included in the next edition of this guide, please write to Steve Cohen, *Adventure Guide to Utah*, c/o Hunter Publishing, 300 Raritan Center Parkway, Edison, NJ 08818. Feel free to include price updates, your opinion on the places you've visited and ways in which you feel we could improve this book for future readers.

Contents

Maps

Introduction

Utah is home to canyons and mountains, desert and abundant waterways, thriving cities and, soon, the 2002 Winter Olympics. The setting for novels by Zane Gray and Edward Abbey, film characters Thelma and Louise and Butch Cassidy, Utah has harsh country for individualists and tamer areas for the meeker at heart. The Beehive State (so called because of the industriousness of its residents) is the geological crossroads of the elevated tableland known as the Colorado Plateau, the western slope of the Rocky Mountains and the Great Basin, the huge expanse of land cradled between the Sierra Nevada and Wasatch mountain ranges.

The state boasts six national monuments, five national parks, countless wilderness areas and thousands of additional acres of public lands accessible for hiking, biking, skiing, rafting, fishing, and much more. Needless to say, these natural spaces provide one of the greatest year-round concentrations of adventurous pastimes.

The preponderance of rugged, virtually primeval terrain lends itself naturally to high adventure. Furthermore, the territory has long been pre-eminent in the pantheon of spiritual places to the native peoples who were first to settle here, and whose ancient mysteries and modern presence are keenly felt today.

If you want to experience the special nature of this exceptional area, and to get out and do things, this book is for you. It provides all the nuts-and-bolts information you need to plan and accomplish an informed trip, as well as specific details on a variety of adventures.

Ride a horse for a day, raft through rapids the next. Climb mountains for a week and know all the best fishing spots in advance. Ski at world-class resorts or snowmobile over hundreds of miles of groomed trails. Climb through ancient Indian ruins. Steer a jeep or a mountain bike over the Wasatch Plateau. Soar above it all in a glider, a balloon, or take a scenic motorized flight. Trek through labyrinthine canyon country with a llama to carry your gear. Snuggle under a blanket of stars while a draft horse pulls your sleigh through the snow. Dip a toe into thermal hot springs. Paddle a canoe or cruise on a houseboat. There's enough to fill vacations for years, and it's no surprise that so many people return year after year.

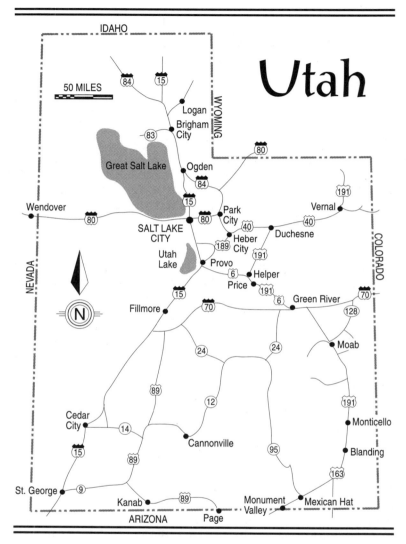

The state's population base is clustered around a 100-mile-long swath of mountains known as the **Wasatch Front**. There you'll find the capitol, **Salt Lake City**, two university towns (**Logan** and **Provo**) that are home to high-tech industries, and the up-and-coming former railroad center, **Ogden**. The cities make great jumping-off places for high-country adventures. Venture beyond the Wasatch and you'll be hard-pressed to find a crowd of people anywhere.

Utah is also home to some of the world's best skiing. Feather-light snow, which dries out over the vast **Great Basin**, frequently slams hard into the Wasatch Range. The result: feet, not mere inches of white stuff, cover the mountains. The majority of resorts are clumped within an hour's drive of Salt Lake City.

Utah contains the modern mountain biking mecca of **Moab**, which seems to grow more popular every year. And there is much more, such as **Arches** and **Canyonlands national parks**, awesome **Dinosaur National Monument**, little-known **Capitol Reef National Park**, better-known **Bryce** and **Zion national parks**, the **San Juan** and **Colorado rivers** flowing into **Lake Powell**, the world's second largest man-made body of water, and the less overrun option, striking **Flaming Gorge National Park**. The **Great Salt Lake** is an underutilized playground and pristine **Bear Lake** offers plenty of elbow room for sailors and motorboaters.

This is to say nothing about the expansive spaces between these landmarks, slickrock trails, multi-colored tiered sandstone formations, snow peaks above clear alpine lakes, and cactus-studded deserts. Towering natural arches and bridges formed over millions of years by the effects of wind and water on stone dot the landscape.

There's plenty of ground to cover, so careful plans are needed to manage the great distances involved yet still have time to do the adventurous things you enjoy. This guide gets right down to the logistics of having fun by connecting you with a multitude of pleasures in this wondrous part of the world.

Geography & History

Long overlooked, Utah has become incredibly popular in the last few years. It evokes visions of Indians and cowboys, snow-capped peaks, buttes and mesas stalked by howling coyotes, wild rivers, and long sunsets. But the state has always been popular with those looking for wide open spaces beneath skies so clear they lend a brightness to the air.

The earliest nomads probably wandered down from Canada and the Bering Land Bridge, settling over time into the first stable populations. Their descendants were the ancient and now extinct Anasazi Indians, whose skillfully constructed and mysteriously abandoned communities are the source of today's ruins. Other descendants were the Hopi Indians, whose oldest inhabited dwellings, just south of the Utah border in neigboring Arizona, look a lot like ruins. The Spanish came upon Navajos and other modern tribes when they explored the Southwest in the 16th century searching for gold.

A pair of Franciscan priests, Fathers Escalante and Dominguez, came through Utah in 1776 while charting a new route from Santa Fe, New Mexico to Monterey, California. The priests' party found the Green River east of today's Dinosaur National Monument. The second wave of European travellers came upon the Great Salt Lake in 1824 when fur trappers, Etienne Provost and James Bridger, made their way to the western side of the Wasatch Range. They were followed by Brigham Young and his band of followers who, fleeing religious persecution in the East, established a new homeland called Salt Lake City in 1847. Mormons, trappers and traders – each had their mission.

Only in the last 175 years has the area experienced modern civilization. First came trappers and traders, then gold-, silver-, or copper-miners, followed by ranchers, cowboys, and business people who created small towns (many of which stayed small or became smaller).

Most of the mines are closed (save for the enormous Kennecott Copper Mine near Salt Lake City), but ranching and the cowboy arts are still widely practiced on vast, open rangelands.

The rugged contours of Southwestern geography haven't changed much throughout the years. Much of Utah, outside the heavily populated Wasatch Front, still resists massive development, although once-inhospitable places are today's pleasure spots. Towns in the wilder hinterlands of southern Utah are still few and far between, but they're here. Confronting modern realities, these towns have survived by mining a mother lode of tourism dollars out of this hard land.

The enormity of the Southwest provides space that cannot be found in urban areas. And, even if you are accustomed to the outdoors, there's no place else where you can find so many diverse geological, historical, cultural, and just plain drop-dead beautiful features. It's a vast canvas on which to paint your own adventure.

In today's rural Utah, the pickup truck is the vehicle of choice for ranchers. Horses continue to serve cowboys who really do wear pointy-toed boots, broad-brimmed hats or, increasingly, baseball caps advertising farm equipment. Dusty jeans and shirts with pearl snaps identify the cowboy style, a pervasive presence here. Except for ceremonial occasions, most Indians wear clothing that looks a lot like cowboy duds. The cities offer a more modern yet still traditional mix of attire.

The unlikely blending of three cultures – Indian, Hispanic, and Anglo – in a still remote, long-isolated environment far from any urban population centers has combined with various natural attributes of mountains, rivers, and deserts, to produce a unique status quo.

Accommodations range from campgrounds and dude ranches – that offer as much time on horseback as you can handle – to deluxe resorts. Dining out in the boonies here is mostly unsophisticated – not the chi-chi grilled avocado and mango salsa one finds in competitive Santa Fe. It's mostly corn dogs and chile, sloppy Joe's and salad bars. In the cities and along the Wasatch Front you'll find some good ethnic restaurants, however. Hearty meals are more the rule than the exception and, in general, you get good value.

As for entertainment, you may be content to gaze at night skies filled with stars, but there are stomping cowboy bars with free two-step lessons or Indian dances. Some of these are ceremonial and restricted to tribal members only, while others are open for all to enjoy. A visit to the capitol city could land you at a Utah Jazz basketball game or a performance by Ballet West. The state has publicly supported the arts since 1899.

There is no shortage of Indian jewelry offered by roadside vendors, trading posts, and galleries. What you'll find on sale ranges from cheap stuff to high-priced objects. Blankets, rugs, baskets, and pottery were once offered as simple trade goods, but even they are pricey these days, reflecting their recent return to the halls of fashion. Country crafts are prevalent in small towns everywhere, on the order of what you'd find in New England.

Activities related to the epic, hard terrain and seasons draw a ski crowd in winter, bikers and river runners in spring. Campers and hikers arrive in summer, leaf peepers and hunters in fall. The Utah outdoors has been claimed by a young, dynamic, fun-loving crowd. You will see sun-tanned hikers and kayakers cruising along in expensive four-wheel-drives with bike or boat racks. Alongside will be cowboys and Indians riding the range on horseback or in battered pickups with gun racks.

Personal values aside, the land remains the dominant force here. Everybody needs to pay close attention to nature's power. In Utah's canyon country the earth reveals deep cracks, dropping precariously to distant rivers. Buttes and mesas are nearby, striped in iron-tinged red and orange colors painted by geological epochs, with mountains, usually snow-capped, looming beyond.

Sometimes, at a quiet moment in a place far from the ordinary, ghosts of those long departed may even pay a visit.

You can go a long way out here without seeing another human being, but you probably won't get far without finding evidence of deer, elk, rattlers, coyotes, eagles, ravens, turkey vultures, or hawks. Less frequently spotted are black bears, mountain lions, pronghorn antelope, bighorn sheep and the occasional bison.

This spectacular landscape was created over eons by the geological forces of volcanoes, wind, erosion, flowing water, and movements of geological plates inside the earth's crust. The result is sometimes phantasmagoric, as displayed by improbably shaped sandstone towers, serpentine canyons, or brooding mountains crowned by massive thunderheads. Water, though sometimes scarce, remains a fashion power as it flows from the snowmelt of high mountains. The streams it forms nourish forests and the giant Colorado River system, which drains the 130,000-square-mile Colorado Plateau. Even in the driest deserts a turbulent downpour can fill thirsty stream beds in a frightening instant. Flash floods can carry away homes, trees, and cars, then subside as rapidly as they appeared, leaving only damp testimony to nature's power.

Of course, many have tried to tame these elemental forces. The area has attracted a long line of explorers and settlers. Indians constructed primitive cities and cultures 1,000 years ago with a sharp eye to the vagaries of nature, yet their dwellings could not protect them from nature's omnipotent energy. Deserted structures – once dwellings and now ruins – pepper the state and attest to ancient conflicts with drought, crop failures, and ensuing famine. Dusty trails may be all that remain of once-productive grassland that was thoughtlessly overgrazed and is now reclaimed by the desert. Crumbling mine structures recall expended mineral resources and dreams.

Modern researchers believe that nomadic hunter-gatherers were predecessors of the Anasazi Indians, presumed to be the area's first settlers 1,500 years ago – coincident with the advent of agriculture and the farming of beans and corn, which became dietary staples. Around 500 years later, another nomadic strain of Athabascan Indians began its migration south through Canada. The earliest of these arrivals began filtering in 600 years ago – at just about the same time the Anasazi were abandoning their cities and disappearing into the sands of time. They are thought to be the ancestors of today's Navajos and Apaches, as well as several other tribes. The term Anasazi actually comes from the Navajo language. Various interpretations give the meaning as "the ancient enemies" or simply "the old ones." From these differing beginnings a variety of cultural conventions emerged, lending distinctive spice to today's Navajo, Hopi and other Native American communities.

The earliest Anglos were ambitious, mostly hunters or traders exploring the territory. In 1825, the United States government purchased 530,000 acres of the Southwest from Mexico, including today's Utah, New Mexico, Arizona, and part of Colorado. Twenty or so years later, after the Civil War, Anglo migration began in earnest. News of gold, silver, and copper discoveries encouraged prospectors. Shopkeepers followed and word of the vast new region spread. By the mid-19th century, the railroads were racing to lay tracks, signaling the end of many centuries of isolation here.

With the rise of Anglo culture, once the government recognized the value of this epic wilderness, Indian interests were ignored or violated, igniting conflicts that would be resolved only after much strife and bloodshed. Eventually, around the same time the railroads chugged into towns like Ogden and then Promontory Summit, there was no turning back.

Unfettered winds and raging waters of the Colorado River have created sculpted sandstone arches, towers, mesas, and scorched canyons on the Colorado Plateau. Mountains are a welcome surprise in the Great Basin, where ranges like the Deep Creek Mountains offer relief from the often bland valleys. From Naomi Peak in the north to Navajo Peak near Arizona, mountains are rimmed by somewhat tortured topography slotted by abrupt canyons. Monument Valley, which stretches across the Utah-Arizona border on the Navajo Reservation, is actually a Navajo Tribal Park with many access restrictions. Its famous buttes rising from the desert are certainly among the most photographed landscapes in all of the Southwest. A string of John Wayne movies in the 1940s and 50s, such as *Fort Apache* and *Stagecoach*, made these vistas widely famous. It was director John Ford's favorite location and an overlook within the park has been named after the Hollywood legend. For more contemporary references just click on your TV. You're bound to see a commercial for a car or a soda that was filmed here.

Nature displays some of its most stunning sculpture in Utah's canyon country. At Lake Powell and Flaming Gorge you can rent a houseboat for a day or a week of unhurried cruising through Glen or Red canyons; at Powell you'll be stunned by the enormous stone span at Rainbow Bridge. West of Lake Powell, the multi-colored turrets and stone monoliths of Bryce and Zion national parks are as close to out-of-this-world as you are likely to find this side of the moon. If Bryce and Zion seem lunar then the red-hot and bone-dry canyons, along with the delicate, fascinating, and unlikely stone arches of Canyonlands and Arches national parks flanking the Colorado River must resemble Mars. To give you an idea of the scale of this region there are three unconnected dead-end roads that lead to different parts of Canyonlands. The entrance to each route is separated by more than 100 miles.

Across southern Utah foliage becomes scarce as canyons deepen below desertscapes. Summer temperatures are fiercely hot all across the Navajo Nation and in the canyons of Dinosaur National Monument. By contrast, the lush green valleys that tumble off the Wasatch Range are home to the state's agricultural industry.

Parts of Utah have never been fully explored and some areas are as close to primal wilderness as you are likely to find in the lower 48 states. Turbulent whitewater rivers churn from snow peaks in springtime. After an average winter with more than 300 inches of snow in the high country, the Colorado River may run 40 feet above normal. Rafters float over rocks they would normally be floating under. Of course, the river comes back down and hardens into blistered, parched lowlands under the unforgiving summer sun. And yes, there are towns and dammed rivers, roads, airports, convenience stores on the reservations, and satellite dishes everywhere, some crowning home lots featuring Navajo hogans made of mud, sticks, and straw.

The roads here are better than in the old mining days, but rugged mountainous areas continue to defy all but idiosyncratic development, as evidenced by abandoned mines and ghost towns. Wildlife, wildflowers, and man all benefit as much from what's not here as what is.

Regarding fashion, the vagaries of style that are in today and laughable tomorrow, Utah and the Southwest may be experiencing its Warholian 15-minutes of fame right now. For those who come in search of adventure, the mountains, rivers, canyons and mesas are very much the same as they were before they were stylish. They change at a glacial pace. They will be here tomorrow.

As always, the essence of Utah is discovered in the way being here makes you feel about yourself on the turf of cowboys, Indians, mountain men, and desert rats. It's a hard country open to all comers, but resistant to easy change.

The Nature Of Adventure

Adventure travel has recently come into its own. It is no longer considered the province only of daredevils seeking the classic hang-by-your-teeth-over-the-jaws-of-death type of adventure, although that sort of trip is surely available in abundance out here. You probably won't have to cheat death unless you choose to, but if you partake in a sampling of this book's suggested activities, you will certainly raise your chances for having a life-affirming experience, without necessarily having a life-threatening one. Adventure doesn't need to be a death march expedition, but it does need to get the juices flowing. At the least, it should provide attainable challenges that any reasonably fit and active participant with an open mind can enjoy.

Inside this book you'll find extensive information on a range of activities, many of which will provide challenges relating to climate, altitude, remoteness, and physical fitness. Others may be less physically stressful while confronting your cultural perceptions.

From easy-to-accomplish soft adventures, family and senior's trips, to daredevil ones that will really get your adrenalin pumping, you can find them here. There are activities you can pursue for an hour, a day, a week, or a month. Whatever your inclination may be the pay-off is in the remarkable regenerative power of a classic river trip, a bison round-up, an Indian ceremony, or an archeological dig.

Utah offers countless miles of maintained trails for you to hike, bike, and ride on horseback. If you're a water-lover, river trips will lure you into canoes, kayaks, and whitewater rafts.

There are evocative backroads for you to explore by jeep and mammoth vistas to gaze upon from the gondola of a hot air balloon. You can visit historic and modern Indian and cowboy sites. You can travel by horse-drawn sleigh, raft wild rivers in springtime, climb cool mountains in summer, and explore canyons and high desert in fall, when mornings and evenings are cool, days warm, and changing leaves enhance the countryside.

How To Use This Book

This book divides Utah into regions. The order of these chapters essentially describes a large circle, presuming that you will begin your journey through the major gateway of Salt Lake City. Each chapter starts with an introduction to the area. This covers climate, history, and culture, along with the main sites and activities. It is followed by a short section called Getting Around, which outlines the main roads and transportation options as well as the general route the chapter will follow. Each region is then broken down into touring sections listed in the same order as they appear on the selected route. These provide information and useful contact numbers such as chambers of commerce, regional United States Department of Agriculture Forest Service offices, Bureau of Land Management offices, National Park Service offices, and airline and rental car services.

After the general touring sections, a separate section detailing specific Adventures within each region follows. These include options for independent travellers or those seeking guided tours. There are many activities to choose from and many more limited only by your imagination. For example, you can generally experience an enjoyable hike on a listed bike trail, or bike on a jeep road.

The following is a brief description of the range and nature of activities covered under "Adventures."

ON FOOT

Hiking/Backpacking/Rock Climbing

Whether you want to go it on your own or with a guided tour, this category will show you where to go and how to do it. There are hundreds and hundreds of miles of hiking trails in the state. Some are strenuous, requiring specialized rock climbing skills and equipment; others are more like a walk in the park. It is impossible to list them all, but you will find a cross-section of the hikes for all levels of ability, from short walks over easy trails to multi-day routes through maze-like canyons.

When hiking in backcountry, the more popular short trails are usually well worn and marked, but it's still remarkably easy to get lost. Don't head out into the wilds on your own without some preparation.

Figure out where you want to go, then consult the Forest Service, BLM, or Park Service for up-to-date topographical maps and information. Discuss aspects of the hike with them. Some adventures in this area can be accomplished easily alone, while others require special gear, permits, and expertise. If you're short on equipment or in doubt about your skills, seek help from the professionals first. This is serious country, often short on absolution. If you question going it alone then you probably should not. Even if you know what you're doing there's no substitute for direct contact with people whose business is understanding the areas and activities you're pursuing. Numerous local contacts are provided in this book. The US Forest Service suggests that all users of the backcountry remember the following:

- ❏ Take no chances. Assistance can take hours or days.
- ❏ Be aware of conditions. Varied terrain exposes you to hypothermia, dehydration, and lightning hazards on exposed ridges. There can be snow fields in early summer.
- ❏ Start hiking early in the day – mornings are generally clear. Later in the afternoon you may encounter storms of varying intensity. An early start gives you time to get to your destination and set up your camp in comfort, not while fighting the elements.
- ❏ Travel with a companion. File a hiking plan with someone who is staying behind and check in with revisions so you can be found if something goes wrong.
- ❏ Be in shape. Don't push past your limits. Allow time to acclimate to altitude.
- ❏ Always take fresh water with you, especially in the desert where heat can be deceiving and water may not be available. A gallon of water per person, per day is recommended for summertime desert travel.
- ❏ Pack extra food just in case something goes wrong and you're out there longer than you planned.

TRAVEL WITH LLAMAS OR HORSES

If you prefer not to be burdened with packs but want to travel into some of the most improbable terrain imaginable, try hiking with packstock. Llamas are employed by several operators. They're not strong enough to carry the weight of an adult human, but they are prodigious hikers and can easily tote 100 lbs of food and equipment in specially designed packs. Other hiking trips are run with horses or mules to carry the gear. Without weight restrictions imposed by the strength of your own back, you can experience deep backcountry with a case of beer or a few bottles of wine, an extra pair of dry shoes, and other heavy and awkward items that will make your trip more enjoyable.

Harder on your bottom than your feet is the venerable primary mode of transportation, horseback riding. Horses are still common out here and trips on well-trained, tractable mounts or high-spirited animals are easily arranged for an hour, a day, or overnight. A number of guest ranches and resorts also offer horseback riding. These are listed under accommodations.

If you want to be a cowhand, working ranches often accommodate guests who can participate in all ranch activities, such as herding and branding, or actual cattle drives, moving a herd from one place to another over several days or longer. Ten to 12 hours a day in the saddle, moving at a slow pace, is hard work, but it is, for some, the ultimate adventure the West offers.

ON WHEELS

Railroads/Jeeps/Stagecoaches & Wagons/Bicycles

There are several train trips offered in Utah on some of the most scenically compelling and historic rail lines in the world. We're not talking about subways here, nor even about Amtrak, though its trains do make several stops along the I-70 corridor.

A jeep or other four-wheel-drive may sometimes be the only motorized vehicle able to negotiate the remote, minimal roads of Utah's backcountry. Please stay on established roads and don't chew up the land by carving your own route.

It's not unusual to see an old-fashioned horse-drawn wagon lumbering down a side road. What is unusual is that some of these operators will take you along for the ride. One local even builds authentic old-fashioned stagecoaches and offers a variety of trips when the equipment isn't being used for a movie or commercial shoot.

Mountain biking is now a mainstream activity throughout the state. High-tech bikes with 18, 21, or more speeds make it possible for just about anyone who can ride to negotiate at least some of the terrain. Mountain bikers move faster than hikers, and knobby tires can transport you into certain regions where motorized vehicles cannot go.

Throughout the region, the topography for biking is testing and picturesque. The assortment of logging roads, jeep routes, and single-track trails on public lands is immense, offering something for everyone, from easy paved bikeways to world-class backcountry excursions.

Again, it's impossible to include all the great biking routes here. The selection offered in this book is to suit varying skills and abilities, along with information sources for further exploration. Guided bike tour operators listed will generally handle the logistical arrangements an independent rider would have to manage alone. Most provide a sag wagon if you really can't make it those last few miles. On a tour or on your own, every rider needs to carry extra food and water, a head lamp, maps, and rain gear. Of course, a helmet is essential.

Local bike rental operators, repair shops, and tour resources are included throughout the text. Experts in local bike shops who know the terrain are valuable sources of information. Make use of them.

Although bike riding is generally supported in Utah, continuing access to backcountry trails is partly dependent on the goodwill of you and other outdoors-folk. The International Mountain Biking Association has established rules of the trail to help preserve mountain bikers' trail rights:

❏ Ride on open trails only. Respect trail and road closures, private property, and requirements for permits and authorization. Federal and state wilderness areas are closed to cyclists and some park and forest trails are off-limits.

❏ Leave no trace. Don't ride on certain soils after a rain, when the ground will be marred. Never ride off the trail, skid your tires, or discard any object. Strive to pack out more than you pack in.

❏ Control your bicycle. Inattention for even a second can cause disaster. Excessive speed frightens and injures people, gives mountain biking a bad name, and results in trail closures.

❏ Always yield. Make your approach known well in advance to others using the trail. A friendly greeting is considerate and appreciated. Show respect when passing by slowing to walking speed or even stopping, especially in the presence of horses. Anticipate that other trail users may be around blind corners.

❏ Never spook animals. Give them extra room and time to adjust to you. Running livestock and disturbing wild animals is a serious offense. Leave ranch and farm gates as you find them, or as marked.

❏ Plan ahead. Know your equipment, your ability, and the area in which you are riding and prepare accordingly. Be self-sufficient at all times, keep your bike in good condition, and carry repair kits and supplies for changes in weather. Keep trails open by setting an example of responsible cycling for all to see.

As for the terrain, even routes classified as easy by locals may be strenuous for a flat-lander. Most downhill routes will include some uphill stretches. Pay particular attention to your personal limits if you're on your own.

ON WATER

Whitewater Rafting/Canoeing/Kayaking/Boating/Fishing

From around mid-May to mid-June rivers rise dramatically and the flows are at their highest, fastest, and coldest. Sometimes by August things are pretty sluggish. It all depends on the winter's snowfall, spring rains, and summer thunderstorms.

In general, at high or low water levels, it takes an experienced hand to negotiate Utah's rivers. Unless you really know what you are doing, it is highly recommended that you consider a river tour, rather than an independent trip. Tour operators also handle the permits that are necessary for certain popular stretches, permits that may only be offered through lottery drawings and are therefore hard to come by. Some stretches of whitewater, such as Westwater and Cataract canyons, can be deadly to all but highly experienced kayakers. Participants are required to take a pre-trip physical fitness test by all tour operators running this stretch. On the other hand, there are mellow stretches of the Green and Colorado rivers that can be enjoyed by almost any boater. There is a river trip for just about everyone, but your enjoyment may be marred if you take on more adventure than you can handle.

For any river trip, the smaller the vessel, the bigger the ride. Be sure to inquire about the size of a raft and how many people it holds. Ask if you'll need to paddle or simply ride along while guides do the work. Listings that mention paddle boats mean you will have to paddle. Oar boats mean a guide does the work. Kayaks accommodate one person, who will obviously do all the paddling. With these things in mind, floating gently through ancient gorges decorated with water-seep gardens, fossils and Anasazi rock carvings, called petroglyphs, or racing along rugged whitewater rivers pouring out of the high country has become justifiably popular. Tours are available for an hour, two hours, half-days, full days, or overnight for up to several weeks.

Lakes and reservoirs throughout Utah have boat ramps for your vessel. Larger bodies of water feature marinas that rent all kinds of boats, canoes, windsurfers, and other equipment. Houseboats affording all amenities for a self-contained vacation are available on Lake Powell and Flaming Gorge.

If you're seeking fishing waters rather than rapids, lakes and reservoirs are suitable for canoe and other boat excursions. There are also innumerable places to fish from the shores of streams, rivers, and alpine lakes. Many waters are well stocked with a variety of fish, including several species of trout, kokanee salmon, northern pike, large- and smallmouth bass, crappie, bluegill, and channel catfish.

ON SNOW

Downhill & Cross-Country Skiing/Snowmobiling/ Dog Sledding/Ice Climbing

You'll find the state's most reliable and sophisticated downhill skiing operations clustered primarily in northern Utah, although the skiing at Brian Head in the south is fantastic too. Cross-country skiing areas are generally more peaceful and less crowded than developed downhill areas. Unless you plan to stick to the easiest groomed trails, it is wise to know what you are doing. You can ski the backcountry for an hour or for days, but snow conditions are often unstable and avalanches are frequent in certain areas or under certain conditions. To help match your abilities with appropriate terrain, it is highly recommended that you consult with ski shop personnel or regional information sources before approaching the backcountry.

The listings in each chapter are some of the safest cross-country routes. Remember that conditions are completely unpredictable and depend entirely on weather conditions that can and do change rapidly. For current snowpack and wind conditions, on-the-spot research is essential before any backcountry ski trip. Dress warmly and carry high energy foods. Though less physically demanding, the same rules apply if you're snowmobiling or dog sledding.

IN AIR

Scenic Flights/Ballooning/Soaring

If you think Utah looks impressive from the ground, you should see it from the air on a scenic flight. A range of options are available, including fixed-wing aircraft, helicopters, gliders, and balloons.

ECO-TRAVEL & CULTURAL EXCURSIONS

This catch-all category includes trips that don't fit elsewhere.

WHERE TO STAY & EAT

Although not expressly an adventure, finding good places to stay and eat in Utah can be a challenge. In some remote areas, there may be only a campground with a fire grill, or a single, shabby motel for many miles. In other places you'll find a number of excellent establishments. All listings are subjective and are included for some good reason, whether for exceptional service, ambience, great food, or good value. Rates range from inexpensive to deluxe choices. Because these services may change rapidly, local information sources may come in handy for updates.

Public campgrounds and information sources are included in this section. You will also find details regarding camping on Indian reservations and remote backcountry campsites.

Travel Strategies & Helpful Facts

Utah's pleasures are many, but they are also quite spread out. Consider whether you will be travelling to one area, say for a week at a dude ranch or a five-day pack trip, or whether you plan to sample several areas. If you've booked a multi-day outfitted trip, the operator may be able to meet you at the closest airport. Otherwise you need a car. Rentals are available in many places.

Salt Lake's international airport is served by most major carriers. There are shuttles to the airports in Vernal and Logan.

An increasingly important factor to consider when visiting Utah is its burgeoning popularity. In many areas, visitations have doubled in the last five years and the effects on privacy and the wilderness environment have resulted in access restrictions on certain public lands at certain times. Consider travelling outside the traditional summer season or the peak winter months. It's uniformly busiest from the Fourth of July through Labor Day. If you're here for the skiing, you may want to schedule trips in December (but not the two busy Christmas weeks), January or early April. Spring skiing is a particularly good idea; the snow is the deepest, the weather at its warmest, and many skiers' thoughts are already turning to cycling and kayaking, so there are fewer folks on the slopes.

Climate

The diverse topography in this area causes wide variations in climate. The season you visit will depend on what sort of activities you wish to pursue, but be aware that summer is not necessarily the most comfortable time. Summer weather is considerably milder the higher you go into the mountains, and it is certainly quite spectacular on a 75°, blue sky day on Mt. Timpanogos. Down below, in the flatlands and arid deserts, it can get dangerously hot, especially if you're hiking in Canyonlands in July or biking around the San Rafael Swell in August. Just the reverse is true in winter. While skiers are snowbound in Alta because the canyon is closed due to avalanche danger, you can head south to Moab. It may be not only warmer, but is likely to be devoid of tourists at that time. There are always trade-offs. Certain outfitting or adventure tour businesses are only open during particular seasons and some lodgings even close during the winter.

If you come in the spring to raft rivers, you need to be prepared to deal with mud in the lowlands, or dust storms in the deserts. Fall is considered by many to be the perfect season. The air is cooler, but not yet cold. Desert areas are once again tolerable after the scorching summer, while mountains boast colorful foliage and fewer crowds. Because of the great ranges in elevation, fall lasts several months – from September in the high mountains, to November in the deserts.

Count on daytime temperatures of 100° in the deserts by July and August. At the same time, temperatures are likely to be 70-80° in Park City or Logan. A drop of 30° after the sun goes down is not uncommon.

Clothing & Gear

Utahans are both casual and conservative when it comes to attire. Shorts and t-shirts are fine for summer days (as long as they aren't too revealing), but long pants and a sweater or jacket may be needed at night, particularly at higher elevations, where it has been known to snow in every month except July. Because conditions can change very quickly, layering your clothes is the best idea. That way, you can remove or add clothing as it gets hotter or colder.

Sneakers may not be rugged enough footwear for backcountry hiking, so heavier, lug-soled boots are recommended. A broken-in pair of cowboy boots may be a good idea for extended horse travel. Hiking boots with heels to catch in your stirrups will probably do for short trips of a few hours to a day.

Find out in advance everything you can about your destination, such as water supplies, restroom facilities, fireplace availability, and restrictions on camping, group size, fires, and wood cutting. Plan your gear accordingly; bring shovels, cook stoves, water jugs, or saws as needed.

Outfitters and tour operators can usually supply any special gear required for specific activities, so check with them regarding rental equipment before buying expensive items. Rafting in spring may call for a wetsuit. In winter, if you're cross-country skiing hut-to-hut, special touring skis with metal edges are highly recommended. Cross-country skiing produces a lot of heat so you can easily work up a sweat, but when you stop moving you will feel how cold it really is out there. Again, layers are the answer. And even in mid-summer on a backcountry bike ride you might start out in 80° weather then run into a thunderstorm that drops the temperature dramatically. If you always plan for the most severe conditions you will be able to weather these changes in fine form.

At any time of the year the sun can be quite strong. Wear a hat, sunscreen, and bring sunglasses which can prevent snow blindness in winter when the glare can be oppressive. Insect repellent is a good idea in the summer, particularly at lower elevations.

Always carry extra food and water on any backcountry excursion.

Driving

To really get out and experience the deserts and mountains of Utah you need a car, and some of the best places to go are not on main roads.

Always inquire of locals about current road conditions. Some backroads may be marked for four-wheel-drive vehicles only. Do not test local wisdom or these signs in your Pontiac coupe. You will be in deep trouble if you travel several miles down an ultimately impassable dirt road and discover you cannot turn around. After rains, dirt roads can become dense, muddy tracks from which there is no easy escape. In the desert, sandy roads can swallow a car up to its hubcaps before you know what hit you. Snow frequently closes main highways (though generally for short periods) and unmaintained backroads may disappear until spring.

Those cowboys in their pickups know what they're doing. A truck or a four-wheel-drive with high ground clearance are the vehicles of choice but, with or without one, precautions are *de rigueur*.

Top up the gas tank wherever you can. The next gas station may be 100 miles away. Smart backcountry winter travel means good snow tires, windshield wipers that work, a couple of blankets, and a shovel in your car.

Local people understand the conditions and will probably help you out if you have trouble, but there may be nobody around for many miles or many hours. A cellular phone or CB radio could make a big difference in getting help. And don't forget to travel with the most up-to-date maps. Reliable maps are available from offices of the Forest Service or BLM. Outdoor stores are also good sources. An excellent driving map called *Indian Country* is published by AAA and is available for sale or free to AAA members.

WEATHER & ROAD CONDITIONS

Always check with local offices of the state patrol and the National Weather Service for current information. Don't be lazy about this. Just because it looks okay where you're standing does not mean it's going to be that way where you're going. Conditions can change fast. Anticipation is the key to success on any wilderness trip.

Special Concerns

The places covered in this book are here for all to enjoy and special care should always be taken to insure their continued existence. Some remote stretches are designated wilderness areas with seriously enforced rules of etiquette, including access limited to those on foot or with pack animals only.

Throughout Utah fishing and hunting are subject to state or tribal law. Certain areas have restrictions on camp fires, and even where fires are allowed, dry weather may lead to prohibitions on open fires. It's always safest to cook on a camp stove. If you need to make a fire, do not cut standing trees; burn dead wood only.

Do not be tempted to pocket an arrowhead or a pottery shard you may find on your travels. Think of the next person who'll be coming along, and remember that artifacts are protected by law. Besides, there have been documented cases of bad things happening to people who steal artifacts!

It's a sound policy to take only photographs and leave only footprints. Before leaving a campsite, replace rocks and scatter leaves and twigs to restore it to a near-natural condition. Pack out all your garbage and any other trash you may find. Take care with human waste. It should be buried 100 feet or more from any water source and not near possible campsites. On most rivers, human waste must be taken along and disposed of later. Use only biodegradable soap and, whenever possible, wash from a bucket of water far from running sources.

Do not travel into a fenced area as the Forest Service or BLM may be protecting it for re-vegetation or protecting you from dangerous conditions, such as extremely wet roads. Private landowners do not need a reason to keep you out; respect private property. Cross streams only at designated crossings.

Watch out for lightning. Especially avoid exposed areas above the treeline during thunderstorms. If you are caught in a thunderstorm, don't hide under a tree or in your tent. Get back into your car, if you can, or look for a cave or a deep protected overhang. If none of these things is available to you, crouch down as low as you can and hope for the best.

Avoid narrow canyons during rainy weather; check weather reports for thunderstorm predictions. Disastrous flash flooding is a real danger.

Drinking water in lakes, rivers, and streams is not exactly the same wilderness treat it once was. Now it's more likely to provide a nasty trick, *Giardia lamblia*, a tiny protozoan that can cause big problems. Animal waste found in many water sources can give you diarrhea and violent stomach cramps, symptoms which may require medical attention that could be far away.

To avoid problems, make sure you always have adequate fresh water. On longer trips this usually means boiling all lake and stream water for 20 minutes or carrying effective water purification paraphernalia, which can be purchased from area sporting goods stores.

The water is fine for swimming, but relying on it as your primary water source without adequate treatment may be painful.

Information

The Bureau of Land Management administers thousands of acres of public lands in Utah. For the good reason that these lands are enormously diverse, these holdings are divided into various regions. Regional headquarters will refer you to local offices which are listed throughout the book, or check the index for specific offices.

Many of these information sources are included in the chapters that follow, but these general sources can be a big help in getting you started before you make up your mind about exactly what you want to do. Most provide free information.

INFORMATION SOURCES

Utah Division Of Parks and Recreation, Council Hall, 1636 West North Temple, Salt Lake City, UT 84116. ☎ 801/538-7221.

Utah Travel Council, Capitol Hill, Salt Lake City, UT 84114. ☎ 801/538-1030.

Canyonlands North Travel Region, 805 North Main, Moab, UT 84532. ☎ 801/259-8825 or 800/635-6622.

Canyonlands South Travel Region, 117 South Main, PO Box 490, Monticello, UT 84535. ☎ 801/587-3235, fax 801/587-2425.

Color Country Travel Region, 906 North 1400 West, Box 1550, St. George, UT 84771-1550. ☎ 801/628-4171 or 800/233-8824, fax 801/673-3540.

National Forest Service, Intermountain Region, 324 25th Street, Ogden, UT 84401. ☎ 801/625-5347.

Ski Utah, 150 West 500 South, Salt Lake City, UT 84101. ☎ 801/534-1779.

Bicycle Utah, Box 738, Park City, UT 84060, ☎ 801/649-5806.

US Bureau of Land Management, 324 South State Street, Suite 301, Salt Lake City, UT 84145-0155. ☎ 801/539-4001.

US Geological Survey, 2300 South 2222 West, West Valley City, UT 84117. ☎ 801/975-3742.

Green River Information Center, 885 East Main Street, Green River, UT 84525. ☎ 801/564-3526.

Bridgerland Travel Region, 160 North Main Street, Logan, UT 84321. ☎ 801/752-2161 or 800/882-4433.

Golden Spike Empire, Union Station, 2501 Wall Avenue, Ogden, UT 84401. ☎ 801/627-8289.

Park City Chamber of Commerce, 528 Main Street, Park City, UT 84060, ☎ 801/649-6104 or 800/453-1360.

Vernal Welcome Center, 235 East Main Street, Vernal, UT 84078. ☎ 801/789-4002.

Northern Utah

If you want to see an area in transition, come to northern Utah. Only an Olympics could spark this much change, excitement and shift away from tradition. A relatively young state, Utah celebrated its centennial on Jan. 4, 1996, although Mormon pioneers had set down roots here a half-century before the area was given its present status.

Utah's population, which flirts around the two million mark, is clustered primarily along the corridor known as the **Wasatch Front,** spanning from Logan near the Idaho border to Nephi in the south. It's no surprise that settlers have traditionally congregated along this 100-mile stretch of mountains and valleys. Water is plentiful, temperatures don't reach the extremes found in the Great Basin and canyon country, and the soil is fertile.

The state has an abundance of badlands and beautiful lands. Forests, heavily weighted with pinyon juniper trees, cover barely a quarter of the terrain. The Sego Lily, the state's flower, thrives because of its ability to adapt to dry soil. Rivers, like the **Green** and **Colorado**, cut deep canyons that weren't considered navigable until charted in 1869 by explorer/Renaissance man John Wesley Powell.

The lands remain wild but, as is true throughout the West, there's an ongoing fight for their soul. Development continues to sprawl away from the urban centers. It's not unusual to see an ugly brown pollution cloud trapped along the mountains of the busy Wasatch Front, where 75% of the population makes its home. Yes, Utah is suffering from growing pains, but a firm foundation provided in part by the Mormon Church, in part by ardent environmentalists, has kept so-called "progress" in check.

Families remain one of the cultures' strongest bases and the influence of the Church of Jesus Christ of the Latter Day Saints – gentiles call it the Mormon Church – cannot be underestimated. While outsiders tend to scoff at Church-inspired restrictions on purchasing alcohol, it is because of the LDS Church that many public spaces remain free of smoke (nicotine is as verboten to members as alcohol and caffeine). A push is on to loosen up the smoking restrictions for the Olympics, but don't look for any radical changes in the near future.

Large Mormon families are sometimes targeted for criticism by non-church members. Yet in this family-friendly atmosphere, job sharing among working women is readily accepted, more so than in more liberal areas. Whether you consider it good or bad, the conservative stronghold remains. For example, while this is certainly the West, people don't dress as casually as they do in Montana or Colorado. By the same token, many residents tend to believe they are better behaved than the average Joe in America, and quietly hope visitors will watch their manners and curb foul language in public. Another area in which traditions are felt is in the Sunday closures of many businesses, which seasoned travellers to resorts may not be accustomed to.

When making your way around northern Utah, watch carefully for your turnoff or final destination. The state agencies produce excellent travel collateral but, unfortunately, signage on the smaller highways is generally so unobtrusive it's easy to miss.

In some rural areas, life continues much as it did 100 years ago. In plain view of high-tech software companies in newly erected and gleaming buildings are the landmark churches and temples that have been the communities' stronghold for 100 years or more. Physically homogeneous – more than half of the incorporated cities have no African-American residents – residents are awakening to the evolution taking place as the 20th century gallops to a close.

After almost 30 years of failed attempts, Salt Lake City was finally awarded the Winter Olympics bid – the world will descend upon northern Utah between February 9 and 24, 2002. And the Games will bring more than just jobs and publicity to the region. Residents realize this and are accepting the monumental event with a grain of salt.

INFORMATION SOURCES

Utah Department of Natural Resources, Division of Parks and Recreation, 1636 W. North Temple, Suite 116, Salt Lake City, UT 84116. ☎ 801/538-7221.

Utah Travel Council, Council Hall, Capitol Hill, Salt Lake City, UT 84114. ☎ 801/538-1467. Volumes of worthwhile, free information are available through this office, located at the corner of 300 N. and State Street.

Bureau of Land Management, 324 South State Street, Suite 301, Salt Lake City, UT 84145. ☎ 801/539-4001.

US Forest Service, Intermountain Region, 2501 Wall Ave., Ogden, UT 84401. ☎ 801/625-5182.

National Park Service, Box 25287, Denver, CO 80225. ☎ 303/969-2000.

Utah Museum Service, 324 S. State St., #500, Salt Lake City, UT
84111.
Utah Wildlife Resources, 1115 North Main St., Springville, UT
84663. ☎ 801/489-5678.

Getting Around

Salt Lake City is the center of the universe when it comes to
accessing the state. **Salt Lake International Airport** is less than a
15-minute drive from downtown on the northwestern edge of the
city, and is served by nine major airlines and two local carriers.
Those in a hurry may fly a commuter carrier to the airport in Vernal,
gateway to Dinosaur National Monument and Flaming Gorge. The
capitol city is also a crossroads for **Amtrak, Greyhound** and
Trailways buses, which spin off in all directions from their
downtown hubs.

Like spokes on a wheel, it's easy to branch out from Salt Lake City
for day trips, overnights or week-long stays. Because of the
distances between attractions and the lack of public transit in rural
areas, a car remains your best mode of transport. **I-70, I-80** and **UT
40** slice their way across the state. **I-15** is the main north-south
connector. Off the busy highways, which residents complain get
more crowded each year, the majority of driving takes place on
narrower, though generally well-maintained backroads.

The suggested itinerary moves counterclockwise, beginning
with the attractions found in **Salt Lake City** and its canyons, then
moving on to progressive **Park City** and its environs. From there
it's a northward movement to **Ogden,** a city founded on railroading
but one that is charging full steam ahead into the 21st century with
a diversified economy. A trip to Ogden wouldn't be complete
without a side trip to **Promontory** and the meeting place of the
Transcontinental Railroad. The lush **Cache Valley,** named for the
mountain men who used to store their pelts in little valleys
surrounding Logan, and the plethora of activities in the northern
Wasatch Mountains, fill another chapter.

The tour returns with a westward gaze to the often-overlooked
Great Salt Lake and the wondrous gem known as **Antelope Island.**
Beyond the water, where the land becomes so flat they say you can
see the earth's curvature, are the **Bonneville Salt Flats,** home to
numerous land speed records. The desert has its own beauty out

here and where vegetation seems unlikely, suddenly there are green-specked mountains mixed with granite peaks.

In the area we call the **southern Wasatch** are **Mt. Timpanogos** and the riveting mountains around Provo. Farther down the pike **Mt. Nebo** makes its statement as the highest point in the range. Shortly thereafter, the Wasatch Mountains come to a quiet close.

Northern Utah

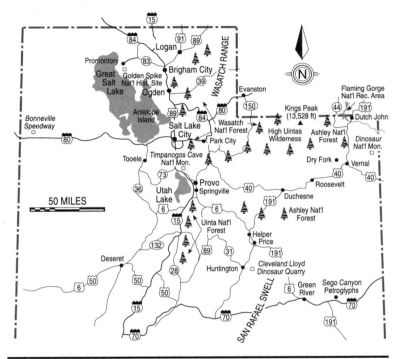

Often overlooked by travellers hurrying northward to the ski resorts or south to the desert is an area of fascinating geology and discoveries between Price and Green River. Indian petroglyphs and bones from ancient beasts like the wooly mammoth were unearthed from the canyons and crater-like lands.

From there, we make a swing north to **Vernal**, rated as one of the top 100 small towns in America. Vernal is more than a hopping-off place for **Dinosaur National Park** and splendid **Flaming Gorge National Monument**, two must-see destinations on any outdoor enthusiast's agenda. Hiking, biking and boating opportunities abound here in the northwestern corner of the state. A trip through the **Uintah Basin** and the fishing-rich **High Uintah Wilderness** area is in order before returning to Salt Lake City.

REFERENCE GUIDES

Hall, Dave. *The Hiker's Guide to Utah*, Falcon Press, 1991.

Hart, John. *Hiking the Great Basin*, Sierra Club Books, San Francisco, 1991.

Nichols, Gary C. *River Runners' Guide to Utah and Adjacent Areas*, University of Utah Press, 1986.

Shelton, Peter. *The Insider's Guide to the Best Skiing in Utah*, Western Eye Press, Telluride, CO, 1989.

Walter, Claire. *Rocky Mountain Skiing*, Fulcrum Pub., Golden, 1992.

Weir Bill. *Utah Handbook*, Moon Publications, Chico, CA. 1st edition, 1988.

Wharton, Tom and Gayen. *Utah*, Discover America Guides, Inc., 1991.

Touring

Salt Lake City

This capitol city, founded in 1847 by Brigham Young and his Mormon followers, is commonly referred to as the "Crossroads of the West" for its diversity as well as its location.

Temple Square is the starting point for the Salt Lake City street system. Confusingly enough, any street south of Temple Square is called a "south street," despite the fact that it runs on an east/west axis. North of the Temple are "north streets."

Street increments are in the 100s, but locals tend to call 200 street "2nd street," etc. Also note that the northeast quadrant of the city has its own street grid system of avenues. The streets in downtown, many of which run one way, are unusually wide. One theory behind this is that they were designed to allow an ox cart to turn around without flipping over or having to back up.

Temple Square actually encompasses three blocks of monuments, church offices, and museums. Brigham Young decided in 1847 that "this was the place" where the church's heart would beat. A half-century later the Mormon Temple, a striking multi-spired monolith that glows with a beautiful light in the evening, was finally completed. Unless you are of a certain standing within the Mormon Church, entrance is restricted once inside the building. But visitors are allowed to take the free 45-minute tour of the Tabernacle and Assembly Hall that runs every 15 minutes. Friendly volunteers staff the visitors center.

Worth attending no matter what your religious leanings are the **Tabernacle Choir** rehearsals on Thursday nights. The actual concerts are held Sunday mornings at 9:30 a.m. Daily tours of the acoustically remarkable Tabernacle, where you can see the famous organ reputed to have 11,623 pipes, are given in several languages. The choir has travelled around the world to perform, even stopping for a concert in Red Square, Moscow.

There's music to be had everywhere. At **Assembly Hall**, hour-long evening concerts are presented regularly by the **Temple Square Concert Series**. ☎ 800/537-9703 for information.

Across the street is the **Family Search Center**, located in the Joseph Smith Memorial Building at 15 East South Temple, ☎ 800/537-9703. The service traces your roots through computerized genealogical data. The 200 computers are often in full use by midday so come early. There is no charge.

Those who can't get enough of the Church's culture should check out **The Beehive House**, 67 East South Temple. Dating back to 1854, this was Brigham Young's family residence for many years. A free guided tour tells the story.

While downtown, scoot on over to **Sam Weller Books**, 254 South Main, ☎ 801/328-2586, to browse through an informative selection of best-sellers, classics, new and used books. Open in the evenings, Sam Weller is a great place to people-watch.

On the same street is the **Off-Broadway Theater**, 272 South Main St., ☎ 801/355-4628, home base for improvisation, spoofs and other reasons for a good laugh.

Ballet West, 50 West 200 South, ☎ 801/355-2787, remains an integral part of the cultural community with frequent performances offered at a range of prices.

Trolley Square, 600 South 700 East, is a touristy retail marketplace in historic trolley car barns. It has plenty of chain stores as well as cinemas and restaurants. A better alternative for shop-til-you-drop types is the **Crossroads Plaza**, 50 South Main, which has Nordstroms as its anchor store.

Salt Lake City

1. Tabernacle
2. Assembly Hall
3. Family Search Center
4. Beehive House
5. Off-Broadway Theater
6. Exchange Place Historic District
7. Delta Center
8. State Capitol
9. Information Center
10. Cathedral of the Madelaine
11. Crossroads Plaza Mall

Exchange Place Historic District, 355 South Main St., was once the major commercial district for non-Mormons. Now, it's a business center that's worth seeing for the Wall Street-style architecture. **The Delta Center**, 301 West South Temple, ☎ 801/325-2500, is where you'll watch the **Utah Jazz** take on their NBA opponents. This sparkling facility is also used for ice skating shows.

The beautiful granite **State Capitol** is appropriately located on Capitol Hill at the northern end of State Street. ☎ 801/538-3000. Tours are offered on Tuesdays, Wednesdays and Thursdays of this Renaissance Revival structure completed in 1916.

Also on Capitol Hill is an excellent one-stop shop for free information: the **Utah Tourism and Recreation Information Center**, 300 North State Street, ☎ 801/538-1467. They offer pamphlets and guides to all of Utah's public lands, state hotels and motels, outfitters, etc. There is free parking in a lot between Council Hall and the chapel.

In the same vicinity is the **Cathedral of the Madeleine**, 331 East South Temple, the Catholic Church's answer to the Mormon Temple. First constructed by a bishop and recently renovated to its turn-of-the-century glory, the cathedral boasts luscious marble, hand-crafted mosaics and two towers.

Bone up on dinosaur history at the **Utah Museum of Natural History**, 215 South 1350 East (on the University of Utah campus), ☎ 801/581-5567. There are rough and tumble rock exhibits, the requisite dinosaur displays, and a comprehensive explanation of Lake Bonneville. The campus, which sits on the city's east side, will house many of the Olympic athletes, trainers and coaches. Opening and closing ceremonies are to be held at Rice Stadium. On the other end of the campus is **Red Butte Garden and Arboretum**, ☎ 801/581-5322. Here you'll find nature trails and botanical gardens. Another option for nature lovers is the **Tracy Aviary** at Liberty Park, 589 East 1300 South, ☎ 801/596-5034, where you can catch free-flying bird shows daily.

Since the pioneer days, the canyons outside the city have offered refuge to worn-out urban warriors. **City Creek Canyon**, a popular walking and bike riding trail, is near the capitol, but is accessed off 11th Avenue and B Street.

Emigration Canyon, site of a popular diner/roadhouse, has near its entrance the **Hogle Zoo**, 2500 E. Sunnyside Ave., ☎ 801/582-1631. A special children's zoo is the attraction's highlight.

Travel past the ski areas in windy **Big Cottonwood Canyon**, which continues 15 miles until it reaches the summer-only

Guardsman Pass Scenic Backway. This partially paved road slices right through the **Wasatch National Forest**, with views up and down the entire mountain range on the way to Park City.

Park City & The Central Wasatch

Drive 20 miles east of Salt Lake on I-80 through Parley's Canyon to Park City's main exit, Kimball Junction. Then head six miles on Hwy. 224 to reach the rowdy former silver-mining town turned ski resort and arts center, Park City.

The city is Utah's only true ski town. It is a crossroads for the ski and film industries. Headquarters to the US Ski Team, it is well-known as the home of the week-long **Sundance Film Festival**, where premiers of non-commercial works draw film lovers and artists each January to screenings at the **Egyptian Theater**.

The locals – Park City's permanent population is almost 7,000 – are a lively and interesting mix of transplants drawn by the old mining town that snuggles against the mountains and the wealth of activities available literally out the back door. Growth in and around Park City can seem out of control at times but, fortunately, the hilly downtown historic district has protections in place. Evidence of the Aspenization of Park City: disheartened locals are moving 20 minutes away to Midway!

Walk up Main St. past the dozens of restaurants and galleries and clubs just bursting with laughter and oozing with good smells. Wind past the old clapboard miner's cabins and through the historic district bordering Woodside Ave., and sense some of those boisterous spirits from days gone by. Free buses run in an around town and a trolley ambles up Main St.

From the heart of downtown, ride the Town Chair to the **Park City Ski Area**, Box 39, Park City, UT 84060, ☎ 801/649-8111, and enjoy 2,200 acres of in-bound terrain. The resort has reliable snowmaking equipment to guarantee the running of early-season World Cup ski races. Park City offers ski terrain for all ability levels, including expert bowls and chutes for those not easily satiated.

Home to ski legend Stein Eriksen, **Deer Valley**, Box 3149, Park City, UT 84060, ☎ 801/649-1000, is for the guest who loves to be pampered. More pricey than its neighbors, it has garnered as much attention for its restaurants and on-mountain valet service as for its actual terrain, which consists of 61 varied runs.

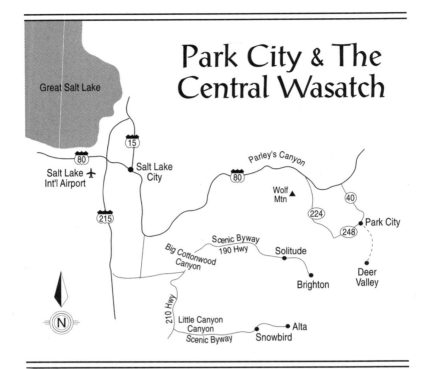

Park City & The Central Wasatch

Wolf Mountain, 4000 Parkwest Drive, Park City, UT 84060, ☎ 801/649-5400, the third local mountain, has night skiing, a laid-back atmosphere and friendly prices. **Utah Winter Sports Park**, 3000 Bear Hollow Drive, Park City, UT 84060, ☎ 801/649-5447, offers recreational ski jumping lessons, rentals and facilities available to the public three times per week in the winter.

Learn more about ski areas in the On Snow section on page 85.

The Kimball Art Center, 638 Park Avenue, Park City, UT 84060, ☎ 801/649-8882, is home to cultural and local functions and serves as a great downtown meeting place. Gallery and studio space are available. The cultural arts hotline is ☎ 801/647-9747.

South of Park City is the rapidly growing agricultural center of **Heber City**. Set halfway between Park City and Provo, Heber is an affordable alternative to the resorts. For visitor information, ☎ 801/654-3666.

Wasatch Mountain State Park, Box 10, Midway, UT 84049, ☎ 801/654-0791, is a lovely retreat for sailing, windsurfing and fishing. Close by is **Deer Creek Reservoir**, south of Midway on US

189, which is bordered by Mt. Timpanogos, one of the most spectacular landforms in the West.

You'll realize how the Heber Creeper Railroad earned its name when it creeps up the hills through Wasatch Mountain State Park and Provo Canyon during the summer and past Deer Creek Dam in the winter. It's now been given the more respectable but less memorable name of **Heber Valley Historic Railroad**, 450 South 600 West, Heber City, UT 84032, ☎ 801-982-3257.

Ogden & The Golden Spike

Ringed by mountains and the Great Salt Lake, this railroad center is enjoying a renaissance as it prepares to host alpine skiing and ice hockey events for the 2002 Winter Olympics.

Ogden's downtown historic district looks snappier than ever, with the upscale restaurants and shops teeming with customers on any given day. Since becoming a primary railroad distribution center in 1869 (following the meeting of the Transcontinental Railroad at Promontory Summit), commerce has been conducted in the shadow of Mt. Ogden and its neighbor, Ben Lomen Mountain (model for the Paramount Pictures peak). Nearby, the confluence of the Weber and Ogden rivers is another reminder that recreation is never far away.

Ogden has been a university town since the founding of Weber State in 1889. It also retains a strong military presence; just south of town in the city of Roy is Hill Air Force Base and to the north near Golden Spike is Morton Thiokol, manufacturers of rocket parts and space shuttle equipment.

Start your tour at the Mediterranean-style **Union Station**, 2501 Wall Ave., Ogden, UT 84401, ☎ 801/629-8444. Built during the Roaring '20s, Union Station is listed on the National Register of Historic Places. There you'll find plenty of free maps and guides to the area. Another recommended stop in the building is the **Utah Railroad History Museum**, where there's a model railroad, informative displays and a visual history of railroading in this country. Union Station also houses a car museum, a vast mineral collection and a firearms collection.

Take 25th St. east of Union Station (between Wall and Grant Avenues) and you'll come to the pride of downtown Ogden. Once a red-light district, **25th St.**, with its artsy shops, bakeries and hot restaurants, is now a respectable destination.

Ogden & The Golden Spike

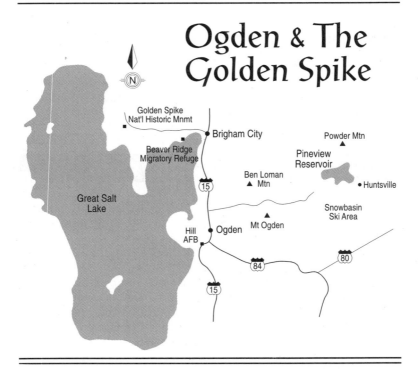

Golden Spike
Nat'l Historic Mnmt

Brigham City

Powder Mtn

Beaver Ridge
Migratory Refuge

Pineview
Reservoir

Ben Loman
▲ Mtn

15

Great Salt
Lake

Huntsville

Snowbasin
Ski Area

Hill
AFB

Ogden   Mt Ogden
▲

84

80

15

One block over is **Ogden City Mall**, 24th St. and Washington Blvd., Ogden, UT 84401, ☎ 801/621-1161. It features a Nordstrom's and other quality stores, such as Rocky Mountain Rubber Stamps, ☎ 801-399-5976, which sells artsy-crafty tools plus any stamp you could ever want. Within the mall is the **Treehouse Children's Museum**, ☎ 801/394-9663, tempting the child in all of us to climb aboard a huge tree or just lounge by its roots, good book in hand. **The Treehouse Theater** presents special events.

Set along the Weber River is **Fort Buenaventura State Park**, 2450 A Avenue, Ogden, UT 84401, ☎ 801/621-4808. Guides dressed in period costume explain the pioneers' lifestyle in this reconstructed fort. Learn about the men who came to this area in the 1840s to trade furs, party and marry Indian women. Buenaventura is one of those Wild West forts that never served its intended purpose.

Before heading into the mountains, take a little time to learn about the national defense and see one of the largest collections of vintage aircraft in the country. Even those who wouldn't normally be enamored by airplanes will be impressed with the B-17 Flying Fortress, the P-51 Mustang and the B-52. The aircraft, missile and bomb displays are at **Hill Aerospace Museum**, Hill Air Force Base, ☎ 801/777-6868. Free.

As is true in other cities laid out by Brigham Young and his followers, navigation here is a breeze. Travel north to 12th Street, turn east and make your way up past the shale and limestone cliffs in Ogden Canyon. On your way up, take a detour to **George S. Eccles Dinosaur Park**, 1544 Park Blvd., ☎ 801/393-3466. Life-size (we think) dinosaurs presented in a park-like setting amid lush ponds and fountains appeal to the kid in all of us. Some of the replicas may be too scary for the youngest family members. Adjacent to a 3.1-mile riverwalk, Eccles also has an excellent playground.

It takes no time at all to access the mountains from Ogden. From the dinosaur park, wind your way up along the Ogden River on Hwy. 39, past the tidy cottages, mountain homes and steep walls to **Pineview Reservoir**, ☎ 801/625-5306, at the head of Ogden Canyon. Boating, fishing, waterskiing and camping are popular here. The towns of Huntsville and tiny Eden lie on either side of the lake.

During the winter there are three ski areas in the Huntsville district. **Snowbasin**, host to the downhill and Super G events in the 2002 Winter Olympics, is the steepest of the three. True-to-its-name **Powder Mountain** has wide-open slopes and a snowcat skiing option. **Nordic Mountain** appeals to locals and families with bargain basement prices. See page 85, On Snow, for details.

Highly recommended is the nine-mile **Trappers Loop Drive** from Huntsville to Mountain Green on Hwy. 167. To return to Ogden, drive west on I-84 into Weber Canyon, following the Weber River back to city limits. A shortcut from Trappers Loop to the Snowbasin ski area will be built in time for the Olympics.

Back in the Huntsville's pastoral valley is the **Holy Trinity Abbey**, 1250 S 9500 E, Huntsville, UT 84317. Attend a Roman Catholic mass or shop for creamed honey nut, raspberry and peach honey spreads or the whole wheat and raisin breads produced on site. The Trappist monks who've resided in Ogden Valley since 1947 are hospitable to the stream of guests who flow through the little gift shop.

Ironically, Huntsville also boasts the oldest continuously working bar in Utah, the **Shooting Star Saloon**, 100 East St., Huntsville, UT, ☎ 801/745-2002. Burgers and more burgers highlight the menu in this funky roadhouse.

Railroad buffs will want to take a separate trip north of Ogden to explore the site of the **Transcontinental Railroad** meeting place.

En route you'll find **Willard Bay State Recreation Area**, a freshwater impoundment between Ogden and Brigham City.

Then comes **Bear River Migratory Bird Refuge**, home to more than 200 types of birds. The 12-mile self-guided loop through salty, marshy inlets and waterways is quite rewarding, although the drive back is on bumpy roads. Pull-offs along the route offer plenty of opportunities to spy egrets, swans, geese, herons and ruddy ducks. The refuge is open year-round. Bring bug repellent if you plan on getting out of the car.

Where West met East in our country's railroad history is the **Golden Spike National Historic Site**, Box 897, Brigham City, UT 84302, ☎ 801/471-2209. Every year, hearty rail buffs re-enact the May 10, 1869 transcontinental meeting of the Central Pacific and Union Pacific railroads, also known as the "Wedding of the Rails" ceremony, at Promontory Summit. Golden Spike is 55 miles northwest from Ogden, via UT 13 in Brigham City and Hwy. 83.

Good and bad came from the meeting, which summoned exploration into some of the last wild lands found in the lower 48 states. Bison hunters ravaged the herds and the Native American way of life.

The **Railroaders Festival** is traditionally held the second Saturday in August. The visitor center shows an excellent film telling of the trials and tribulations of building the rails. Outside are replicas of the *Jupiter* and 119 locomotives that arrived at Golden Spike. The site itself, located in barren hills near the Morton Thiokol plant (where there is a rocket display for enthusiasts), is a little disappointing to those expecting a glorious landmark.

Two auto tours, the two-mile **East Tour** and the seven-mile **West Tour**, are available. Either may be navigated on mountain bike or by foot. The West Tour chugs up a shallow grade past parallel tracks, sidings and the limestone formation known as Chinaman's Arch to honor the many laborers who worked on the Central Pacific. There is a sign noting the 10 miles of track that were laid in less than 12 hours by Central Pacific rail workers. The East Tour cuts past the Big Fill and trestle site.

The wedding of the railroads became a moot point when the Southern Pacific Railroad built its own above-water crossing on a trestle and rock causeway over the Great Salt Lake. In 1941, the rails around Golden Spike were dismantled to provide equipment for the war effort. A year later there was an "Undriving of the Last Spike" ceremony.

Golden Spike continues to draw rail buffs, as evidenced by the 14,000 visitors who turned out in 1994 for the 125th anniversary of the Transcontinental Railroad.

If returning to Ogden, take a slight detour to the **Crystal Springs**, 8215 North Hwy. 69, Honeyville, UT 84314, ☎ 801/279-8104. Here you'll find hot and cold pools, a mineral pool and waterslides. Water temperatures range from 85 to 112°.

Logan, Cache County & The Northern Wasatch

Logan is an ideal jumping-off spot for climbers, boaters, hikers and other recreationalists more interested in what they're seeing rather than who is seeing them do it. The surrounding mountains – the steep Wellsville Range to the southwest, dominated by the Wellsville Cone and Box Elder Peak – rise high from their narrow base. The other natural border is the Bear River Range that charges northward towards Idaho. Home to a half-dozen or more cheese factories, the lush Cache Valley is the bridge between these two mountain ranges.

Logan, Cache County & The Northern Wasatch

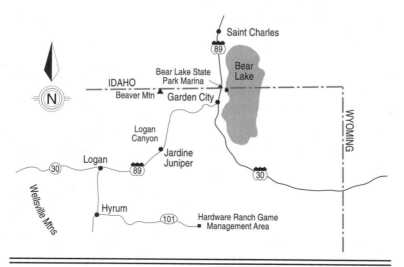

Logan, 80 miles north of Salt Lake City, sits perched atop a terrace created by historic Lake Bonneville. **Logan Temple**, with its 170-foot tower visible from throughout the Cache Valley, sits where Native Americans used to hold healing ceremonies.

One block away is the pastel **Logan Tabernacle**, a snappy blend of Gothic, Byzantine and Roman styles, with a splash of New England thrown in for good measure. Surprise, surprise, it was built by pioneers from Scandinavia, Great Britain and Western Europe. In the basement there is a satellite office of the **Family History Center**, open to anyone interested in tracing their family lineage. Upstairs are stained glass windows, pillars and, of course, a pipe organ complete with 194 gold leaf pipes. A 1989 restoration brought back the original color scheme for the walls and ceiling, including scroll work that was designed from oil cloth patterns.

Logan has a friendly downtown with shops that haven't been squeezed out by huge chains. On Center Street is the **Lyric Theater**, one of the city's two historic theaters. Originally built in 1913 by the Thatcher family, the building (reputed to be haunted) is home each summer for the **Old Lyric Repertory Company**. Sunbirds flock here to escape the summer heat of Arizona and to enjoy the seasonal concerts which literally fill the hills. Both the **Utah Festival Opera** and the **Festival of the American West** set up shop on campus during these months.

Utah State University students run the **Ronald V. Jensen Living Historical Farm**, Hwy. 89-91, Wellsville, UT 84339, ☎ 801/245-4064. Farm equipment, draft horses and farm animals are the primary draw at this farm, circa 1917.

Like the rural alpine valleys of Switzerland, Cache Valley is known for its local dairy products. The most famous of the cheesemakers is **Cache Valley Cheese**, 6351 N. 2150 W. Amalga, ☎ 801/563-3281.

The highlight of your stay in the area extends northeast of downtown. **Logan Canyon** is a 40-mile-long climbers' playground with steep limestone walls stocked full of fossils, trails and fun. Biking, hiking and fishing are accessible within a short walk from the road. The **Beaver Mountain ski area** regularly enjoys good snow conditions. In early autumn the canyon is a favorite spot for leaf peepers.

Logan Canyon is home to a famous juniper tree that's said to be one of the world's oldest. **The Old Juniper** was discovered in 1923 by a Utah State botany student. It stands on a rock ledge near the mouth of Cottonwood Creek. The juniper has been the subject of numerous study and visitation and was even the cover shot for a box of chocolates at the Bluebird Restaurant in Logan.

After the canyon summit, you'll almost literally drop into 20-mile-long **Bear Lake**, on Hwy. 89 in Garden City, ☎ 801/946-3343; campground reservations ☎ 800/322-3770. The water is so blue that tourists have asked if dye is used to give its color! Credit should be given instead to the limestone particles that reflect the sunrays and give the lake its iridescence. A fine time to visit is early August, when the raspberries are harvested and a festive mood abounds. Undoubtedly, someone will talk you into drinking a fresh raspberry shake.

South of Logan about six miles is **Hyrum Reservoir State Park**, a popular boating and camping area on the road to **Blacksmith Fork Canyon**. The spectacular canyon is home to a huge elk refuge at Hardware Ranch and other assorted big game that are likely to rear their heads as you meander the 18 miles up the canyon. Sleigh riding and snowmobiling are popular in the wilds surrounding Hardware Ranch.

Great Salt Lake

Looming large from almost everywhere on the Wasatch Front but by and large ignored by its brethren, the Great Salt Lake remains an under-used, under-loved amenity.

This mythological body of water is all that remains of ancient Ocean Bonneville. Seventy miles long and about 25 miles wide at its present state, the Great Salt Lake expands and recedes regularly because it has no outlet.

The best place to experience the lake is from **Antelope Island State Park**, 4528 West 1700 South, Syracuse, UT 84075, ☎ 801/773-2941. Take I-15 north of Salt Lake City to the Layton City exit. Drive west on Hwy. 108 across the seven-mile causeway to Antelope Island. A marina and information center sit near the causeway's end.

Antelope Island is where the buffalo (actually, they're bison) roam. It's also where the deer, elk and a handful of antelope play.

Fifteen miles long by 4½ miles wide, the island covers 28,000 acres, although only 2,000 acres are open year-round. Antelope was privately owned until earning state park status in 1981. It now sees 300,000 visitors each year who come for the lavender sunsets, pure white sand beaches and to catch a glimpse of those wooly beasts who roam freely across the island.

Bridger, Buffalo and **White Rock bays** on the north end of the island are all accessible destinations anytime of year. Bridger Bay is where you'll find the beach facilities and the best camping. There is a small gift shop and snack stand featuring lean buffalo burgers at the viewpoint, and a group site overlooking White Rock Bay. The corral where the bison are herded each year sits near the road to the campsite.

A dozen or so weekends each summer and fall the historic ranch on the eastern shore is opened for public tours. It's definitely worth visiting the property and this little-seen section of the island. The ranch gets all gussied up for oxen-shoeing demonstrations, candlemaking, story telling, quilting, Dutch oven cooking, even saddle making. Tour the blacksmith shop, which is still in its original state. The white adobe bunkhouse was built in 1849 by Fielding Garr, Antelope's first resident. Constructed of mud and straw, the home has withstood almost a century and a half of use, many residents and, now, a steady stream of visitors.

If time is limited on your visit, at least take the short hike up to the **Buffalo Point Overlook**. Looking west, the islands of the Great Salt Lake, some of which are actually extensions of the Stansbury and Oquirrah mountain ranges, seem to float in the haze. Those with more time should try the hike from White Rock Bay to Bridger Bay along the **Lakeside Trail**.

One of the best ways to see the island is on horseback. Every year 450 equestrians come to help round-up the bison, which have numbered as many as 750 head. The horseback riders assemble at the ranch then travel to the south part of Antelope Island where they spread out to capture the beasts. With the aid of helicopters and trucks, it takes several days to herd the animals to the corrals up north. Spectators are welcome to sit in the bleachers and watch the late fall round-up.

Many people are reluctant to take a dip in the Great Salt Lake because of its high salt content. There are no outlets from the lake, and when water evaporates it leaves behind the salt. But salinity varies greatly depending upon location and Antelope Island offers excellent bathing facilities at Bridger Bay.

The upside of all this salt is a fine breeding ground for brine shrimp, but little else.

There's a push to keep Antelope Island from being overrun, a formidable task considering its proximity to the majority of Utah's population. The lake's most visible recreation area remains **Salt Lake State Park**, accessed off I-80 at exit 104, with its Taj Mahal-style building, a smattering of amusement rides and spartan concessions. The pavilion looks like one you'd find in Blackpool, England or on the New Jersey Shore.

Originally completed in 1893, the once-fabulous **Saltair Pavilion** hosted dance competitions, a bath house and other recreational activities during its heyday early this century. But a fire in the 1920s burned it to the ground. The structure was rebuilt in a more modern style only to be overrun by floods on several occasions.

Great Salt Lake

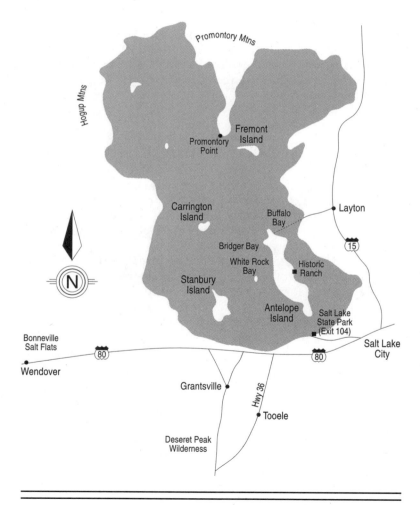

Consecutive years of flooding in the 1980s almost completely washed away the beaches – and left a yucky smell due to the brine flies remains in its aftermath. It is doubtful that the recreation area will ever recover.

The large marina here is home to sailboats, picnic facilities and a canoe sculling group. Sailing is the sport of choice in the Great Salt Lake. Kayaks and canoes get buffeted by winds and waves but can be kept under control near the shore. For the boatless visitor uninterested in wading through muck to access the water, Salt Lake State Park remains a distant second place to Antelope Island.

Legislators have tossed around the idea of building a causeway from the park to southern Antelope Island, which could revitalize the area. For now, that remains just talk.

On the west side of the lake, above the Hill Bombing Range, are the Hogup Mountains, accessed off Highway 30. Here you'll find **Hogup Cave**, said to be inhabited by man 6,000 years ago. Rough roads out here in the desert and the dearth of good maps make this a questionable detour.

BONNEVILLE FLATS

The sweeping desert area west and south of the Great Salt Lake is considered bleak by some and starkly handsome by others. Relief from the expanse of roan-colored hills, white ash badlands and Air Force test centers comes in the form of mirage-like images created as salt rises from the earth.

For a student of geology or ancient history, the Bonneville Salt Flats and their surrounding areas are an interesting case study. The flats were formed by the evaporation of ancient Lake Bonneville, which left large concentrations of salt on the land. The ancient Ice-Age lake that developed on the Great Basin (the expanse of desert valleys and narrow mountain ranges bounded by the Sierra Nevada Mountains in California and the start of the Rockies east of Salt Lake City) was roughly the size of present-day Lake Michigan.

Massive flooding and warming of the earth robbed Bonneville of its greatness. What remains is a shrunken remnant of the past, a too-salty badland where the high mineral concentration stunts plant growth. Yet conditions here are ideal for man and his machines; numerous land speed records have been set on this natural racetrack since the early part of the century.

To reach the Bonneville Salt Flats from Salt Lake City, take I-80 west, following the railroad tracks and the southern boundary of the Great Salt Lake. In the sand and the salt you'll see stone graffiti, messages, names and hearts decorating the highway.

The farther west you go, the flatter the landscape becomes. There's a tennis ball tower on the north side of the interstate called the **Tree of Utah**. Installed in 1981 by Karl Momen who was struck by the area's flatness and its lack of growth, the Tree of Utah reaches 87 feet toward the sky. The six spheres are said to be coated with natural minerals and rocks found in the region. The pods below – what look like broken tennis balls – symbolize the changing of the seasons.

The Silver Island Mountains welcome the visitor to the Wendover area and the outskirts of **Bonneville Speedway**. Use exit 4 for Bonneville Salt Flats and follow signs north.

Everything in these badlands of the Great Salt Desert looks like a mirage, caused by the combination of salt and dust rising. The Floating Island Mountain to the north is one such example.

Named for an early military explorer, the flats' racing potential was realized around the turn of the century by W.D. Rishel. Carriages and bicycles first raced here followed by Ferg Johnson's Packard in 1911. A signpost at the flats reads: "In 1914, Teddy Tetzlaff reached 141 mph in his Blitzen Benz."

The big push came in the 1930s when speed aficionado Ab Jenkins set the first of many speed records. Jenkins gained so much notoriety that he swept to an easy victory as Salt Lake's mayor during the next decade.

By 1940, its reputation ever-growing, jet and rockets cars appeared on the speedway. In 1965, the Summers Brothers raced to 409 mph, setting the world land speed record for a multiple engine car. That record was only matched recently by Al Teague, who tied the 409 mph mark for a single engine vehicle in 1992. A needle-nose competition coupe with a Simca body hit 307 mph in 1994. Batmobile-style Streamliners remain the fastest cars on the track.

Studebakers, Camaros, Firebirds and motorcycles have all had their day on Bonneville's seven-mile straightway. Some less orthodox vehicles have also dabbled in the flats. Speed skier Kirsten Culver once held a tuck atop a race car so she would know what it was like to go 130 miles per hour on skis.

The Bonneville Speedway takes up 10 miles of the firm salt flats which one member said are so fast "because there's nothing to hit!" Stray too far off the beaten path, however, and and you can sink down to your axles in the soft sand. As it is, the salt builds up on the wheel wells.

Only car club members can race (contact **Utah Salt Flats Racing Association**, 540 East 500 North, Pleasant Grove, UT 84062, ☎ 801/785-5364), after first having passed a technical inspection and driving test. Races are usually held in July, August and September.

Come early and savor the lovely sunrises on the Salt Flats and the quiet, ethereal beauty that can be enjoyed on either end of the day.

Looking for the speedway museum on Wendover Blvd? It's been closed for several years. Cheap meals and bountiful buffets can be had in Wendover, NV, but be prepared for plenty of cigarette smoke in the casino restaurants.

ON FROM BONNEVILLE

Testing zones south of Interstate 80 in Skull Valley and its environs have made much of the area unwelcoming. However, a little investigation nets huge rewards. Take Hwy. 138 through Grantsville, where you'll pass the Bonneville Sea Base, a place where divers can earn their certification but certainly not a place to choose over Ambergris Key.

The **Deseret Peak Wilderness** in the Stansbury Mountains, is a happy spot of green that rises dramatically from the flat valley expanse. There are steep vertical canyons to South Willow and the Mill Fork Trail, whichs climb about four miles to 11,031-foot Deseret Peak. East of Deseret Peak is the **Benson Grist Mill**, State Route 138, Tooele, UT 84704, ☎ 801/882-9160, which was constructed by early pioneers and redone by later residents. Listed on the National Historic Register, the mill site has a blacksmith shop, log cabin and farm equipment.

Farther south are the boom and bust towns like Gold Hill and Callao. Difficult to reach, the solitary beauty of these Great Basin towns and the mountains they access may appeal to some. As its name would imply, Gold Hill was a short-lived gold mining community. The gateway to the majestic Deep Creek Mountains is in this vicinity.

Ibapah Peak, rising 12,087 feet from Cottonwood Canyon, looks perennially snow-capped, but that is just because of its white-washed granite. Bristlecones can be spotted on the limestone, and bighorn sheep and pronghorn antelope are a few of inhabitants. It's flanked by **Haystack Peak** of **Red Mountain**, which stands around 11,500 feet. There is good hiking in this remote area and streams teeming with cutthroat trout.

Access to the Deep Creeks is through Wendover south over Gold Hill and through Callao; or west from Delta over Marjum and Cowboy passes. Respect Goshute Indian lands. Contact the BLM for maps and access to the Deep Creeks and the even more remote House Range, more typical of the desert mountains found in the Great Basin.

Provo & The Southern Wasatch

The farther south you go in the Wasatch Range, the more dramatic and beautiful the mountains become. In this transition from mountain to desert, alpine peaks gradually change into spires and canyons more typical of the Colorado Plateau.

Spanish explorers looking for a better trade route between Mexico and California first traipsed through here in the 18th century. One hundred years later the area was settled by Mormon pioneers who realized the rich lands and abundant water supply would be ideal for agricultural purposes. The area's appeal continues to this day.

Begin your tour of this region from the **Alpine Loop** which, as its name suggests, offers some outstanding mountain scenery. The Alpine Loop starts at the mouth of American Fork Canyon and winds its way 25 miles up and around stair-stepped Mt. Timpanogos, some famous caves, the Sundance Ski Resort and past a huge waterfall before finishing in Provo.

The **Timpanogos Cave National Monument,** ☎ 801/756-5238, Hwy. 92, seven miles east of American Fork, is comprised of man-made tunnels that wend through numerous formations. Jackets are needed in the chilly cave, which remains 45° year-round. The 1½-mile hike to the cave may be too arduous for some family members.

The **Cascade Springs Scenic Highway** is a 7½-mile paved spur of the Alpine Scenic Loop. Raised walkways offer views of springs cascading down the limestone slopes into little pools and terraces. By continuing on a bumpy, dirt road at the end of the trail you can finish in the town of Midway.

The careful melding of environment with resort is **Sundance,** Box A-1, Sundance, UT, 84064, ☎ 801/225-4107, a respectable ski area in a gorgeous setting that has evolved into an outpost for film students and think tank for protectors of the environment. First established in 1969 and named for owner Robert Redford's favorite leading character, Sundance also hosts outdoor and children's theater productions.

By turning east on Hwy. 189 in Provo Canyon and following the Provo River past many blue ribbon fly-fishing spots, you'll end up at Deer Creek Reservoir and the lush Heber Valley. Turn west on Hwy. 189 and drive beneath the jagged rock walls towards the **Bridal Veil Falls Tramway,** ☎ 801/377-5780, to see the Provo Canyon's double waterfall. The tramway, which soars more than 1,700 feet from the canyon floor, is one of the steepest of its kind.

Provo and its suburbs are home to not only the country's largest private college but to computer software makers WordPerfect and Novell, Inc. The high tech buildings standing in stark contrast to the verdant fruit fields nearby that provide more than three-quarters of the state's peaches, cherries and other fruits.

In the heart of Provo is **Brigham Young University.** With an enrollment topping 28,000 students, Brigham Young is the largest private university in the nation. For public tours, ☎ 800/537-9703. Stop in at the **Earth Science Museum** on campus, ☎ 801/378-3680, for a look at wooly mammoths, dinosaurs and ancient forms of sea life unique to this area. Lucky enough to visit during football season? If you can possibly secure a ticket, come watch the program that produced Jim McMahon and Steve Young.

West of Lehi on Highway 73 in the foothills of the Oquirrh Mountains is **Camp Floyd and the Stagecoach Inn State Park,** ☎ 801/768-8932. That's where you'll find a 19th-century cemetery and army commissary left over from 1858. It's a jumping off place for the **Pony Express Trail,** which continues west of here through the Great Basin.

Resting in the shadow of Mt. Timpanogos across the Interstate from the city is **Utah Lake State Recreation Area,** 4400 W. Center, Provo, UT 84501, a long, shallow body of water that's popular for waterskiing, boating and, in the winter, ice skating. Reconstructed after flooding in 1982/83, the lake is heavily used and open year-round.

Just south of Provo via Hwy. 89 is the **Springville Museum of Art,** 126 East 400 South, Springville, UT 84663, ☎ 801/489-2727. Considered the leading art museum in the region, Springville has 11 galleries and at least one major exhibition per month. The area's art movement harkens back to the turn of the century, although the building didn't go up until 1937. The museum remains true to its roots and continues to focus on Utah artists.

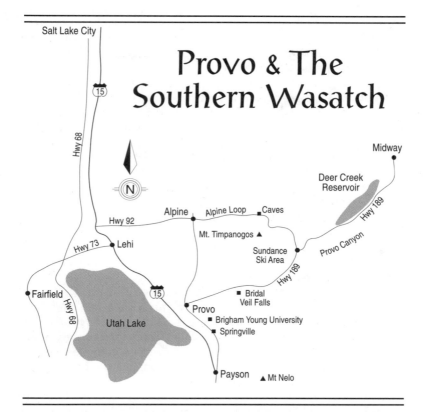

Provo & The Southern Wasatch

Salt Lake City

Hwy 68

Hwy 92

Hwy 73   Lehi

Alpine   Alpine Loop   ■ Caves

Mt. Timpanogos ▲

Midway

Deer Creek
Reservoir

Hwy 189

Provo Canyon

Sundance
Ski Area

Hwy 189

Fairfield

Hwy 68

Utah Lake

■ Bridal
Veil Falls

Provo

■ Brigham Young University
■ Springville

Payson   ▲ Mt Nelo

Mountain peaks stretching to 11,000 feet above sea level continue south of Provo in the **Uintah National Forest**. Begin at Payson for access to 11,877-foot Mt. Nebo, tallest in the Wasatch. Pines and aspen along the 38-mile byway are splendid in the fall. Take a side trip to the **Devil's Kitchen Geologic Interest Site**, which offers red rock that's a stark contrast to the mountain greenery. The multi-faceted route, offering many options for short excursions, is closed in winter. The loop ends in Nephi, a town named for a Book of Mormon prophet, that is notable for its diversity in architecture, adobe structures, brick and stone places and log homes.

Canyon Country to Green River

Rolling hills, desert grasslands and sparse trees are typical of the lands spanning the high alpine mountains and red rock country. This tour starts east of Provo on Hwy. 6 and weaves through the forests and deep canyons like a storyteller spinning a good yarn. Sparsely populated, at times it seems there are more dinosaur bones here than people.

Near the junction with Hwy. 89, little remains of the once tiny town of Thistle, buried by mud and landslides following the heavy snow season of 1982/83. The 100-mile drive atop the Wasatch Plateau, called the **Skyline Drive Scenic Backway**, starts near here. Offering mountain and valley views, it cuts through the Fishlake National Forest and Manti LaSal National Forest before ending up near Interstate 70. Most people take the drive in small sections rather than bite off more backcountry driving than they can chew. For information on the drive, ☎ 801/283-4151.

A spur off the Skyline Drive called the **Mayfield-Ferron Scenic Backway** is a 50-mile gravel road that climbs to 10,700 feet and is well used to access the backcountry. Camping, hiking and, in winter, snowmobiling start from here. The town of Ferron is known for its peach crop and pageant held every September.

Back north is the **Huntington Canyon Scenic Byway**. Start in either Huntington or Fairview and climb past aspen and pine forests to 10,000-foot summits. There is a side road to **Huntington Reservoir**, where the remains of a wooly mammoth were unearthed in 1988 by a backhoe operator. Initially, he noticed just one huge bone. Eventually 98% of the mastadon's bones were uncovered from what was once an Ice Age lake.

Near the town of Huntington off Hwy. 155 is the **Cleveland-Lloyd Dinosaur Quarry**, ☎ 801/637-5060, located near the northern edge of the San Rafael Swell. The quarry has netted four dozen allosaurus skeletons from the Jurassic Period. More than 70 different animals were pulled from here, many of which are proudly displayed at museums around the world. On-site visitors will find an information center and a nature trail.

It's said that Butch Cassidy and the boys set up shop in the hills south of Castle Dale. **Emery County Pioneer Museum**, 93 East 100 North, Castle Dale, UT 84513, ☎ 801/381-5454, is actually a fully stocked mercantile, recreated with items early settlers and bank robbers might have used.

The region's most dominant geological feature, the **San Rafael Swell**, 75 miles long by 30 miles, is a site to behold. Tall slanting spires and anticlines – upward thrusts of rock pushing forward from the valley floor – join sandstone formations and little-visited streams. More than 2,000 square miles of public land are among the reasons to discover the swell.

The San Rafael Swell may be accessed from downtown Castle Dale via Hwy. 10 to a dirt road that runs through a log corral. After a dozen miles over lands which are home to an antelope herd is the Buckhorn Flat Well Junction. Continuing south through the Buckhorn Draw will take you to the **Wedge Overlook**, also called "Utah's Little Grand Canyon." This is your hopping-off point to **Black Dragon Canyon** (named for an Indian panel), Crack Canyon, Iron Wash and other winding canyons of the swell.

If coming from Interstate 70, find the Black Dragon by taking the highway west for 19 miles to a dirt road just slightly past Mile Marker 145. Follow the road for one mile to a streambed for the Black Dragon Wash. Turn left for a half-mile to the canyon entrance. Access the Wedge Overlook from a road off Highway 6 or by taking I-70 west of Green River 19 miles.

After winding around the rock and the San Rafael Reef, head back to **Price**. If returning to Hwy. 6, you'll come to Hwy. 96 and the turnoff to Price Canyon Recreation Area. Price's fortunes were boosted by the coming of the railroad, plus coal mining and farming. Price is also home to the **College of Eastern Utah Prehistoric Museum**, 155 East Main St., Price, UT 84501, ☎ 801-637-5060, which houses the aforementioned huge Huntington Mammoth. There is a "hall of dinosaurs," including the Utah raptor (remember Jurassic Park?) and scary fossil marine animals.

Back on Hwy. 6, head northeast from Wellington into the Tavaputs Plateau to **Nine-Mile Canyon** (it is actually closer to five times that size). The name could have come from one of John Wesley Powell's map makers or from a family named Miles that had seven children, hence the "nine Miles." Loaded with pictographs and petroglyphs from the Fremont and Ute periods, it is considered one of the best collections of its kind. It's certainly one of the most well-preserved because of the dry climate and relatively inaccessible location. Approximately 26 miles from the Wellington turnoff is the first rock cliff near the entrance. There you'll see a giraffe-necked mountain sheep, one of hundreds of rock panels.

There's some great nothingness in the 60-mile stretch between Wellington and Green River. At times it seems as though you've stumbled upon the craters of the moon. The rather faceless Book Cliff Mountains run east into Grand Junction, Colorado, and provide coal deposits that are used by the local industry. This area looks like badlands where dinosaurs dragged along.

Canyon Country to Green River

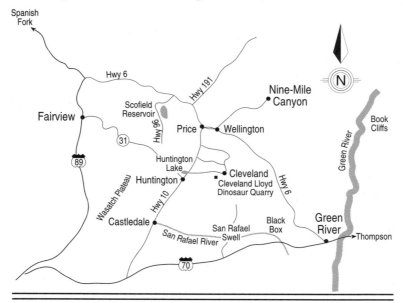

Spanish Fork

Hwy 6

Hwy 191

Nine-Mile Canyon

N

Book Cliffs

Fairview

Scofield Reservoir

Hwy 96

Price   Wellington

Green River

31

89

Huntington Lake

Wasatch Plateau

Huntington

Cleveland

Cleveland Lloyd Dinosaur Quarry

Hwy 6

Hwy 10

Castledale

San Rafael River

San Rafael Swell

Black Box

Green River

Thompson

70

Approximately 16 miles north of Green River is the gravel road 29 miles long to the Buckhorn Flat Well Junction and the San Rafael Swell. After what seems like a longer drive than it actually is, you reach Green River.

Green River started as a mail relay station between Ouray, Colorado and Salina, Utah. Now it's a base for river runners, melon lovers and others who might happen along to this sparsely inhabited stop along Interstate 70. It's named for the Green River, which starts in the Wind River Mountains of Wyoming before joining up with the Colorado River south of here. The town is known, in addition to being a truckers' stopover, for producing the world's best watermelons.

Appropriately seated on the Green River is the **John Wesley Powell River History Museum**, 885 East Main St., Green River, UT 84525, ☎ 801/564-3526. The museum tells the history of the many moods of the canyon country carved by the mighty rivers as well as a little insight into explorer John Wesley Powell. A former geology professor at Illinois Wesleyan, Powell was first a war hero who lost his right arm in a battle. That he was able to navigate these difficult waters is further evidence of his steely strength. Respected for his ability to work with the Ute Indians, his expeditions of the Green and Colorado rivers in 1869 and again in 1871 were invaluable to future explorers.

East on I-70 towards Colorado is a must-see canyon chock full of Indian ruins. Take the Thompson turnoff north of town, cross the railroad tracks and continue about three miles to the **Sego Canyon ruins**. The rock art represents a cross-section of Barrier Canyon-style art that dates back to the year 500 BC, 1,000 year-old Fremont art and traditional Ute art. Bug-eyed alien-looking people, snakes, buffalo and ghost-like figures line the walls. An evocative site in a haunting setting.

VERNAL

Vernal is a cool little town having gained a spirited injection from all the sports people who have come for clean waters, bountiful fishing and still affordable living. Poised for a boom, it has been discovered by senior citizens too, landing as number 100 on the list of best small towns in America. It's the kind of place that *Outside Magazine* would, and probably already has, embraced.

The locals take a humorous look at their legacy, the dinosaur, and you'll see comic renditions of him all over town, at campgrounds, mini-golf courses and car rental agencies.

Downtown Vernal is a fun, roughly 10-block-long strip with period neon on the movie theater and a 7-11 diner. It has fun little gift shops downtown and a solid museum. The **Utah Field House of Natural History**, 235 East Main St., Vernal, UT, 84078, ☎ 801/789-3799, boasts a dinosaur garden along with comprehensive mineral exhibits.

It smells of eucalyptus, potions and all things wonderful. At **A Boutique**, 45 South Vernal Ave., Vernal, ☎ 801/789-2433, owned by Patsy Sardiner and Shirley Freestone, glassware, cards, and cherubs remind one of the holidays.

Glass teardrops catch the eye and suddenly you're wandering into a pottery, card and stained glass emporium known as **Trailway Art Shop**, 65 East Main, ☎ 801/789-9220, to buy tasteful Utah-made gifts. On the eastern outskirts is the suburb at **Naples**, which has a few good antique stores along the highway before greater Vernal.

DINOSAUR

Many million years ago, there was a flash flood or some other tumultuous occurrence that trapped a dinosaur colony living near present-day Green River into the surrounding canyon. Earth and water conspired to entomb this pack of dinosaurs in a sandbar where they would have remained indefinitely had intrepid paleontologist Earl Douglass Ford not spotted eight tail bones of a brontosaurus sticking out of the earth during the summer of 1909. During the next 15 years, he was to excavate 1,000 tons of bones, most of which had been preserved in pristine state.

This real-life Jurassic Park sits on the Utah/Colorado border in **Dinosaur National Monument**, Box 128, Jensen, UT 84035, ☎ 801/789-2115, or 4545 Highway 40, Dinosaur, CO 81610. (Colorado's headquarters has no fossils at its visitor center.)

Obviously, the monument offers far more than just footsteps from the past. At Dinosaur you can find solitude, scenery and, of course, all those bones.

About 17 miles east of Vernal, via Hwy. 40 and Hwy. 149, is the infamous quarry and an excellent museum, which hints at the domination these fascinating beasts had 150 million years ago. The quarry is where dinosaurs were actually entombed in their mud mausoleum and is where more than 1,600 bones were excavated from an ancient river bed. Past joins the present in a kind of surreal Stone-Age-meets-Space-Age experience. There are brontosaurus bones, a reconstructed allosaurus and the hump-backed stegosaurus.

Woodrow Wilson established Dinosaur National Monument as an 80-acre preserve in 1915. In a 13-year period, more than 350 tons of bones were shipped to the Carnegie Museum in Pittsburgh.

The park is diverse in many ways. It's the meeting place of the desert, Great Plains and Uncompaghre cultures and has been occupied in one form or another by humans for more than 9,000 years. Dinosaur National Monument is biologically diverse, as well. The Yampa and Green rivers meet here and the water courses helped carve through these rugged canyon lands. It's a rough, tough land, with temperature extremes and sparse vegetation.

Dinosaur is a good place to see a golden eagle or a peregrine falcon, but visitors are usually enticed by the prospect of seeing all those bones.

Plenty of rewards are available to the first-timer in a very short period of time. Although a week is necessary to see the park for all its worth, it is possible to gain the essence through only a day trip.

The monument's wild lands, including the confluence of the two rivers, were annexed to the park in 1938. They remain best seen by river. A permit is required for boating either river in Dinosaur and is doled out on a lottery basis. ☎ 970/374-2468 for an application.

Vehicular access to the park is available from both the Colorado and Utah sides. From Hwy. 40 in Colorado, six miles east of the town of Dinosaur, is monument headquarters and the visitor's center. That's the start of the road to Harper's Corner.

In a few miles you'll pass Plug Hat Butte and Blue Mountain. The road continues to weave towards the monument, straddling the Utah/Colorado state line en route to Harper's Corner.

At the **Canyon Overlook** and picnic area is the rugged country of the rivers, which twist and wind through goosenecks. Those interested in geology will see examples of Uintah quartzite and Weber sandstone. Continue to the trail's end and take the hiking path to enjoy views of the Green River, which may really be rumbling at this point. To the north is Wild Mountain, which well-describes the area and the nearby fabled rapids of the Gates of Lodore.

Echo Park Campground and a 13-mile side trip on the unimproved road to **Echo Park** is a turnoff from the Harper's Corner scenic drive. **Echo Park Road** plunges deep into the monument's heart. It features prehistoric rock art, views of the two rivers and landmark Steamboat Rock. Between the historic Chew Ranch and Echo Park are the **Pool Creek petroglyphs** which, strangely enough, are very different from the park's other petroglyphs. **Whispering Cave** may also be seen from this route.

The Gates of Lodore, accessible from Hwy. 318 west of Maybell, Colorado, is tough to reach but worth the effort. Considered one of the most beautiful stretches of the Green River, its red canyon walls are sprinkled with lodgepole pine and fir trees. **Lodore Canyon** is packed with churning rapids boasting names like Hell's Half Mile and Disaster Falls. Take the short trail to the overlook and watch the river run.

That very same Hwy. 318 will take you across the Green River on a swinging bridge where waterbirds can be viewed.

Yampa Bench Road is 25 miles one-way and impassable when wet. It sidles alongside the Yampa River, offering great views before it meets up with the Green. The road can be accessed from Echo Park of Hwy. 14 at Elk Springs in Colorado.

Those coming in from Utah should start at the quarry, turn left at the junction and head towards Split Mountain, a popular put-in place for river runners. Along the way is a marker telling the story of the Green River Valley. At Split Mountain Campground turn left and drive down to the river. Near the boat ramp is a John Wesley Powell Memorial marker.

Tour of the Tilted Rocks is the name of the self-narrated 22-mile round-trip drive. Pictographs and prairie dogs, Split Mountain, and the Elephant Toes Butte may be spotted from the paved road. Pick up a copy of the *Tour of the Tilted Rocks* brochure for more information.

A side journey to **Josie Morris' cabin** in the Cub Creek Valley is well worth the effort. The remains of Josie's homestead, located behind Split Mountain, demonstrate her self-sufficient and industrious nature. Runoff and springs provided her essential water. A chicken coop and fruit orchard provided food. Morris' cattle were kept in natural corrals, the steep box canyons with near-vertical walls. More well-trod these days than in Josie's heyday, the area still emits a calm aura.

There are other options from the Utah entrance. **Island Park Road** to Rainbow Park meanders past colorful badlands and follows on the other side of Split Mountain. At McKee Spring are some of the park's best petrolgyphs: huge, human-like figures etched into the sandstone cliffs. To reach the Island Park Road, follow Brush Creek Road five miles towards Vernal after leaving the monument. Then go 16 miles northeast.

Pets must be leashed and carefully monitored for heat prostration and dehydration in this deceptively harsh climate. Winter days here can hit 40° below when cold settles into the basin and there are scalding 104° days in July. Oddly enough, most visitors choose to come in the heat of summer, rather than waiting for better weather that accompany the wildflowers of spring and fall colors.

Dinosaur's offerings are many and the the question remains: What secrets or other species lie in these lands, frozen in time by calamity or some other fate?

Uintah Basin & High Uintahs Wilderness

The Uinta Mountains (basins and landforms may be spelled Uintah) run east-west from Brown's Park near the Colorado border to the Kamas area east of Park City. The mountains have gained a sort of notoriety for their east-west heading, unusual but not unique in the lower 48 states. The earliest inhabitants were probably the Ute Indians.

It's an area of high mountains and alpine basins filled with more than 500 lakes and thick stands of conifers. Headwaters for four of the state's major rivers, the basin provides critical habit for moose and mountain lion, among other creatures. Hunters manage to bag their prey with little effort and can do so almost without leaving their cars or trucks. Fishers have a heyday in the high altitude lakes.

ATV users may enjoy the **Yellowstone ATV Trail**, covering about 30 miles of varying terrain in the canyon 10 miles north of Altamount.

To keep the area from being loved too much, Congress in 1984 established the **High Uintah Wilderness**, which bans motorized vehicles. Hiking and horseback riding remain the best mode of transport. This is where you'll find Utah's highest mountain, 13,528-foot **Kings Peak**.

Farmers and ranchers work the lands on either side of the mountains. Guest ranches cater to hunters, families and others who need to get away. There are rumors of rich gold veins in the hills, but you won't see the pragmatic locals out there looking to get rich quick.

If approaching from US 40 in the south, don't be dismayed by the drab brown mountains that appear to hide the high peaks. Behind the foothills lie the rugged wilderness and some classic, rustic hunting and fishing resorts that are best described as dude lodges on the edge of the wilderness.

The most popular access route to the High Uintahs is via Hwy. 150, through the town of **Kamas** to **Mirror Lake**. En route you'll pass Castle Peak, Provo River Falls and a smattering of lakes near Mt. Watson before reaching the 10,687-foot summit near Bald Mountain. From there, the road descends to sheer Mirror Lake. Fly fishers may want to stop and drop a line in the Provo River, which the highway parallels for much of its route. At times this 33-mile drive is very busy, but the traffic thins out as you continue towards Wyoming.

On the eastern edge of the Uintahs cuts the **Drive Through the Ages**, which takes off north of Vernal on US 191 and culminates approximately 40 miles later at Flaming Gorge. It is a geological timeline with plenty of turnoffs and opportunities for day excursions. The road is quite windy straight out of Vernal with more than a dozen switchbacks in just nine miles.

Steinaker Lake State Park, a popular boating and picnicing place, is five miles north off Hwy. 191. Another five miles in the same direction takes you to the unusually shaped landforms and the crimson sandstone ships which lend their name to **Red Fleet Reservoir** and a camping area.

Past a homely open pit mine, the road continues to wind up the hill leaving behind the cedars for sagebrush, pine and aspen.

Enter **Ashley National Forest** at the top of the rise. Aspens and spruce appear at higher elevations. Near the 8428-foot summit of the pass is the eastern boundary of the Uintah Mountain Range.

There is the **Stringham Cabin Historic Site** and then back-to-back campgrounds, **Red Springs** and **Lodge Pole**, within the next five miles as you descend to the Flaming Gorge turnoff. If it's fall, the roadsides will likely be lined with hunters. The road continues six miles from Greendale Junction to **Flaming Gorge Dam**.

Adventures abound at turnouts along the highway to **Flaming Gorge**. If you have a sturdy vehicle, take a left onto the **Red Cloud Loop** (18 miles north of Vernal) and head into the pines for caving, camping and views of 12,000-foot mountains such as Leidy Peak.

The fishing is said to be good in Big Brush Creek, which runs past the Brush Creek Cave. It's about a half-mile from the road.

There is a campground at **Kaler Hollow**, 10 miles past the turnoff from Hwy. 191. Kaler Hollow was a government camp in the 1930s.

Just three miles past the campground is the turnoff to **Oak Park Reservoir**, where fishing and camping facilities are available. Ashley Creek wanders next to the road. A steep descent into Brownie Canyon follows after Lookout Point.

The loop continues into the old town of **Dry Fork,** one of the Ashley Valley's early settlements. In another 2½ miles is the exit for **McConkie Ranch** and **Indian petroglyphs**, an impressive display in an area known for its rock art. The Red Cloud Loop eventually returns to Vernal near the county park.

About halfway between Vernal and Flaming Gorge, on the east side of the highway, is the detour to **Diamond Mountain** and the **Jones Hole Hatchery.** Diamond Mountain's name comes from a famous hoax that was perpetuated in the 1870s by two men, John Slack and Philip Arnold, who claimed there were plentiful diamonds in this gulch.

After investors sunk their monies into a $10 million mining corporation, what was unearthered was anything but precious. Apparently the diamond finders had planted some native South Africans gems in the gulch, but the natural land was not abundant with riches. Arnold was said to have returned the money to the investors while Slack fled without a trace.

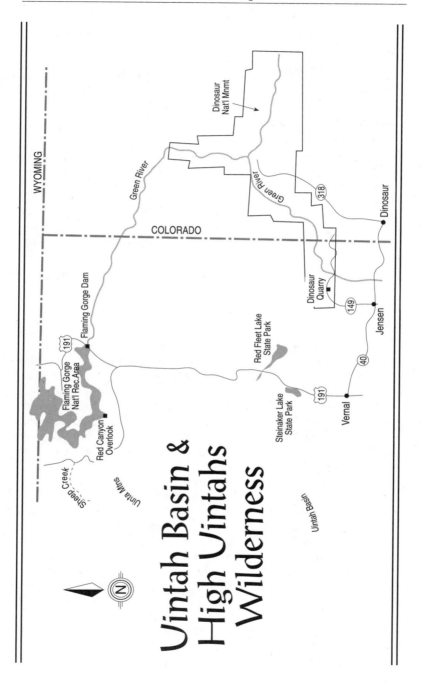

Continuing across the plateau past the turnoff to Crouse Canyon and Brown's Park is the descent into **Jones Hole**. The dramatic drive, offering views of the Green River and Dinosaur National Monument, dips down about nine miles to the fish hatchery where trout are bred for stocking streams, reservoirs and lakes in the tri-state area. The ambitious may take the hiking trail down to the Green River.

Access to the foothills of High Uintahs Wilderness Area is available from paved and unpaved routes on the northern and southern ends. Once inside the wilderness, travel must be completed on foot or horseback. There area is known for its backpacking. (See page 67.)

For information on the Uintah Basin contact **Duchesne County Area Chamber of Commerce**, 48 S. 200 E. Roosevelt, UT, ☎ 801/722-4598. The US Forest Service has an office on West Highway 40 in Roosevelt, UT, ☎ 801/722-5018.

FLAMING GORGE

Call it Flaming Gorgeous for the blazing red cliffs and crimson sunsets. Adventurer/explorer/renaissance man John Wesley Powell, who made his first expedition through this section of the Green River way back in 1869, is credited with having bestowed the enchanting name upon the gorge.

The damming of the Green River created a 91-mile reservoir, perched on the Utah/Wyoming border. It provides hydroelectric power and water storage to seven states. After six years of construction, a 502-foot dam was completed in 1964, with the **Flaming Gorge Recreation Area** established four years later. These days, Flaming Gorge, which is managed by the US Forest Service, sees more than two million visitors per year.

The geology is as interesting as you'll find anywhere. On the northern end of the Colorado Plateau, Flaming Gorge shares some of the same biological characteristics as the Grand Canyon and Zion national parks. Located halfway between Yellowstone and Canyonlands, it also has elements of Rocky Mountain habitat, borne out in the lodgepole pines that dot the neighboring Uinta Mountains.

Cliffs, canyons and lush forests characterize the heavier-used Utah side of the lake. Farther north in the desert-like badlands of Wyoming are low hills dotted by shrubs.

Lake activities are best confined to summer and fall. Winds can whip through here seemingly on a moment's notice, creating serious waves and substantial headaches for boaters. The lake's headwaters, which start in the Wind River Mountains of Wyoming, achieve only a tepid status at their warmest. Swimmers (more truthfully, splashers) dip into the cool waters only during the height of summer. There are swimming beaches at **Lucerne Valley** and also at **Sunny Cove**, north of the dam near Mustang Ridge Campground.

In the dead of winter, it's not usual for the lake to freeze over and diehard fisherman, toasty beneath their moveable shanties, dangle their lines. Why endure a January afternoon on the lake? The 51-pound record trout gives an idea.

Unlike Lake Powell, whose views are most satisfying from a boat, Flaming Gorge offers plenty of attractions for the landlubber.

The best place to start a tour is at the **Flaming Gorge Dam Visitor Center** on US 191, two miles southwest of the community of Dutch John. To get there you'll first cross the protractor-shaped **Cart Creek Bridge**, an engineering marvel unto itself. Guided tours of the dam are offered during the summer, with self-guided tours available other times of the year.

Dutch John is one of two towns providing services to the recreation area. It was established in the late 1950s to house construction workers building the dam and still has the sparse look of a government town. There is an airport, gasoline, a small camp store and, in the summer, a tackle shop.

From Dutch John you can either follow the Green River's spillway below the dam, to the **Little Hole Recreation Area** (a popular fly fishing hole), or cruise northwest up to **Antelope Flat**, where nice views of the Flaming Gorge cliffs may be had. Farther north, on US 191, it's not unheard of to see roaming packs of wild horses.

Looping back past the dam and Cedar Springs Marina is **Swett Ranch Historic Site**, a half-mile north of the intersection of Highways 191 and 44. A pioneer homestead circa 1909, Swett Ranch has a woodshed, granary, workshop/barn and root cellar, most of which are still in their original locations. The site is open weekends from Memorial Day to Labor Day, but visitation is limited to preserve the historic buildings. If starting your tour on water, **Cedar Springs Marina** is the closest spot to the dam. In addition to a full-service marina, it has boat trailer parking and two campgrounds. There are two other marinas, one near Manila, and one at Buckboard Crossing, Wyoming.

The Red, Hideout, Kingfisher and Horseshoe canyons are most appealing to pleasure boaters not only for the spectacular scenery but the protection from high winds these areas afford. In the open and exposed sections of the lake, whipping winds can make for big waves.

Back on shore, Highway 44 roughly follows the watercourse upstream. At the intersection with Hwy. 191, head west towards Manila and look for the turnoff to **Red Canyon**. Here you'll find easy access viewing of Flaming Gorge's heart and soul. Stair-stepped cliffs and cardinal-red benches rise directly from the water below. A level walkway allows everyone in the family to enjoy maximum viewing pleasure.

From Red Canyon Junction, the road veers away from the gorge as it sidles along the edge of the Ashley National Forest, where numerous little streams and creeks beckon to fly fishermen and women. Rolling hills border the rock and, at times, one is reminded of the ocean bottom history of this land.

If time allows, take a detour at Elk Park to the **Ute Lookout Tower**, the first fire tower in Utah. Two miles down the road is Browne Lake, and approximately 13 miles beyond is Spirit Lake, where cabins and a restaurant operate during the summer.

There's a spur to the **Sheep Creek Geological Area**, which showcases different layers and formations of rock from towering spires to smooth sandstone cliffs. The area is famous for wildlife viewing, offering sightings of tropical migrants like warblers. Big Spring is fed from a cave and is a Kokanee spawning spot. It's a land of dogwood trees, streams and, as its name would suggest, sheep.

From the Sheep Creek Loop, turn north towards the town of **Manila**, where the open sage hills present an entirely different landscape. Located 34 miles from the dam, Manila has an airport and other services for vacationers, such as two groceries, a smattering of diners and a US Forest Service information center. Eight miles north is the **Lucerne Valley Marina**, which draws not only boaters but, strangely enough, pronghorn antelope.

Returning back towards the dam, a stop at **Dowd Mountain Overlook** and picnic area for awesome views of the spindly canyon below is highly recommended.

Scenic, unspoiled **Brown's Park** is 25 miles east of the dam via Hwy. 191 and the maintained gravel road known as Clay Basin Creek that dips for about two miles into steep Jesse Ewing Canyon.

Here, in addition to one of the West's remaining remote outposts, is the historic John Jarvie property. A cluster of Jarvie's century-old buildings remain, including a blacksmith shop, stone house and corral built from hand-hewn railroad ties.

INFORMATION SOURCES

Information sources abound. The Bureau of Reclamation operates the dam and the US Forest Service runs the recreation area. As aforementioned, reams of material are available in the visitor's center at the dam. Alternately, try:

District Ranger's Office, US Forest Service Office, Box 279, Manila, UT 84046, ☎ 801/784-3445.

For the **BLM John Jarvie Site**, call ☎ 801/789-1362.

Adventures

Northern Utah is ripe for adventuring. In this seemingly dry land, boating possibilities are plentiful in Flaming Gorge National Recreation Area and Dinosaur National Monument. Reservoirs speckled along Hwy. 40 beckon to pleasure boaters and fisherman, while the Great Salt Lake is a surprisingly good place to sail.

Trails abound in the High Uintah Wilderness, along the Wasatch Front and even in unexpected places like the Great Basin. Mountain bikers can choose from the rolling hills of Cache Valley to the single-track trails near Park City.

The possibilities are as great as the contrasts of red rock to turquoise water. Before setting out on any adventure, make sure you're adequately prepared with current maps, a first aid kit and plenty of water.

On Foot

SALT LAKE CITY & ITS CANYONS

Roll out the state capitol and land in scenic City Creek Canyon. In just four miles you can ascend 2,000 vertical feet to the City Creek Meadows.

The **Brighton Lakes Trail** starts behind the Brighton Lodge in Big Cottonwood Canyon. This self-guided nature trail is good for the whole family.

Okay, maybe this is cheating a little bit, but if you ride the **Snowbird Tram** to the summit of **Hidden Peak** you can meander along the ridgeline with little effort. Alternately, take the trail down Peruvian Gulch and pass the rock walls and cliffs that you'd probably ski in the winter. Maps are available at the resort in Little Cottonwood Canyon.

The steep trail to **White Pine Lake** starts about five miles up Little Cottonwood Canyon and gains more than 2,000 feet in 3½ miles.

The flat 15-mile **Perimeter Trail** connects Hailstone to Rock Cliff at Jordanelle Reservoir. Access at press time (it may improve in the future) was via the frontage road through the Keatley Mine and up a short gravel road.

OGDEN & THE GOLDEN SPIKE

The **Indian Trail** offers excellent views of steep, slender Ogden Canyon. The footpath starts on the east end of 21st St. in Ogden and, after winding through oak, fir and spruce trees, finishes 4.6 miles later in Ogden Canyon.

Beus Canyon starts easy and ends steep as it ascends up the western slope of Mt. Ogden. The views from this seven-mile (one-way) hike extend west beyond the Great Salt Lake and to the lush river valleys of the east. The hillsides are chock full of wildflowers during the summer. Start the hike at the east end of 4600 S. Street. **Locals warn:** beware of rattlesnakes!

The trip up **Ben Lomond Peak** is seven miles one-way, but relatively easy. Start from the North Fork Park Campground and gear up for the 23 switchbacks ahead. Mountain bikers share this trail with you.

There is a self-guided 1½-mile walk along the **Union Pacific** and **Central Pacific Railroad** grades at Golden Spike. Pick up trail guides at the Big Fill Walk parking area.

LOGAN, CACHE VALLEY & THE NORTHERN WASATCH

The two-mile **Crimson Trail** starts at Guinavah Campground, approximately 6½ miles northeast of Logan via Hwy. 89. It follows the south side of the China Wall section of Logan Canyon. There are steep sections along the route and some loose rock. The trail may also be reached from the Spring Hollow Trailhead.

Wind Cave Trail, just 1.3 miles one-way, also showcases part of the China Wall geologic formation. This trail starts on the north side of Logan Canyon across from the Guinavah-Malibu Campground. You may see fossils along the route to the cave. Rattlesnakes in the area are common.

A trip to Logan Canyon wouldn't be complete without a visit to the **Jardine Juniper**, estimated to be several thousand years old. The 4.4-mile trail starts 12 miles up Logan Canyon on Hwy. 89 on the north side of the highway. Park at the Wood Camp Campground.

The **Lakeside Trail** meanders 4.2 miles from the Bear Lake Marina to Ideal Beach. The paved trail, which runs alongside Bear Lake, draws many runners and cyclists, too.

The **Naomi Peak Trail** winds through meadows full of wildflowers en route to the highest point in the Bear River Range. Take the Tony Grove turnoff 19.2 miles from Logan and follow the seven-mile road to the lake. The trail itself is about three miles long.

A hike in the **Wellsville Mountains** starts south of Mendon off Hwy. 23. It's two miles to Stewart Pass from the watering trough starting point. You'll pass tiny Coldwater Lake and maple and aspen trees en route. An additional 1½ miles of hiking will bring you to Stewart Peak.

Climbing

Climb on the sunny or the shady side of the street in **Logan Canyon**, northern Utah's newest hot spot. North- and south-facing cliffs start at 4,500 feet. There are more than 275 limestone and quartz routes. The best climbs are within 15 miles of the mouth of Logan Canyon, between First Dam and Temple Fork. But word is getting out and favorite routes can be crowded on weekends.

The Long Wall is on the right side of the canyon above Bridger Campground. The hike up an open scree slope to the black cliff face takes over a half-hour. This face also goes by the name Hamburger Hill.

The Promised Land starts at Mile Marker 378 and is a two-rope climb. It is very steep and can be difficult.

There are over 30 climbs in the area called **Fucoidal Quartzite**, located at Mile Marker 383.2.

Adventure Sports, 51 South Main St., Logan, UT 84321, ☎ 801/753-4044, has quality climbing gear, recommendations and a climbing wall.

A locally published book, *Logan Canyon Climbs*, is available at shops and the tourist bureau for $10. (No author is given, but it appears to be written by Tim Monsell.) It lists the climbs in detail.

GREAT SALT LAKE

There is a nine-mile backcountry loop road covering much of the northern section of **Antelope Island**, with a three-mile spur open to hikers, bikers and horseback riders.

A nice easy path that sidles along the northwestern shore is the **Lakeside to Bridger Bay Trail**. The three-mile, one-way trail offers views of Stansbury Island and the Lakeside Mountains.

Lady Finger Point is a quarter-mile trail along a ridge overlooking Buffalo Bay.

If you only have time for a short jaunt, make sure it's up to **Buffalo Point**. The trail starts behind the gift shop, climbs rather steeply for several hundred yards, then flattens out as it wanders around huge rocks. Catch the sun setting over the lake, as colors bounce off the Stansbury and Promontory mountains.

Climbing

Big and Little Cottonwood Canyons draw seasoned climbers to their rugged glacier-carved canyon walls. **Snowbird Ski Area** has a climbing wall and series of competitions for climbing's elite.

The mid-summer Sports Festival draws climbing's elite to The Bird. There are all sorts of sports at this outdoor festival, which takes place annually in July. The actual date changes each year. The pinnacle of the Snowbird event remains its invitational climbing competition where past winners compete on the 12-story Cliff Lodge wall. Climbers of all abilities can contend in this event.

A mountain biking race tests riders who wheel their way up, then descend the rocky slopes of the Snowbird Ski Area. Meanwhile, the latest athletic gear is showcased in an on-going two-day sports exposition at the Snowbird Event Center. Call ☎ 801/742-2222 for information.

BONNEVILLE & MOUNTAINS

In the Deseret Peak Wilderness section of the Stansbury Mountains, **Mill Fork Trail** offers a pleasant climb through the trees. It skirts the circumference of Deseret Peak before splitting

into the **South Willow** and **Deseret Peak trails**. The trail winds
about 3½ to 4 miles over a saddle to South Willow. From 11,031-foot
Deseret Peak you can see into Antelope and Hickman canyons. The
dirt road that squeezes past narrow vertical walls en route up to
the Loop Campground. It is recommended only for heavy duty
cars.

In the Deep Creek Mountains south of Wendover and Gold Hill
there is good hiking around the mineral rich **Ibapah Peak** and
Haystack Peak. The higher peaks have bristlecone pine and alpine
characteristics. The Granite Creek area receives the heaviest use.
The best route up Haystack Peak is through Indian Farm Canyon.

PROVO & THE SOUTHERN WASATCH

There's good reason why the **Mt. Timpanogos Trail** is so
popular – it's convenient and it's gorgeous. Limestone and quartz
are dominant in the glacial formations that make up these cirques.
Reach the trailhead from the Alpine Loop Road to the village of
Aspen Grove. The trail starts in aspen trees before opening up. The
final stretch is steep. The alternative route up Timpanogos, the
Timpooneke Trail, is longer but easier.

Considered strenuous, the **Nebo Bench Trail** leads to the summit
of Mt. Nebo, highest peak in the Wasatch. The trail climbs 5,000 feet
in five miles through meadows and forests. From Nephi, turn east
on Hwy. 132 about six miles to the Nebo Salt Creek Road. After
three miles, bear left to the trailhead.

PRICE TO GREEN RIVER

A fine day hike, the **left fork of Huntington Creek** starts 20
miles southwest of Price via Hwy. 10 and Hwy. 31. Pick up the trail
near the Huntington Creek Campground. There is hardly any
elevation gain as the trail winds alongside Scad Valley Creek.
Views are offered of the Candland and Seeley mountains.

Navigating the Lower and Upper Black Box of the San Rafael
River requires some work and the will to get wet. Start at **Sinkhole
Flat Trail,** whose trailhead is about five miles north of I-70. Detailed
maps are needed to chart this remote route that follows the San
Rafael River as it cuts through sandstone rock.

VERNAL & DINOSAUR

Dinosaurs first walked where tourists now leave their imprint upon the land. There are many trails you can hike without seeing another soul. Dinosaur is not a backpacking park and it has no trail system. It's best to take day hikes and use the beautiful campgrounds.

The topography coupled with the heat extremes mandates you take lots of water. Both short jaunts and longer trips require preparation.

The moderately difficult **Desert Voices Nature Trail** is two miles long and offers sweeping views of Split Mountain and the Green River. Nearby is the **Sound of Silence Route**, on Cub Creek Road, two miles east of the dinosaur quarry, that rewards hikers with uplifted rocks.

Harpers Corner Trail allows expansive views of the deep canyons and is great for almost anyone. The trailhead is at the end of Harpers Corner Scenic Drive.

In Box and Hog canyons, settler Josie Morris lived a good life, as a visit to her old cabin demonstrates. Josie used to keep her livestock here with a simple fence and by utilizing the natural canyon boundaries.

There's an easy, well-trod hike across the parking lot from Josie's place, and other trails meander through the property.

FLAMING GORGE

The **Swett Ranch Loop** starts near a cluster of historic buildings and winds six miles through aspen trees, alongside streams and into open sage meadows. The **Canyon Rim Trail** has it all: Views, wildlife (are moose and elk wild enough for you?) and breathtaking views of Red Canyon. Flat, with only one hill, the five-mile one-way route connects the Red Canyon Visitor Center to the Greendale Overlook, where the wildlife viewing is primo.

The three-mile round-trip hike to **Tamarack Lake** starts from the Spirit Lake Campground. It's a moderate ascent to the lake. By continuing west from here you enter the High Uintahs Wilderness.

Meander along the Green River below the Flaming Gorge Dam on the **Little Hole Trail**, where you're likely to see fishers casting their flies. Access the trail from below the dam spillway off Hwy. 191 or at the Little Hole Recreation Area.

UINTAH BASIN & THE HIGH UINTAS

Some of the state's best day hikes and backpacking are available in the High Uintas Wilderness off Mirror Lake Highway (Hwy. 150). To access from the south, try the Upper Stillwater Reservoir road north of Duchesne or the Moon Lake Road north of Roosevelt. The other main entry point to the area is from Hwy. 191 north of Vernal and Sheep Creek Canyon east of Flaming Gorge Reservoir. Less convenient access is possible through Mountain View and Lonetree, Wyoming.

From Hwy. 150, the heavily used **Highline Trail** takes off two miles north of Mirror Lake and cuts through the heart of the range near 13,528-foot Kings Peak. The ambitious, well-equipped backpacker could conceivably hike near 100 miles and end up near Vernal. Day hikes to destinations like Four Lakes Basin are more common. Start at the trailhead east of Hayden Pass and make the easy cruise to Scudder Lake, then Wilder, Wyman and Packard lakes. Further exploration leads to more peaks and more views.

The **Uinta Trail** to Atwood Basin and Kings Peak starts in the pine and aspen north of Neola. Lovely in the fall, the trail is shared with horses.

Golf Courses

Wasatch Mountain State Park, ☎ 801/654-0532, offers 27 beautiful holes in a splendid setting on the eastern slope of the Wasatch Range. Accessible via Hwy. 224 in the city of Midway.

Park City Municipal, ☎ 801/649-8701, is an 18-hole course located within the city limits.

Ben Lomond Golf Course, 1600 N. 500 W, ☎ 801/782-7754, is a 18-hole public course with short par 4s, but the par 3s are quite demanding.

Monte Golf Course, 1300 Valley Drive, Ogden, ☎ 801/629-8333, is set against the mouth of Ogden Canyon. The nine-hole course is full of rolling hills.

At the 18-hole **Mount Ogden Golf Course**, 3000 Taylor Ave., Ogden, ☎ 801/629-8700, the views are sharp and the greens are tough.

Bear Lake Golf Course, 2176 Bear Lake Blvd., Garden City, ☎ 801/946-8742, has nine holes, a driving range, lessons and club rentals.

Tri-City Golf Course in American Fork, has 18 holes. ☎ 801/756-3594. **Seven Peaks** offers an 18-hole course in Provo, ☎ 801/375-5155.

The **Carbon Country Club**, located on Hwy. 6 between Price and Helper, ☎ 801/637-2388, has an 18-hole golf course that is open to the public. The club is home to the annual Black Diamond Open.

The **Dinaland Golf Course**, 675 S. 2000 E, Vernal, ☎ 801/781-1428 has 18 holes for your golfing pleasure and spectacular views of the Uinta Mountains. Tee times may be reserved a week in advance. Special prices for senior citizens.

Uinta Golf, 560 East 2100 South, Salt Lake City, ☎ 801/487-8233, sells golf equipment and accessories as well as maps of all the golf courses in the state.

· On Water

Though dry and deserty by nature, Utah has many reservoirs and lakes to catch all that precious water as it flows off the mountains.

Flaming Gorge accommodates primarily house boats and power boats. Bear Lake and the Great Salt Lake are well suited for sailboats and whitewater rafters, who may also enjoy stretches of the Green and Yampa rivers. Shorter runs are available in the urban canyons.

SALT LAKE AREA

Big and Little Cottonwood canyons flow west from the Wasatch into south Salt Lake City. Below the mouth of **Big Cottonwood** is a short river run that's best boated in spring. From the old mill to 6200 South there can be large waves. Below that are several bridges that need to be scouted.

The white gold that covers the Alta and Snowbird ski areas all winter and spring becomes liquid gold as it blasts down **Little Cottonwood Canyon**. Late May and early June are the best times to boat through this glacial canyon.

PARK CITY

One of the first federal water development projects in the West, **Strawberry Reservoir** was created by the Soldier Creek Dam. Today this expanse of water, located 23 miles southeast of Heber, holds up to 17,000 acres. Be aware of large waves that can develop quickly when winds kick up. Pick up maps at the huge visitors center. During the summer, there are evening campground programs offered at the Strawberry Bay Amphitheater.

There are boats ramps at Strawberry Bay, Soldier Creek, Renegade Point and Aspen Grove. The Strawberry Bay Marina has all the basic supplies and services, including dry boat storage and a café.

Jordanelle Reservoir, Box 309, Heber City, UT 84032, ☎ 801/649-3602, opened in June of 1995 and immediately exceeded the expectations of the state parks department. Jordanelle's proximity to a large population center meant crowds and too much trash during its inaugural season. Hopefully, those glitches have been worked out because it is a lovely, well-situated facility.

At the **Hailstone Recreation Site**, on US 40 between Park City and Heber, there is an eight-lane boat ramp. Hailstone also has a visitor center, day-use cabanas and three separate camping areas. At the **Rock Cliff Recreation Site**, two miles west of Francis on Hwy. 32, the water is more shallow and not really suitable for launching power boats. Rock Cliff has a nature center, group-use pavilions and three walk-in campgrounds.

Deer Creek State Park, Box 257, Midway, UT 84049, ☎ 801/654-0171, is set in the scenic Heber Valley and is favored by sailors because of its predictable afternoon winds. Fishing is popular, too. There is a concrete boat launching ramp, restrooms and a 32-unit campground.

OGDEN & THE GOLDEN SPIKE

The **Ogden River** below Pineview Reservoir is mellow below the dam, but quickly gains momentum. Too narrow for rafts and often rocky, the river gets large waves and rapids ranging from Class II to V. Four-mile-long **Pineview Reservoir**, Hwy. 39, Huntsville, is tucked into the bucolic Ogden Valley. The earth and rock dam was constructed in 1937. Boating, swimming, windsurfing and fishing are popular here. There are two boat ramps.

Willard Bay State Park, 650 North 900 West, Willard, UT 84340, ☎ 801/734-9494, is a 9,900-acre freshwater inlet on the Great Slat Lake flood plain. The facility is best suited to boating, waterskiing and fishing.

LOGAN & CACHE VALLEY

The **Logan River** offers a continuous stretch of Class II to Class V rapids for kayakers. It may be easily scouted by car because the road sidles alongside. The Rick's Spring to Preston Valley Campground run is eight miles.

Bear Lake has 172 square miles of water for motor and sailboats. Species of cisco and cutthroat fish are found here and nowhere else in the world. There's also a Loch Ness-type monster that's been rumored since pioneer days!

The lake straddles the Utah-Idaho border. The **Bear Lake State Park Marina**, 1065 N. Bear Lake Blvd., Garden City, UT ☎ 801/946-2717, has a ramp, slips, campsites, showers and a visitor's center.

South on Hwy. 30 is **Blue Water Beach**, where Bear Lake Sails (☎ 801/946-8611) rents boats on site.

Rendezvous Beach State Park, near Laketown, has 1¼ miles of sandy beach and is a good place for launching smaller boats. Rentals are available here through Bear Lake Sails. There are three campgrounds accommodating more than 130 sites and RV hook-ups available.

At **Eastside**, 10 miles north of Laketown, there is fishing, boating and, due to the fact that the water depth drops to 200 feet, scuba diving.

The lake crosses into Idaho where you'll find the **Eastside State Park**, which has a boat ramp, camping, hookups, and North Beach, a day-use area. Also across the Idaho border is the not-to-be-missed **Bear Lake National Wildlife Refuge**, spanning more than 17,000 acres of grasslands, marsh and water. Sandhill cranes, white pelicans, Canadian geese and many different species of duck summer here.

Bear Lake Sails Boat Rental, ☎ 801/946-2900 (Rendezvous Beach) or 801/946-8611 (Blue Water Beach), has motorboats, sailboats, canoes, Jet Skis and more. Free lessons are also offered with each rental.

GREAT SALT LAKE

Floods during the high-water years of the early 1980s wreaked havoc upon the beaches of the **Great Salt Lake State Park**, which is accessible off Interstate 80. The marina gets plenty of use, with sailors heading towards Antelope and Stansbury islands.

Antelope Island's marina is near the end of the causeway. Sailboats are the vessel of choice and boaters cruise in Bridger and Buffalo bays as they look towards the Promontory Mountains or back east at the Wasatch Front.

PROVO AREA

The **Provo River** may be boated with a raft or kayak. The river is mellow from Soapstone to the North Fork. You'll have to portage here to get around the logjams. The upper section is primarily Class II. The six-mile run from Deer Creek Reservoir to the first diversion jam is easy, scenic and popular, featuring views of Mt. Timpanogos. The river picks up steam near the Bridal Veil Falls and there's a good drop at Canyon Glen Park.

Contact **High Country Tours**, ☎ 801/645-7533, for raft trips.

Surrounded by the Cedar Valley Mountains on the west and the Wasatch to the north and east, **Utah Lake State Park**, 4400 West Center Street, Provo, UT 84601, ☎ 801/375-0731, is a 96,000-acre lake used frequently by speedboats, sailboats, canoes and kayaks. Four boat ramps, a 30-acre marina and 78 slips are available. Originally called Provo Boat Harbor, the facility was donated to the Utah Division of Parks and Recreation in 1967. It was totally rebuilt following a flood in 1983. Located five miles west of Provo, off I-15.

PRICE TO GREEN RIVER

The **San Rafael River** slices through the Swell of the same name. Rafts only are recommended on the upper section, though smaller boats can savor the sheer walls and occasional sand waves. One of its tributaries, **Cottonwood Creek** west of Castle Dale, is considered among the state's toughest runs for kayaks. **Straight Canyon** is mostly Class IV. Dam controlled, the run is typically best in June. **Ferron Creek** is another boatable tributary of the San Rafael River.

Millsite State Park, Box 1343, Huntington, UT 84528, ☎ 801/687-2491, is a secluded 400-acre lake at the mouth of Ferron Canyon. There is a sandy beach, boat launching ramp and campground.

Scofield State Park, Box 166, Price, UT 84501, ☎ 801/448-9440, is a 2,800-acre lake on Hwy. 96. In the winter it serves as a base for snowmobiling and cross-country skiing.

VERNAL

Steinaker Dam and Reservoir outside Vernal has sandy beaches, boating and a good waterskiing lake located halfway between two national parks. **Red Fleet State Park,** 10 miles north of Vernal on Hwy. 191, has boating, watersports and fishing amid a picturesque backdrop of red slickrocks. Dinosaur tracks were recently discovered in the area.

House and speed boats are most popular at **Flaming Gorge Reservoir,** but be aware that wetsuits are needed by waterskiers throughout most of the year. Inconsistent winds make it undesirable for sailors and boardsailors. For canoeists and kayakers, the short side canyons of **Red Canyon** and the lakeside campgrounds are most friendly.

There are three marinas at Flaming Gorge offering mooring, fuel, limited repairs and some rentals. **Cedar Springs,** Box 337, Dutch John, UT 84023, ☎ 801/889-3795, is a full-service facility leasing pontoon, ski and fishing boats. Located two miles west of the dam. Lucerne Valley Marina, Box 10, Manila, UT 84046, ☎ 801/784-3483, rents houseboats, pontoon and fishing boats. South of Green River, Wyoming is the **Buckboard Marina,** Box 100, Green River, WY 82935, ☎ 307/875-6927, offering motorized and ski boats. Rates drop before mid-May and after mid-September. Boat ramps are located at Sheep Creek Bay, Antelope Flat and Mustang Ridge.

Watercraft may also be rented through **Blue Mountain Motor & Marine,** 2217 N. Vernal Ave., Vernal, UT 84078, ☎ 801/789-5661; **Flaming Gorge Recreation Services,** Box 367, Dutch John, UT 84023, ☎ 801/885-3191; and **York Motor Sports,** 591 S. 1500 W., Vernal, UT 84078, ☎ 801/789-7463.

Whitewater river trips are the best way to enjoy the **Dinosaur National Monument.** A permit is required for all boating in the monument, on both the Yampa and the Green. Apply for one before Feb. 1 by calling the River Ranger office at ☎ 970/374-2468. Permits are doled out on a lottery basis.

River trips in Dinosaur can range from a day to a week. An outstanding journey for experienced river runners is the 45-mile trip through the colorful **Gates of Lodore**, (the name is borrowed from a poem by Sotheby), taking out at Split Mountain. In high water, the canyons of Lodore's Disaster Falls and Hell's Half-Mile are gnarly. The Green River's releases are controlled at Flaming Gorge Dam.

A popular day trip is **Split Mountain Gorge**, nine river miles with a few fun rapids and the shortest canyon in the monument. The stretch between Rainbow Park to Split Mountain, dominated by mostly Class II and III rapids, sees a half-millions visitors annually.

Kayakers love to play in the **Moonshine** and **Schoolboy rapids**. Below the gorge, the waters mellow until revving up again in Desolation Canyon

The free-flowing **Yampa River**, running from extreme western Colorado into eastern Utah, is only runnable early in the season and is usually too low by mid-July. The trip through Dinosaur National Monument cruises through the hanging sandstone cliffs of Yampa Canyon. **Warm Springs Rapid** provides the most excitement; in high water it's been rated a Class V rapid. It's 72 river miles from Deerlodge Park to Split Mountain, or about a three- to five-day river trip.

Farther down the **Green River**, south of Vernal on Hwy. 88 near the town of Ouray, is the start of Desolation and Gray canyons. Boaters make their way past the tamarisk trees to the Sand Wash ranger station for the put-in.

The 95-mile trip first run by John Wesley Powell in 1869 begins in mellow waters and slowly builds momentum. The Fremont Indians left behind rock art near Flat Canyon, Indian granaries at Florence Creek. Mother Nature created a likeness of Egyptian Queen Nefertiti near Swasey Beach. By the time you hit Green River, you will have boated through 60 Class III rapids. But wildwater isn't the attraction here; people opt for this trip to enjoy the historic old cabins and skiffs alongside the banks and the legends about outlaws hiding in the hills.

During the height of summer, be prepared for some scalding hot days on the cold river. Be sure to bring along insect repellent when boating these sections of the Green River.

As is true in downtown Moab, river outfitters line the main drag of Vernal looking for your business. Most offer mild and wild trips of varying length through Dinosaur National Park and into Desolation Canyon.

Dinosaur River Expeditions is at 540 E. Main St., ☎ 801/781-0717. They feature oar boats. There's also the **Green River Boaters** at 68 East Main St., Vernal, ☎ 801/789-5535, and the family-owned **Hatch River Expeditions** at 55 East Main St., Vernal, ☎ 801/789-4316.

Adrift Adventures, Box 192, Jensen, UT 84035, ☎ 801/789-3600, offers one- to five-day raft trips in Dinosaur on the Green and Yampa rivers. Adrift also has Indian rock art and fossil tours.

Chapoose River & Trails, Box 141, Ft. Duchesne, UT 84023, ☎ 800-854-4364 specializes in multi-day trips through Green River's Desolation Canyon.

Boaters who need a shuttle service should check in with the **Flaming Gorge Lodge**, US 191, Dutch John, UT 84023, ☎ 801/889-3773, and **River Runners' Transport**, 126 S. 1500 W., Vernal, UT 84078, ☎ 801/781-1180.

FISHING

Fishing regulations are published in a booklet from the State of Utah Natural Resources, available at US Forest Service offices and other tourist information places.

The record cutthroat trout was taken out of Strawberry Reservoir. This is heaven for the recreational fisherman and "The Berry" is known for its production of trout.

Park City Fly Shop, ☎ 801/645-8382, is a full-service operation also offering guided winter trips.

The **Causey Reservoir**, on the South Fork of the Ogden River, is trout central. Rainbow, brown and brook may be captured here. Rocky Mountain whitefish are plentiful in the **Weber River** and smallmouth bass are stocked in the lower Weber west of I-15.

Largemouth bass, catfish, yellow perch and tiger muskie make their home in **Pineview Reservoir.**

Bear Lake is best in early spring and late fall for trophy cutthroat trout fishing. It's also the place for ice fishing. The Cisco fish spawn at the end of January and early February on the lake's eastern shore or near the rockpile at Ideal Beach. Wind breaker huts are available by phoning ☎ 801/946-3226.

The **Logan River** receives less people-pressure than other places on the Wasatch Front despite its convenient location along the highway.

To paraphrase Forrest Gump's pal Bubba, there are enough shrimp in the Great Salt Lake to fry, dice, boil, bake, bread or barbecue. Shrimping companies regularly haul prodigious loads out of the water.

The *Salt Lake Tribune* rated the Provo River tops for trout fishing in the state. Contact **Provo River Outfitters**, 51 West Center, #304, Orem, UT 84057. There are also fly-fishing schools offered at Sundance.

Fishing is bountiful at **Utah Lake**. Walleye, white and black bass and several species of panfish are swimming in Utah's largest freshwater lake. There is a fishing area accessible to those with handicaps. The park is five miles west of Provo.

Deer Creek Reservoir, west of Heber City, offers anglers many choices, including bass, perch, walleye and, of course, trout.

There is excellent fishing in **Uintah Canyon**, north of Neola on Hwy. 121 and in **Moon Lake**, about 40 miles northwest of Roosevelt.

The **North Fork of the Duchesne River** is another hot spot.

Falcon's Ledge, Altamount, ☎ 801/454-3737, is a high-end lodge offering fly fishing.

Flaming Gorge is full of Kokanee salmon, Mackinaw and smallmouth bass. As the reservoir straddles the Utah-Wyoming state line, fishing licenses are required for both states.

Fly fishers have long-known about the wonders of Red Canyon in Flaming Gorge. **Little Hole Recreation Complex**, located seven miles below the dam on the Green River, is another hot spot for day trippers. The section of the **Green River** between the dam and Little Hole sees the most anglers. There is lighter use between Little Hole and Brown's Park and even less between Brown's Park and the Gates of Lodore.

An upside to the cold winters which can settle in is the thick slab of ice that typically forms on **Flaming Gorge** making it ideal for ice fishing. Head to the Wyoming side where the ice is thicker.

Cedar Springs Marina, Box 337, Dutch John, UT 84023, ☎ 801/889-3795, offers guided fishing trips to Flaming Gorge and its environs. So does **Flaming Gorge Lodge**, US 191, Dutch John, UT 84023, ☎ 801/889-3773 and **Lucerne Valley Marina**, Box 10, Manila, UT 84046, ☎ 801/784-3483.

Mike Tafoya came from Anaheim to open his fishing haven, **Double-Haul Flyfishing**, 110 W. Main St., Vernal, ☎ 801/781-1333. He offers knowledgeable advice, custom rods and flies, and guided trips.

Dinosaur imposes fishing regulations for everyone over the age of 12. On the Colorado side, that limit is 15 years old. Catfish are most likely caught in the Green; Jones Hole is best for trout fishing; and in Jones Hole Creek, only fly fishing is allowed.

On Horseback

Homestead Resort Sleigh Rides, Midway, ☎ 800/327-7220, and the Park City Sleigh Company, ☎ 800/820-2223, offer sleigh rides with Western dinners or rides on your own. Soak in the hot springs after your ride.

At the Bear Lake Livery and Chuckwagon, ☎ 801/946-8623, a team of Clydesdale horses will do the pulling. Dinner from a Dutch oven is followed by Western entertainment.

Bear River Outfitters, 500 Loveland Lane, Fish Haven, ID 83287, ☎ 801/752-4183, has horses for trail rides and hunting. Bear Lake Buggys, 100 North Bear Lake Blvd., Garden City, ☎ 801/946-2980, has horse-drawn sleigh rides by reservation.

Beaver Creek Trail Rides, Hwy. 89, ☎ 801/753-1076, offers guided tours and trail rides. The stables are a half-mile east of Beaver Mountain.

Horse-drawn sleigh rides to the 800 head of elk may be taken in the day or evening at Hardware Ranch Elk Refuge, ☎ 801/245-3131. Dinner packages and all-you-can-eat nights are popular. Located in Blacksmith Fork Canyon, 18 miles east of Hyrum.

The Stables at Sherwood Hills, ☎ 801/245-5054, has horseback rides, supper rides and hay rides. Situated in Sardine Canyon between Brigham City and Logan.

The Highline Trail is popular for horseback riding in the High Uinta area. Access the trailhead off the Mirror Lake Highway.

Antelope Island has a weekend round-up of bison every fall; it's a rare opportunity to enjoy seldom-seen parts of the island. Equestrians assemble at the historic ranch to begin their round-out of the furry beasts. Contact: Antelope Island State Park, ☎ 801/773-2941.

The Shaman Lodge, 3645 W. Gordon Creek Road, Price, UT 84501, ☎ 801/637-7489, has guides, horses, all meals and equipment for outfitting trips.

San Rafael Trailride, Box 7, Elmo, UT 84521, ☎ 801/653-2372 offers pack-trips, day rides and catered Dutch-oven dinners.

U-Bar-Ranch in Neola, ☎ 801/645-726, operates from May through October and has six guest cabins. You may stay as long as you choose. Packages available for singles, families and corporate retreats. Located on the Uintah River, the ranch offers all-day and multi-day horse rides into the High Uintahs Wilderness.

Customized rides are available through the All 'Round Ranch, Box 153, Jensen, UT 84035, ☎ 801/789-7626. There are also four-and six-day cowboy horseback adventures that come complete with instruction.

The J/L Ranch, Box 129, Whiterocks, UT 84085, ☎ 801/353-4049, has backcountry trips into the High Uintahs and special photography outings. Many cabins come with full kitchens. The horse ranch is surrounded by public lands, which means easy access to wilderness areas.

Horses may be rented at the **Red Canyon** and **Flaming Gorge** lodges for use on the system of trails that winds through the national recreation area. The **Sheep Creek Ranch** has trail rides into the geologically astounding Sheep Creek area.

On Wheels

SALT LAKE CITY

Road riders will enjoy the 15-mile climb up **Big Cottonwood Canyon** to Brighton. Begin at Wasatch Boulevard and 7200 South. Bikers are welcome to cruise around the ski area, but there's no lift access. Neighbor **Solitude** does have lift-served terrain as does **Snowbird Ski and Summer Resort** in Little Cottonwood Canyon, where clinics and special events make it a fun place to ride.

Easily accessible from downtown, **City Creek Canyon** is a pleasant six-mile getaway through cottonwood, pine and maple trees. There are restrictions on the trail during high-traffic periods, so check before setting out.

Try **Guthrie Bicycle**, 731 E. 2100 South, Salt Lake City, UT 84106, ☎ 801/484-0404, for your biking needs.

Fishlips, Box 2203, SLC, UT 84110, ☎ 801/467-8911, builds handmade framesets and sells other high-quality parts.

PARK CITY

Daly Bowl, the canyon atop Main Street, remains a favored place (as long as it continues to fend off development). Start at the bottom of Main Street and climb up Daly Avenue, following a dirt road until the trail begins.

Deer Valley has more than 20 miles of trails for lift-served biking. Silver Lake Village on the upper mountain is the likely starting place. Neighbor **Wolf Mountain** offers 10 miles of trials on the ski area.

The Rail Trail, a converted railroad line, begins at Prospector Square in Park City and continues 25 miles northeast to Echo Reservoir. Plans call for it to eventually connect to Jordanelle Reservoir. At Jordanelle, there is the 15-mile Perimeter Trail connecting the park's two main camping areas.

There's a good ride along **Strawberry Ridge,** which peers into Strawberry Reservoir.

Jans Mountain Outfitters, 1600 Park Avenue, Park City, UT 84060, ☎ 801/649-4949, has rentals and a full line of quality equipment.

OGDEN & THE GOLDEN SPIKE

Easy and pretty, **Wheeler Canyon** starts below Pineview Reservoir on the south side of Hwy. 39. Follow Wheeler Creek along the shrub- and wildflower-covered route past little waterfalls and pools. Connect to the Upper Wheeler Canyon/Maples Trail at the Maples Campground.

A steep trail starting from **Snowbasin's** upper parking lot passes under the Becker and Wildcat lifts and winds up toward lower Ogden Bowl. Steep and rocky as it climbs toward the Mt. Ogden, you'll enjoy views DeMoisey Peak up high and Pineview Reservoir below.

The two-mile **Green Pond Trail** takes off from the Snowbasin Ski Area's upper lot. Follow the dirt road out of the lot to the south. This is considered a difficult trail. A much easier ride is the 18-mile loop around **Pineview Reservoir.**

At the **Bear River Migratory Bird Refuge** there is a 12-mile loop around the marshes. While you'll have to share the road with the occasional car, pedal power allows you to creep up on flocks of egrets and herons.

Riding conditions are ideal around **Golden Spike National Historic Site.** Because of their remoteness, be sure to bring a tire repair kit and at least one spare. The west and east auto tours at Golden Spike, which climb up and over the gravel railroad grade, are a viable option for a shorter day.

Those interested in a longer ride should consider the **Transcontinental Railroad** backcountry byway. The 90-mile narrow roadway that follows the old Central Pacific Line on the northern shore of the Great Salt Lake is loaded with trestles, culverts and waterside views. The trail starts west of Golden Spike and terminates near the Nevada border at Lucin.

Bingham Cyclery, 3259 Washington Blvd., Ogden, UT 84401, ☎ 801/399-4981, carries all the top brands and has high-end rentals.

LOGAN, CACHE COUNTY

The Cache Valley is kind to cyclists, with country roads, quiet highways, and dirt trails in bucolic settings with plenty of peaks as backdrop. There's a hardcore cycling contingent here who enjoy the steep climbs into the Wellsvilles and the ride through **Logan Canyon**. The serious don't miss the double century ride to Jackson, Wyoming.

The 18-mile ride along the **Blacksmith Fork River** is a popular trip. Road riders will end at Hardware Ranch, but mountain bikers may ride 10 more miles and complete the **Left Hand Fork Loop**.

The **Upper River Trail** in Logan Canyon follows the river to the third dam, while the **Green Canyon Ride** climbs six miles up to the Mt. Naomi Wilderness boundary.

The Bridgerland Tourist Bureau puts out a good map. **Sunrise Cyclery**, 138 N. 100 E. Logan, UT 84321, has been serving the area since 1981.

BONNEVILLE & THE GREAT SALT LAKE

Start in Tooele and ride into the Oquirrh Mountains on the 11-mile **Middle Canyon Trail**. Views include most of northern Utah, the Deseret Peak Wilderness and the unsightly copper mine. Nearby Butterfield Peak has scores of single-track trails. The other canyon overlooking Tooele is Settlement Canyon, which features the **Bear Trap Loop**.

Mountain bikers come to Antelope Island in spring because the snow melts early. The 15-mile **backcountry loop trail** doesn't have much shade. **The Lakeside Trail** to Bridger Bay is a flat, easy trail. Moonlight bike rides are held annually on Antelope. Call ☎ 801/773-2941 for dates.

PROVO & SOUTHERN WASATCH

Wasatch Mountain State Park has 24 miles of relatively flat trails. A spur climbs Cascade Springs Road to Mt. Timpanogos, eventually returning via the steep Snake Creek Road. The shaded 12-mile **Provo River Parkway** connects Provo Canyon to Utah Lake via local parks. Pavement, dirt and gravel greet the cyclist along the way. At the lake you'll find the **Utah Lake Loop**, which winds around on a frontage road. Start at the Bridal Veil Falls exit in Provo Canyon.

Squaw Peak Road rollercoaster-rides its way on the asphalt and dirt between Provo and Hobble Creek canyons. Get ready for a wild downhill ride near the end. Access it seven miles north of Provo, via Hwy. 89.

Try the **Bike Peddler**, 24 East Main, American Fork, ☎ 801/374-5322, for your cycling needs.

PRICE TO GREEN RIVER

The **Skyline Drive**, with views of canyons, mountains and spectacular Mt. Nebo, is a fine bike ride along the Wasatch Plateau. Ride the 100-mile trail in several sections.

In **Nine Mile Canyon** there are two popular trails, **Sheep Creek Canyon Trail** (the easier of the two) and the **Harmon Canyon-Prickly Pear Loop**, which lives up to its name. Take your mountain bike into the maze of canyons inside the San Rafael Swell. **Black Dragon Canyon** is a 16-mile ride on dirt roads. Access the trailhead from a dirt road off I-70, about 15 miles west of Green River.

VERNAL, FLAMING GORGE & DINOSAUR

South of Vernal are BLM lands filled with lots of dirt roads. Take your bikes out and ride in the open desert. You're frequently on your own out here, so bring plenty of water and, of course, a repair kit.

The **Upper Bonanza Loop** is entirely paved. It starts at Highway 45, four miles west of Vernal. Ride seven miles south of Vernal to the Green River. Another nine miles further brings the rider to a junction. Turn left and soon the road will be paralleling the river, where you might spy some sandhill cranes hovering near the water or antelope on the hillside. Return the 13 miles to Vernal. Best taken in the spring or fall as there is little shade.

The East Park Loop is a 32-mile intermediate ride on paved, dirt and gravel roads. Find it by taking Hwy. 191 north from Vernal to the Red Loop Road. Start your ride at the junction of Forest Service Road #018. Ride on this paved road the 9½ miles to the East Park Campground. Here, the road turns to gravel and starts meandering over rolling hills and into Trout Creek Park. The route crosses Big Brush Creek before going another four miles back to the start.

There is a **mountain biking festival** in early August near the shores of Flaming Gorge. The rest of the year locals head to the **Gonzo Loop** near Swett Ranch for six miles of mostly double-track riding through aspen trees and open sage meadows.

The rolling road out past the **Ute Fire Lookout Tower** welcomes bikers to pedal the two miles to Browne Lake or another dozen to Spirit Lake. Accessible from the Sheep Creek Loop, or drive to the fire tower for a shorter trip.

Sheep Creek Canyon Loop covers 19.7 miles of primarily paved road, taking riders past the historic Dowd grave site on into narrow Sheep Creek Canyon. Start at Sheep Creek Gap and Forest Service Road #218. At the Big Spring, water spurts from a canyon wall. Ahead are views of the Uinta Fault, which can be seen as the road switches back up the hill. At the highway intersection turn left and cruise along until you see the splendid views of Sheep Creek Bay. There's a long downhill with several switchbacks before the round-trip is completed. Avoid in the summer when traffic on Hwy. 44 may be high.

Mountain biking is prohibited within the confines of Dinosaur National Monument, but road bikes are welcome on the paved roads.

The route through **Dinosaur National Monument** and **Chew Ranch Road** begins in the parking lot of the entrance station. It is an intermediate ride that rolls 24 miles on pavement and dirt. Follow the main road in the park 5½ miles across the Green River, then another 2½ miles farther. Take a right and go past the #10 marker. Up the hill to the right is a dirt trail, then a wood fence and finally a Dinosaur Boundary marker. A half-mile later the road forks; go right. Head down the hill, across the creek, and up another hill for a total of five miles until you reach the pavement again. Back on Hwy. 40, ride until the intersection at Jensen and the finish.

Dinosaur River Expeditions, 540 East Main, Vernal, UT 84078, ☎ 800/247-6197, takes cyclists on mountain bike tours of Dinosaur National Monument, the Flaming Gorge area and into the Uinta Mountains.

Bicycles may be rented at the **Flaming Gorge Lodge**, 155 Greendale, Dutch John, UT 84023, ☎ 801/889-3773, and at the **Red Canyon Lodge**, Hwy. 44, Dutch John, UT 84023, ☎ 801/889-3759.

HIGH UINTAHS

Off the Mirror Lake Highway is the popular **Beaver Creek Trail**, a single track that skirts through the aspen trees along the base of the Uintas. Many fat tire riders like to cruise along a jeep road that climbs to Piute Creek and offers views of the Kamas Valley.

Bicycle Utah, Box 738, Park City, UT 84060, ☎ 801/649-5806, publishes an excellent free guide book to the state's trails.

Hunting

Pleasant Valley Hunting Preserve, Box 3736, Myton, UT 84052, ☎ 801/646-3194, is a 3,200-acre hunting preserve with guides and dogs available to guests. Similar services are offered by **LC Ranch**, Box 63, Altamount, UT 84001, ☎ 800/354-8729.

Bison hunts thin the herd on **Antelope Island**. Nine lucky permit holders can pay a flat fee that includes five days of guiding, meals and "clean it, skin it, load it." Odds in bagging a permit for this once-in-a-lifetime hunt have been as good as 1 in 10. The hunt takes place in December. **Information:** ☎ 801/773-2941.

No hunting is allowed in Dinosaur National Monument, but along Hwy. 191 between Vernal and Flaming Gorge, hunters have a heyday and barely need step from their cars to find elk and deer.

Licenses: Utah Division of Wildlife Resources, Northern Regional Office, 515 E. 5300 S., South Ogden, UT 84405.

On Snow

Northern Utah is known world-wide for its voluminous snow, wide-open ski slopes and cheap (when compared to the rest of the West) lift tickets.

The **Wasatch Range**, stretching from near Idaho to south of Provo, offers consistent snow, long seasons and the convenience of being near metropolitan areas. Utahns claim it is one of the snowiest places in the world. Decide for yourself: Area totals range from 350 to 500 inches, large by any yardstick. The incredibly light snow is formed as moisture dries out over the deserts of Nevada and western Utah before smacking into the mountains.

While skiing has long been a draw for tourists, the coming of the 2002 Winter Olympics has given all the resorts the impetus to add spit and polish to their facilities. But, with the exceptions of Deer Valley and, to an extent, Park City, you won't find the slickness of facade that characterizes many ski resorts in the Rocky Mountains and Lake Tahoe. You also won't find the smorgasbord of nightlife available at Vail, Aspen or Tahoe, either. An après ski cocktail, hearty meal and hot tub are usually the extent of the evening's entertainment.

Another advantage the resorts of northern Utah have over their better-known competitors is convenience to an airport, with nearly all the resorts located within an hour of Salt Lake International.

A bias still exists at many resorts against snowboarders, although it's possible these bans could be slowly lifted in the coming years. Park City, for example, will host the Olympic snowboarding events, but in the meantime is prohibiting boarders from its slopes!

LITTLE COTTONWOOD CANYON

Alta Ski Area, Box 8007, Alta, UT 84092-8007 (☎ 801/742-3333; snow report, ☎ 801/572-3939), has so much to offer – steeps and open cruising, trees and, of course, powder. Intermediates can learn the finer points of powder skiing on wide, open slopes from the acclaimed Alf Engen Ski School, now under the direction of P.J. Jones. Meanwhile, experts savor precipices like High Rustler and the Baldy Chutes. Terrain is rated 25% beginner, 40% intermediate and 35% advanced.

Alta boomed with a silver strike in 1865 and was once a raucous party town. In a typical powder season, the lights go out early as tired bods, well-seasoned by the hut tub, surrender to the land of nod. In contrast to its gleaming, modern next-door neighbor Snowbird, Alta offers a mellow experience. A congenial, family atmosphere is created by visitors who opt to stay in this 19th-century mining town turned ski village. A distinct advantage to staying in one of the handful of on-site lodges is that you don't get skunked on big powder days when the canyon may close due to avalanche danger. Lift tickets are always among the cheapest in the nation, but then again, the resort continues to offer only slow-speed chairs (six doubles, two triples and four surface tows).

Snowboards are not allowed. As they like to say, "Alta is for skiers." Senior citizens earn free passes when they hit a ripe 80, not the typical free-for-70 program.

As vertical and powder-blessed as Alta, its neighbor in Little Cottonwood Canyon, **Snowbird Ski and Summer Resort**, Snowbird, UT 84092 (☎ 800/453-3000; snow phone ☎ 801/742-2222, ext. 4285), offers excellent steep skiing, bowls, and moguls plus a wide beginner area called Big Emma. Bassackwards is a fine cruiser, located where most of the intermediate level skiing is in the Mid-Gad region.

Snowbird is best enjoyed by advanced and expert skiers who savor precipices like Great Scott, the Gad Chutes and Wilbere Bowl. If you are an intermediate, don't commit to the tram unless ready for a challenge (or be relegated to Chip's Run, the bailout trail that can be a traffic jam). The quick tram speeds you to the 11,000-foot summit at Hidden Peak for lap after lap of joy.

Snowbird is a gem of a resort. Launched in 1971 with its avalanche-proof buildings, high tech tram and modern village design, it was soon considered among the world's most sleek and contemporary resorts. Its spare, utilitarian structures are, somehow, timeless. Come April, Snowbird is a big party as conditions range anywhere from slush bumps to huge dumps. Ski bums flock here well into May. Snowboards are permitted.

Utah Powderbird Guides, ☎ 801/649-9739, flies skiers deep into the helicopter-accessed powder.

Ski up to five resorts in one day by taking a guided tour with the **Utah Interconnect**, 150 West 500 South, Salt Lake City, UT 84101, ☎ 801/534-1907. The guide program takes skiers on backcountry trails between Big and Little Cottonwood canyons and the Park City area. Shorter tours are for less hearty souls. Prices include a well-deserved private luncheon and return transportation to the resort where you started.

BIG COTTONWOOD CANYON

Friendly, family-oriented **Brighton**, Star Route, Brighton, UT 84121 (☎ 800/873-5512; snow phone, ☎ 801/359-3283), lets kids ski free in this pretty alpine resort 30 miles southeast of Salt Lake City. Its 8,750-foot base elevation is highest in the Wasatch.

Two mountains feature 60 runs with a well-balanced mix for different abilities. Beginners have huge choices of terrain off the Mary lift. Intermediates head to Snake Creek or Millicent areas, the latter serving up the cruiser Evergreen. Experts make the hike to

Mary's Chutes (when open) for some sky-high vertical runs. Snowboarding is welcomed.

Brighton is a great place to learn to ski because the prices are among the region's cheapest. Virtually ignored by advanced and expert skiers, Brighton can hold secret stashes of powder long after the snow is played out elsewhere.

Solitude Ski Resort, Box 21350, Salt Lake City, UT 84121-0350 (☎ 801/534-1400; snow phone, ☎ 801/536-5777), gives just what you'd expect on spacious slopes in Big Cottonwood Canyon. The backyard ski area for Salt Lake area residents since 1957, Solitude offers plenty of powder, a 2,047-foot vertical drop and rarely crowded trails. Intermediate runs comprise half the lift-served terrain. The best choices include Inspiration and Sunshine Bowl, located off the Eagle Express lift. The choicest expert skiing is in Solitude Canyon off the Summit chair, one of seven lifts at the resort. Novices have the short Link and Moonbeam II lifts almost to themselves.

For even more Solitude, try the off-piste, double-diamond skiing in Honeycomb Canyon. There you'll find chutes with names like Voltaire, Black Bess and Black Forest. The only drawback is the long runout back to the base.

Development of a base village during the mid-1990s means there's finally some on-site lodging. Solitude sells a combined area ticket with neighbor Brighton. Snowboarding is allowed here only Monday through Thursday.

The Solitude Nordic Center, ☎ 801/534-1400, between Solitude and Brighton, has 20 km of trails and snowshoeing opportunities through the trees. Ski to the Yurt and enjoy some fine dining.

PARK CITY

The charm of historic **Park City**, PO Box 39, Park City, UT 84060 (☎ 801/649-8111; snow phone, ☎ 801/647-5335), the only real ski town in Utah, is paired with a mountain that features excellent bowl skiing, fine intermediate cruisers and a guaranteed early season thanks to an efficient snowmaking system. Home to the US Ski Team and the 2002 Winter Olympics, Park City boasts a 3,100-foot vertical drop on 89 trails. Park City is one of three resorts in Parley's Canyon, east of Salt Lake City.

Modern-day Park City, first called the Treasure Mountain Resort, features a great variety of trails and several classic steep bowls, including a stunner named Jupiter. A dozen chairs and gondolas serve the undulating terrain that seems to fall off the aspen-lined mountain from every angle. There are fine cruisers off the King Con Chair and Pay Day, which is also open for night skiing, remains a classic intermediate run. You can't help but love the Mid-Mountain Lodge, restored to its original splendor and relocated three-quarters of a mile from its old location by the Pioneer Chair Lift.

Look for the ban on snowboarding to loosen as the Olympics draws nearer.

Park City Powder Cats, ☎ 800/635-4719, offers guided cat skiing for all abilities. The fee includes a day of deep snow, transportation and lunch.

Deer Valley, PO Box 1525, Park City, UT 84060 (☎ 801/649-1000; snow phone, ☎ 801/649-2100), invented the ski valet and brought resort opulence in this country to a new level. Double-medalist from the 1952 Olympics, Stein Eriksen lends an air of refinement through his joint roles as director of skiing and ambassador of goodwill. He's behind the Stein Eriksen Lodge, where the family's good taste is evident in everything from the decor to the shopping to, most notably, fine dining.

Three mountains of skiing – Bald, Bald Eagle and Flagstaff – and 2,200 feet of vertical drop are served by 13 lifts and snowcats. Lower Bald Eagle Mountain has gentle terrain for beginners and lower intermediates. Olympic mogul events will be staged here on Know You Don't and the slalom races will be run on Big Stick.

The summit of Bald Mountain, at 9,400 feet, provides great views of downtown Park City. Perseverance and Mayflower Bowls are where you'll find some challenging skiing. Bald Mountain also features some long cruisers. When there's new snow, head up here for some fine tree skiing. Flagstaff Mountain has bowls and glades for different ability levels. The next planned area of expansion, the multi-faceted Empire Canyon, may be sampled via snowcat.

Deer Valley's skiing has always been overshadowed by its elegant reputation and emphasis on luxury services. For those willing to pay the premium, there are refined accommodations aplenty. Deer Valley is known for its good grooming on and off the slopes. Deer Valley prohibits snowboarding.

Oldtimers may remember when **Wolf Mountain**, 4000 Park West Drive, Park City, UT 84060, ☎ 800/754-1636, was called Park West. But the mountain gained an identity of its own a few years back and with it came the re-naming of its lifts for threatened species like spotted owls and golden eagles.

Wolf offers 64 trails on three skiable peaks. Terrain is rated 24% beginner, 34% intermediate and 42% expert. In contrast to its neighbors in Park City, Wolf welcomes snowboarders to its five half-pipes and snowboard park, which features rails, hips and log slides. There is also a specially dedicated snowboard school. Whereas Deer Valley caters to the wealthy, Wolf Mountain is friend to the no-frills skier. Night skiing is also available.

Homestead Cross-Country Ski Centers, Box 99, Midway, UT 84049, ☎ 801/654-1102, has 12 kilometers of groomed trails for beginners. Located 20 minutes south of Park City.

The White Pine Touring Center, on the Park City Golf Course, ☎ 801/649-8701, has 18 kilometers of nordic skiing. Tours into the Uinta Mountains are available.

Utah Winter Sports Park at Bear Hollow (☎ 801/649-5447), five miles from Park City on Hwy. 224, has four ski jumps (the grandaddy of them all is a proposed 360-foot jump), a half-pipe hill for snowboarders, a bobsled and luge track. There is also an area for freestyle training. The park has gentle jumps and instruction for beginners. During the summer, watch Olympic hopefuls practice their freestyle maneuvers into a pool.

OGDEN AREA

Powder Mountain, Box 450, Eden, UT 84310 (☎ 801/745-3772; snow phone, ☎ 801/745-3771), has so much open skiing (a total of 4,000 acres) that the lift-served terrain must be augmented by a snowcat and shuttle bus. Powder, which benefits both from storms that hit the Wasatch and fronts rolling in from southern Idaho, lives up to the highest expectations. Average annual snowfall is 500 inches! The bulk of the terrain is rated intermediate, but experts will certainly be challenged by the backcountry trails. Night skiing is offered at the Sundown Lift; return in the daytime for views of the Great Salt Lake.

Snowbasin, Box 460, Huntsville, UT 84317 (☎ 801/399-1135; snow phone, ☎ 801/399-0198), site of the women's and men's Olympic downhills and Super G races, will become much more accessible when the new spur from Hwy. 167 is completed. Then it will be an easy drive from both Park City and Salt Lake International Airport. Located 17 miles east of Ogden, through Ogden Canyon and windy State Road 226, the resort owned by the firm that operates Sun Valley Ski Resort bursts with development potential.

Snowbasin sits cradled beneath the rocky summits of Mt. Ogden, the Needles, DeMoisey Peak and Strawberry Peak. It's also located in a snowbelt that can produce 400 inches annually. Up top are great steeps off the Middlebowl lift, which tower to 8,800 feet above sea level. Excellent intermediate terrain is found in the thrilling Wildcat Bowl found near the lift of the same name. Beginners should opt for the Becker and Littlecat chairs. The mountain has a 2,400-foot vertical drop and 1,800 acres of terrain for all ability levels.

On the road to Snowbasin is cross-country skiing. To reach **Maples**, start from the lower parking lot. The three-mile **Green Pond Trail** takes off from the upper lot.

Everywhere you look around Ogden there's skiing. In addition to the three alpine areas are cross-country trails, both tough and easy. The ski to **Ben Lomond** is five miles one-way, with a 4,000-foot elevation gain. Mt. Ogden Park can be a short or long excursion.

Snowshoers and nordic skiers like to meander through the **Ogden Nature Center**, 966 W. 12th St., Ogden, UT 84404, ☎ 801/621-7595, where there are tours and special programs.

Though it sounds like a resort for cross-country enthusiasts, **Nordic Valley**, Eden (☎ 801/745-3511), operates two double chairs serving 16 trails. Prices remain low in order to attract families; kids might especially enjoy the intermediate trail called Charlie Brown! It's near to both Powder Mountain and Snowbasin in the snowy Ogden Valley. Appropriately enough, the closest town, a beauty, is named Eden. Night skiing is a big draw.

LOGAN

Ever hear of **Beaver Mountain**? Didn't think so. Logan's backyard ski area, Beaver, Box 3455, Logan, UT 84321 (☎ 801/753-0921; snow report, ☎ 801/753-4822), offers a respectable 525 skiable acres and three lifts, but remains a quiet, down-home area. That's great for skiers and snowboarders who can take over the 26 runs and three double chairlifts. Beaver has a steepness tougher than its 1,600-foot vertical would belie.

The Seeholzer family has run the resort since 1939. Harry's Dream lift, reaching the 8,800-foot summit, pays homage to its founder and it's where you'll find most of the runs. Beaver has nice open areas and glades, too. Night skiing is available "by arrangement," meaning tons of fun for private groups.

There are groomed trails for nordic skiing in beautiful Logan Canyon. Maps are available from the Logan Ranger District by calling ☎ 801/753-2772.

Outfitter Powder Ridge Ski Touring, 500 W. 3200 S. Nibley, UT 84321, ☎ 801/752-7853, offers backcountry getaways in private yurt huts. Trips venture into the Mt. Naomi Wilderness in the Northern Wasatch Mountains.

PROVO AREA

Robert Redford's love of skiing and the environment come together at **Sundance**, Box A-1, Sundance, UT 84064, ☎ 801/225-4107. Redford bought the former small ski area called Timphaven back in 1969, re-naming it after his best-loved film character. He's gradually made upgrades to this diamond-in-the-rough. Itendures a low elevation (an 8,250-foot summit) but benefits from a bounty of north-facing slopes.

Sundance rests beneath magical Mt. Timpanogas and has 41 trails and 450 acres of skiing. The two peaks that make up Sundance are called Front Mountain and Back Mountain. And now a base-to-summit lift makes it a snap to ski both sections of the area without a lot of hassle.

Front Mountain is where you'll get your feet wet on the mostly intermediate slopes such as Maverick and Outlaw and the handful of green trails near the base. Back Mountain has the steep stuff, such as the gnarly Grizzly Ridge, the wide expanse called Far East and the blue/black Bishop's Bowl. Snowboards are not allowed.

Tastefully appointed cottages and homes line the base of this retreat that's a welcome break from the hustle-bustle of hectic society. The Sundance Institute here helps filmmakers develop their works in a nurturing setting. The facilities are also available for rental by groups. All visitors benefit from the arts on-site as there are film screenings in the Sundance theater every Friday and Saturday night.

The Sundance Nordic Ski Area has 6.2 miles of trails that wind through aspen groves and alpine meadows in an area called the Elk Meadows Preserve.

SNOWMOBILING

Everybody gets out into the backcountry in Utah, even the less physically inclined. Snowmobiles can cover a lot of ground in still pristine country.

Snow-sport enthusiasts interested in exploring the backcountry via motorized transport have many choices in the **Wasatch Mountains**. It is popular in the **Ogden Valley** around Pineview Reservoir and in **Huntsville**.

Snowmobile rentals are available at **Chris'**, 7345 E. 400 S. Huntsville, UT 84317, ☎ 801/745-3542; **High Adventure Rentals**, 2470 N. 750 W. Ogden, UT 84414, ☎ 801/782-7860; or **Big Boys Toys**, 2529 N. Hwy. 89, N. Ogden, UT 84414, ☎ 801/782-6125. There are guided tours to the Hardware Ranch available through **Snowmobile Adventures BCD**, 1240 Harrop St., Ogden, UT 84404, ☎ 801/394-5448.

Up north near Logan Canyon there is the **Bridgerland Trail System**, off Highway 89 east of Logan. Farther up the canyon near Beaver Mountain are the **Beaver Creek** and **Sinks** trailheads. For those with backcountry experience, there is the 220-mile **Great Western Trail** connecting to Yellowstone. Start your trip at Beaver Creek Lodge in Logan Canyon (or add a day to the typically five-day jaunt by starting farther south at Hardware Ranch).

Snowmobilers ride sections of the Great Western Trail north out of Logan Canyon, through southeastern Idaho and into the community of Bone. There, it may be necessary to trailer the snow machines for a short distance. The trail continues outside of Idaho Falls through Harriman State Park and eventually into West Yellowstone.

A map of the trail is being developed. For information on the Utah portion, contact Scott Mehunin at Utah State Parks, ☎ 801/538-7342. For the Idaho section, ☎ 208/334-4180.

The **Beaver Creek Lodge**, 25 miles northeast of Logan on Hwy. 89, ☎ 801/753-1076, and **Bear Lake Funtime**, 1217 S. Bear Lake Blvd, Bear Lake, ☎ 801/946-3200, rent machines.

Highly recommended is the 63-mile loop trail that starts near the **Hardware Ranch** winter-feeding station for elk. The trail traverses Ant Flat, through Monte Cristo, Curtis Creek (to the norht) and then heads back to Hardware. The ranch itself has 150 miles of groomed trails with a guide service available.

At Hardware Ranch, check in with **High Adventure Rentals**, ☎ 801/782-7860. Overnight snowmobile adventure packages, dinner and snowmobile rentals and gasoline service are available through **Hardware Ranch**, ☎ 801/245-3329.

West of Salt Lake City in the Tooele Mountains are the **Middle Canyon** and **Settlement** trails. Both start near the town of Tooele.

Highline Trail (before Flaming Gorge) is a great place to ski.

Cross-country skis may be rented through the **Vernal Athletic Club**, 1180 North Vernal Ave., Vernal, UT 84078, ☎ 801/889-3759.

The **Mirror Lake Trail** complex boasts nearly 200 miles of trails, some of which climb more than 10,000 feet in elevation. Access the main trailhead by taking Hwy. 150 east of Heber. There are trailheads into the Wolf Creek areas at Woodland, Tabiona and

Mill Hollow. During the winter the Mirror Lake Highway is plowed to Soapstone.

Wasatch Mountain State Park is a favored place for snowmobiling. Located just five miles from Heber via Hwy. 40, it offers 70 miles of trails in some of the state's most rugged mountains. From Wasatch Mountain there are trails connecting Pine Creek to Park City, Snake Creek Canyon to Cummings Parkway, the Alpine Loop and American Fork Canyon.

Daniel Summit Lodge and general store, Box 490, Heber City, UT 84032, ☎ 800/519-9969, rents snowmobiles. You'll find it near the starting point for 200 miles of maintained trails.

The Red Canyon Lodge, 790 Red Canyon Road, Dutch John, UT 84023, ☎ 801/889-3759, leases snowmobiles in the Flaming Gorge area.

There is **ice skating** at **Garden City Park** in Bear Lake. For skate rental information, ☎ 801/946-3277. In Logan, spin the light fantastic at the **Merlin Olsen Park**, 300 South East Canter, ☎ 801/750-9877.

In Air

Point of the Mountain, south of Salt Lake City, is an excellent place to learn how to hang glide and paraglide. Experienced pilots enjoy great flights off this flat-topped formation, which allows you to take off and land at essentially the same place.

Glider and airplane rides above the Heber Valley and Park City are available through **High Valley Aviation** in Heber, ☎ 801/654-5831.

Park City Balloon Cooperative, ☎ 801/647-0888, has hot air balloon flights above the old mining town.

Arrow West Aviation, Carbon County Airport, Price, ☎ 801/637-9556, has customized scenic trips to see the San Rafael Swell, Nine-Mile Canyon and the rest of the northern canyon area.

Dinaland Aviation, 830 East 500 South, Vernal, UT 84078, ☎ 801/789-4612, offers charters, scenic flights and river shuttles of the Dinosaur and Flaming Gorge areas.

The **Dutch John Airport** has a 6,600-foot paved runway sitting 6,561 feet above sea level. There are tie-downs and hangar storage.

Flaming Gorge Flying Service, Box 368, Dutch John, UT 84023, provides shuttles from the Vernal and Rock Springs airports, but mostly is a fishing guide service on the Green River.

Hot Air Balloon Rides, Vernal, UT 84078, ☎ 801/789-3432, offers sunrise flights, breakfast and balloon flight combos and first-time flyer certificates. Group rates available for three or more people.

Eco-Travel & Cultural Excursions

Anyone fascinated with the Old West will want to see Eli Anderson's buggy and carriage collection at **Bear Lake Buggys**, Hwy. 89 in Garden City.

Reflections on the Ancients, Box 444, Wellington, UT 84542, ☎ 800/468-4060, offers eco-tours, archaeology insight and photo safaris in the prehistoric landscapes around Price by certified avocational archaeologist Jeanette Evans.

Where to Stay & Eat

Accommodations

SALT LAKE CITY

All over Utah you're likely to find hotel rooms that are typically larger than usual to accommodate those families that are larger than the national average.

Little America Hotel and Towers, 500 S. Main St., Salt Lake City, UT 84101, ☎ 801/363-6781, is a sprawling complex occupying an entire city block. Colonial-style, florally appointed, expansive rooms are welcoming after days on the road. A nice spa plus indoor and outdoor pools are a plus. The lovely lobby with a well-used piano bar are icing on the cake.

Peery Hotel, 110 W. 300 South, Salt Lake City, UT 84101, ☎ 801/521-4300, was built in 1910 for the Peery Family of bankers and merchants. The hotel regained its historic look and feel following a 1986 remodelling. It's conveniently located downtown near the train station and most popular sites.

Inn At Temple Square, 71 W. South Temple St., Salt Lake City, UT 84101, ☎ 801/531-1000, is a first class European inn featuring 90 Queen Anne-style rooms, health services and Crabtree & Evelyn soaps and lotions.

The **Shilo Inn**, 206 South West Temple St., Salt Lake City, UT 84101, ☎ 801/521-9500, has a heated swimming pool and sauna plus a coffee shop on site. Free fruit and continental breakfast are welcomed as is the location, across from the Salt Palace.

PARK CITY & CANYONS

Alta Lodge, Alta, UT 84092-8040, ☎ 801/742-3500, is family run and friendly. Known for having some of the best food in the area, the lodge also features a popular afternoon tea. Its proximity to the lifts is a big plus.

Stein Eriksen Lodge, Box 3177, Park City, UT 84060, ☎ 801/649-3700, is located mid-mountain in the area of Deer Valley called Silver Lake Village. Luxury is the operative word here, as you can get pretty spoiled with the daily newspaper service, comfortable lobby, raoring fire and the old-world Norwegian charm.

The **Cliff Lodge and Spa** in Snowbird, ☎ 801/742-3300, is as luxurious as Little Cottonwood Canyon gets, with large rooms that face either the ski area or the steep, deep canyon. For single or budget travellers, this fine dwelling offers dorm rooms too. Guests have full run of the rooftop pool, whirlpool and fitness center.

All Seasons Condominiums, Park City, ☎ 801/649-5500, are well-appointed one- to three-bedroom units, most of which have great views of the ski area. The **Snow Flower Condominiums**, ☎ 800/852-3101, are situated right on the Park City Ski Area runs.

Set in a historic building in downtown Park City, **The Washington School Inn**, Box 536, Park City, UT 84060, ☎ 801/649-3800, is an upscale bed and breakfast.

The **Yarrow Hotel**, 1800 Park Ave., Park City, UT 84060, ☎ 801/649-7000, is a full-service resort offering all the basic amenities in a convenient location near the slopes. A nice heated pool, whirlpools and sauna are welcome after a hard day on the slopes. Ask about room specials, which seem to be offered frequently.

OGDEN

Ogden Park Hotel, 247 24th St., Ogden, ☎ 801/627-1190, or 800/421-7599, has all the amenities the leisure and business traveller need. Reasonable packages to skiers heading up to nearby Snowbasin are available during the winter. Located a half-block from the hopping 25th St. district and a half-block from the Ogden City Mall.

The historic Radisson Suite Hotel, 2510 Washington Blvd., Ogden, ☎ 801/627-1900 or 800-333-3333, has been restored to its former grandeur and is conveniently located downtown near all the city attractions. Original art was uncovered during the restoration of this spiffy downtown railroad-era inn. Worth a look-see, even if you aren't staying here.

Comfort Suites of Ogden, 1150 W. 2150 S., Ogden, UT 84401, ☎ 801/621-2545, offers large rooms and a continental breakfast. Discount ski passes are available upon request.

Jackson Fork Inn, 7345 E. 900 S, Huntsville, UT 84317, ☎ 801/745-0051, sits in the beautiful Ogden Valley. Ski packages and snowmobile rentals are available to guests.

The Snowberry Inn B&B, 1315 N. Hwy. 158, Eden, ☎ 801/745-2634, is within a snowball's throw of Nordic Valley and Powder Mountain. A little farther away is Snowbasin.

LOGAN

Location, location, location and reasonable prices are key to the Comfort Inn, 447 N. Main St., Logan, UT 84321, ☎ 801/752-9141. Just a mile from the Cache National Forest, 25 miles from Beaver Mountain and a nibble away from those yummy Cache Valley cheese factories, the Comfort Inn offers comfortable rooms, a heated pool complex and facilities for large groups.

Super 8 Motel, 865 South Hwy. 89-91, Logan, UT 84321, ☎ 801/753-8883, is clean and cheap with free HBO.

Beaver Creek Lodge, Logan Canyon (Hwy. 89), ☎ 801/753-1076, is a new hideaway featuring pine beds and sporting activities at your front door.

Inn of the Three Bears, ☎ 801/945-8590, is just a hop, skip and a jump from Bear Lake. Three cozy rooms, a hot tub and afternoon tea are included in this bed and breakfast.

Ideal Beach Resort, 2176 S. Bear Lake Blvd., Garden City, UT 84028, ☎ 801/946-3364, offers two- and three-bedroom condominiums and hotel rooms with queen beds. On site are two heated pools, saunas, a hot tub and tennis courts.

PROVO

The **Sundance Cottages and Mountain Homes**, Hwy. 92, Provo, ☎ 801/225-4107, are appointed in Ralph Lauren-influenced Southwestern-style furniture. In a colony that's clustered yet private, the suites all have gas fireplaces. Larger groups should opt for one of the mountain homes. Free screenings of films from the Sundance Institute are open to all guests.

The East Bay Inn, 1292 S. University Ave., Provo, UT 84601, ☎ 801/374-2500, is a comfortable motel with a Western motif located opposite the town golf course.

Best Western Paradise Inn, 1025 S. Main St., Nephi, UT 84848, ☎ 801/623-0624, has 40 rooms, a sauna, exercise equipment and phones in the rooms. Renovated in 1992.

CANYON COUNTRY TO GREEN RIVER

The **Manti Country Village Motel**, 145 N. Main. St., Manti, ☎ 801/835-9300, has 23 rooms, cable TV, a spa and on-site restaurant.

The **Carriage House Inn**, 590 East Main St., Price, ☎ 801/637-5660, with arguably the best accommodations in town, has free HBO, an indoor pool and Jacuzzi tubs.

Recently renovated **Budget Host Inn and RV Park**, 145 N. Carbonville Rd., Price, ☎ 800-283-4678, has rooms and suites, a heated pool and laundromat.

Robber's Roost Motel, 225 West Main St., Green River, UT 84525, ☎ 801/564-3452, is clean and simple with free coffee in the morning.

VERNAL & DINOSAURLAND

Best Western Dinosaur Inn, 251 East Main, Vernal, ☎ 801/789-2660, is cheery and spotless with a great pool and dino-filled gift shop. Vernal's top spot for lodging.

There's never a shortage of rooms at the expansive **Weston Plaza Hotel**, 1684 West Hwy. 40, Vernal, ☎ 801/789-9550, which has wings spanning each direction from the parking lot.

Red Canyon Lodge, Hwy. 44, Dutch John, UT 84023, ☎ 801/889-3759, has 16 comfortable cabins equipped with queen beds and wood stoves. Some cabins are simple and basic; others are more luxurious.

The other option for on-shore lodging at Flaming Gorge is the **Flaming Gorge Lodge**, 155 Greendale, Dutch John, UT 84023, ☎ 801/889-3773. The lodge is open year-round and offers one-bedroom condos and motel rooms. Located four miles south of the dam and three miles from the Cedar Springs Marina. Pets are not allowed.

The **Spirit Lake Lodge**, 1360 Hallam Rd., Francis, UT 84036, ☎ 801/783-2339, has rustic cabins tucked away in the pines of the Uinta Mountains. The accommodations appeal to the outdoorsman with hiking, backpacking, hunting and fishing just out the door. Open seasonally.

Restaurants

Utah seems to be constantly revising and updating its liquor laws, in spite of the few conservative lawmakers who would prefer that alcohol remain difficult to get. The state's answer to a neighborhood watering hole is a number of private clubs that require a nominal guest membership, $5 at press time, good for two weeks. For longer stays you should buy an annual membership, usually $15-20. Those fees entitle the bearers to bring along guests.

To get around the confusion, ask doormen or maitre d's at restaurants if you can be "sponsored." That allows you to come in on someone else's card.

If you are buying food, there's less of a problem, as most restaurants now can sell wine and mixed drinks with your meal.

Restaurants in rural Utah get a bad rap as purveyors of artery-clogging country meals. But there is some wholesome and sometimes healthful food to be found outside the city centers. A word of advice: while "scones" are sold about everywhere, they are more akin to deep fried sopapillas than the traditional muffin-like cakes.

Some places lack charm because of their size (meant for large groups and families). The great American drive-in, gone in many places, lives on in Utah.

SALT LAKE CITY

Lamb's Café, 169 S. Main, ☎ 801/364-7166, draws the city's power brokers who meet at this old time establishment for breakfast, lunch or an early supper. The counter remains great for single diners. You can't go wrong with the day's special, a sandwich or some comfort food.

At the **Rio Grande Café**, Rio Grande Train Depot, Salt Lake City, ☎ 801/364-3302, *carnitas* and *enchiladas* are the specialty of the house. The Rio Grande is a dress-down art deco-style diner in the downtown Amtrak station. Local's sniff that it's touristy, but the place merits a stop if only to see the photo or art collections.

Red Rock Brewing Co., 254 S. 200 W., Salt Lake City, ☎ 801/521-7446, is handsome, with its modern wood and brick interior. Pizza remains the specialty of the house. You should, of course, order one of the homemade beers.

Café Trang, 818 S. Main, Salt Lake City, ☎ 801/539-1638, serves huge portions of Vietnamese food, such as spring rolls, *saté*, noodle and hot pot dishes at a good value. What it lacks in atmosphere it makes up for in price.

Try the **Bombay House**, 1615 S. Foothill Drive, ☎ 801/581-0222, when you're feeling the urge for some chicken tandoori, *dal*, or basmati rice. Located near the university district.

Kabul, 260 S. Main, Salt Lake City, ☎ 801/355-3653, entices with *lam*, *hummus* and other wonderful middle eastern and Mediterranean spices. The restaurant features good breads in an out-of-the-ordinary experience.

Baci Trattoria, 134 W. Pierpont, Salt Lake City, ☎ 801/328-1500, has a trendy and imaginative menu. For the time being, it is the place to be seen.

The Old Spaghetti Factory, Trolley Square, Salt Lake City, ☎ 801/521-0424. So shoot me, but I still love the dependable food and cheap prices of this chain restaurant.

La Caille at Quail Run, 9565 S. Wasatch Blvd., Sandy, ☎ 801/942-1751, is a pricey French country estate that has withstood the test of time. Some feel it's pretentious, but others call it the most romantic restaurant in Utah. Those frightened away by the dinner prices can splurge instead on Sunday brunch.

Mulboon's (multiple locations around the city) has heaping bowls of shrimp that are included with all dinner entrées. Portions of steaks, chicken, halibut and prime rib are all oversized and the items are a little overpriced to cover all that free shrimp.

Favorite **Brackman Brothers Bagels** has merged with the Einstein chain but remains a good bet at various locations around town.

SALT LAKE CITY

Ruth's **Diner**, 2100 E. Emigration Canyon Rd., Salt Lake City, ☎ 801/582-5807, is an old roadhouse dishing up huge helpings of continental cuisine. A Bloody Mary makes the perfect partner to Sunday Brunch, but *huevos rancheros* and *chile relleno* are good anytime in this renovated trolley car with a unique atmosphere.

PARK CITY & THE CANYONS

Café Mariposa in the Silver Lake Lodge is Deer Valley's premier restaurant. An elegant rustic setting. The menu is always inventive.

Grappa, 151 S. Main St., Park City, ☎ 801/645-0636, serves Italian cuisine and wood-fired pizzas. A favorite for locals and visitors.

Wasatch Brew Pub, 250 Main St., Park City, ☎ 801/649-0900, has excellent sandwiches, soups and fish and chips. Catch a game on the big screen in the Slickrock Sports Bar.

Locals like **Miletti's Restaurant**, Park City, ☎ 801/649-8211, and so will you. Try the Texas shrimp, wrapped tightly in bacon, which crackles under the broiler.

OGDEN

Farr **Better Ice Cream Company**, 274 21 St., Ogden, ☎ 801/393-8629. Only ice cream at this modest but popular favorite.

Gray Cliff Lodge Restaurant, 508 Ogden Canyon, Ogden, ☎ 801/392-6775, is five miles up Ogden Canyon. Continental cuisine. Sunday brunch is popular and features homemade cinnamon rolls.

Delights of Ogden, 258 25th St., Ogden, ☎ 801/394-1111, is a friendly lunch place offering homemade soup and sandwiches.

Enjoying a thick steak while sitting in a covered wagon can be one heckuva good time at the **Prairie Schooner Steak House**, 445 Park Blvd., Ogden, ☎ 801/392-2712.

Hot bread and cookies stream out of the **Great Harvest** bakery on 25th Street. Visitors are usually greeted with a slab of fresh warm bread.

For healthy helpings of pasta, chicken or fish dishes, try **Roosters 25th St. Brewing Company**, 253 25th St., Ogden, UT 84401, ☎ 801/627-6171. The atmosphere is contemporary.

LOGAN

Mandarin Garden, 432 N. Main St., Logan, ☎ 801/753-5789, is not afraid to use its spices. Surprisingly good food is served in a plastic booth typical of Chinese restaurants.

Gia's Restaurant, 119 S. Main, Logan, UT 84321, ☎ 801/752-8384, is the quintessential Italian restaurant and a longtime local favorite.

Any visit to Logan wouldn't be complete without a trip to the **Bluebird Restaurant**, 19 North Main St., Logan, UT 84321, ☎ 801/752-3155. Stop to see the marble soda foundation and photos from the past. A handmade chocolate (or two or 10!) would be fitting.

On warm summer days, it seems as if everybody in Bear Lake is slurping down a raspberry shake, the town specialty. There are several drive-ins along the side of the road, **LeBeau's** being notable among the pack.

PROVO TO GREEN RIVER

The Tree Room at Sundance, RR 3, Sundance, UT 84604, ☎ 801/225-4107, spoils its guests with inventive cuisine like apple smoked duck breast and bucatini pasta, baked mussels in Focaccia and marinated quail. The Tree Room's menu continually strives to be fresh and exciting. A casually upscale atmosphere with attentive service and warmth. It's the best restaurant in the state, some people say

China City Café, 350 E. Main St., Price, UT 84501, ☎ 801/637-8211 offers Chinese and American cuisine in a comfortable setting. Specialty of the house: prime rib!

Looking for a huge Las Vegas-style buffet? Try the **Pantry Restaurant**, 1257 E. Main, Price, UT 84501 ☎ 801/637-5512.

Cathy's Pizza, 184 West Main St., Green River, ☎ 801/564-8122, has more than just pies. Submarine sandwiches, shakes, chicken and sack lunches are served well into the evening.

Serving boaters for more than 50 years, **Ray's Tavern**, 25 South Broadway, Green River, serves huge burgers, great nachos and sandwiches. Diners graze on large log tables inside the bar or out in the "boneyard." Ray is long gone, but his tradition of feeding hungry river runners lives on.

VERNAL, FLAMING GORGE & DINOSAUR

La Cabana at the Sage Hotel, 54. W. Main St., Vernal, ☎ 801/789-3151, has great *chile verde* and *enchiladas* and even better prices. Don't miss a bowl of rich and creamy guacamole. A la carte items are suitable for the average appetite, while the famished seek out the large full dinners.

Spoof's Coffee and Tea Shop, 38 E. Main St., Vernal, ☎ 801\789-1154, has absolutely delicious espresso, steamers, latte, tea and plain old coffee. The high-octane coffee is served in gigantic bowls requiring double fisted drinkers.

7-11 Café, 77 East Main, Vernal, ☎ 801/789-1170, features hearty home cooking for large appetites. This 60-year-old downtown hangout has a friendly crew, a pie spinner and great neon.

Last Chance Café, 3340 N. Vernal Ave., Vernal, ☎ 801/789-5657, serves heaping big breakfasts in a smoky truck-stop atmosphere.

The adjacent supper club offers steaks, chops and the like.

Niki's Inn at the Gorge, Manila, ☎ 801/784-3117, has gut-busting burgers and steaks, as well as boat lunches for those on the go. My companion warned to opt for the French fries over the leaden "English chips."

Down Home Pancake House at the Weston Lamplighter, Vernal, is the place to carbo-load for your river trip. All-you-can eat pancake breakfasts sell for less than some Sunday newspapers.

The town roadhouse, The Sorry Nag, Roosevelt, offers Mex and American "vittles" in a local's atmosphere.

Marion's Variety and Confectionery in Roosevelt has been making thick malts and filling burgers since 1933.

The Red Canyon Lodge, Hwy. 44, Dutch John, UT 84023, ☎ 801/889-3759, overlooks East Greens Lake and serves country meals, prime rib and nightly specials. During the winter, the restaurant serves dinner only on Friday and Saturday.

Camping

The extensive list of public camping areas that follows is offered because of Utah's splendor and the scarcity of decent accommodations in certain areas. Camping may be the preferred alterative in some cases or the only possibility for many miles in remote stretches. During the busy summer season, limited accommodations, even not very good ones, may be filled. The information agencies in Utah are extremely well organized and helpful to boot. The **Utah Travel Council**, Council Hall, Capitol Hill, Salt Lake City, UT 84114, ☎ 801/538-1467, is an excellent resource. For information about any of the campgrounds, contact the **Inter-Mountain Region Office**, 324 25 th Street, Ogden, UT 84401, ☎ 801/625-5182.

Camping in national forests, national parks, recreation areas, and on BLM land is generally first-come, first-served. For state parks, call ☎ 801/322-3770 or 800/332-3770. Mail in applications can be sent to **Utah Division of Parks and Recreation**, 1636 W. North Temple, Salt Lake City, UT 84116. If you pay for a camping reservation with a major credit card, you receive an instant confirmation. Most of Utah's state park campgrounds are well kept, and some, like the one in Snow Canyon, are exceptional.

For **national forest reservations**, ☎ 800/283-2267.

Overnight camping or day-use fees are charged at most public campgrounds. Primitive sites are generally free, but backcountry permits are usually required. These are available free from the administering agency. Backcountry restrictions regarding fires and off-road vehicles apply in certain areas. Check first with the administering agency.

There's usually room to pull in an RV at public campgrounds, but hook-ups are not often available. Numerous private campgrounds on the outskirts of public lands can generally provide full service to RVs. Camper-van rentals are available from the following source: **Adventure Werks Utah VW Camper Rentals**, mailing address, 3713 Seeley Street, Bellingham, WA 98226, ☎ 206/738-1159 or 800/736-8897, fax 206/738-1062.

SALT LAKE CITY AREA

Little Cottonwood Canyon climbs quickly away from the urban landscape to towering peaks. The following are all national park campgrounds. **Tanners Flat Campground** is four miles up from the intersection of Highways 209 and 210. Seven miles further up the canyon leads you to **Albion Basin Campground**, another fee site. Its season is short due to the high elevation.

In Big Cottonwood Canyon, **Spruce Campground** is nine miles from the canyon mountain and sits at an elevation of 7,400 feet.

PARK CITY AREA

At Jordanelle State Park, Box 309, Heber City, UT 84032, ☎ 801/649-3602, **Keetley Point Campground** has 41 tent sites nestled in a scrub oak draw. Sites include a grill, fire pit and tent pad. There are five sites accessible to disabled campers. **McHenry Creek Campground**, also in Jordanelle, has 42 sites with most of the above amenities. There are restrooms and showers available at a camp service center. There is also an **RV Campground** with 103 developed sites overlooking the reservoir. Each site includes an aluminum table, grill, fire pit and hookups. Reservations may be made one year in advance by calling ☎ 800-322-3770.

Strawberry Bay offers single, family and group sites along with parking for boats. **Soldier Creek Bay** and **Aspen Grove** have large sites and boat site. During the summer there are nightly campground programs at the Strawberry Bay Amphitheater. Campsites are mostly run on a first-come, first-served basis. **Information:** ☎ 800-280-CAMP.

Wasatch Mountain State Park, two miles northwest of Midway, has 139 camping sites, group-use buildings, modern restrooms and utility hookups. **Reservations:** ☎ 800-322-3770.

Deer Creek Reservoir, seven miles southwest of Heber, has 32 sites, restrooms and water. Make reservations through the Utah State Parks system, ☎ 800-322-3770.

OGDEN, LOGAN & BEAR LAKE

Pineview Reservoir offers two campgrounds along the southeast edge of the lake. There are seven developed campgrounds on the south fork of the Ogden River east of Huntsville. **Monte Cristo Campground**, along the river's edge, has 47 individual and two group sites with a flush toilet.

Willard Bay has 62 sites, modern restrooms, showers and sandy beaches in the north marina, located 15 miles north of Ogden off I-15. At the south marina, eight miles north of Ogden, there are 30 sites with restrooms.

Rendezvous Beach at Bear Lake has a wide sandy beach, showers, water and a few sites. It's located two miles north of Laketown. Reservations are taken at ☎ 800-322-3770.

There are 19 National Forest campgrounds in **Logan Canyon**.

Call ☎ 800/283-2267 to reserve a space at any of the above campgrounds.

At **Hyrum Reservoir**, 405 West 300 South, Hyrum, UT 84319, ☎ 801/245-6866, there are 40 fee campsites with nearby boating, watersports and fishing. The lake is 15 miles from Hardware Ranch.

GREAT SALT LAKE & BONNEVILLE

On Antelope Island, **Bridger Bay Campground** (☎ 800/283-226) has 12 individual sites and killer views of Promontory Point. Drinking water and excellent private showers.

There is camping at **Great Salt Lake Park**, Box 323, Magna, UT 84044, ☎ 801/250-1898, but if you want a better experience on the lake, head to Antelope Island. If a night's rest off I-80 is all you're seeking, this park 16 miles west of Salt Lake City will suffice.

In the **Deseret Peak Wilderness** south of Grantsville there are lovely campsites in the trees at the **South Fork of Willow Creek** with good hiking nearby. Popular on the weekends, you can have the place to yourself most any other time. Call ☎ 800/283-226.

PROVO & THE SOUTHERN WASATCH

There are plenty of fee sites, with names like Little Mill, North Mill, Granite Flat and Altamont, located in **American Fork Canyon** on the Alpine Loop. Granite Flat has been recently renovated. Call ☎ 800/283-226.

The Timpooneke site, on the Alpine Loop, is where you'll find a trailhead to Mt. Timpanogos. **Theater-in-the-Pines** is a group campsite near Sundance, about 14 miles north of Provo on Hwy. 92. For reservations, ☎ 800/283-2267.

Utah Lake, five miles west of Provo off I-15 on Center Street, has 71 campsites available near Utah's largest freshwater lake. ☎ 800-332-3770.

Close to the northern end of the Mt. Nebo loop is the **Payson Lake Campground**, a summer and early fall-only site that sits at an elevation of 8,000 feet. Call ☎ 800/283-226.

Those needing hookups should check into the **Wagon Wheel Trailer Park**, 500 S. Main in Springville, ☎ 801/489-4783.

PRICE TO GREEN RIVER

Huntington State Park, Box 1343, Huntington, ☎ 801/687-2491, nestles at the base of the Wasatch Plateau. Camping and picnic sites, restrooms and showers are available.

A BLM campground with restrooms is maintained in the northern section of the **San Rafael Swell**. ☎ 801/637-4584 for more information.

Scofield State Park, Box 166, Price, UT 84501, ☎ 801/448-9449, has two state-owned facilities. **Mountain View** has a 34-unit campground, restrooms and a boat launch. **Madsen Bay**, on the northern end of the reservoir, has a 40-place campground.

Green River State Park, Box 637, Green River, UT 84525, ☎ 801/564-3633, offers a 42-unit campground, hot showers and an amphitheater. The attraction is the popular boat launching ramp.

UINTAS AREA

Red **Fleet**, 10 miles north of Vernal, is a fee site amid slickrock formations in the land of the dinosaurs. Facilities include 29 campsites and 32 covered picnic tables.

Steineker, Hwy. 191, seven miles north of Vernal, is close to boating activities and is accessible to all. The park offers 31 trailer sites and 31 spots for tents.

Starvation Reservoir, Hwy. 40, Duchesne, has 26 RV sites and 28 tent sites. There is a 14-day limit.

Reservations for any of the above state campgrounds, which are open year-round, may be made by calling ☎ 800/322-3770.

The following camprounds can all be reserved by calling ☎ 800/283-226.

Campsites at **Whiterocks** offer space for RVs and tents, along with all the necessities to make your stay enjoyable. Located north of town, the site is open from mid-May through late-October.

Moon Lake has RV and tent sites available from late May through early September at this high-altitude site 35 miles north of Duchesne. ☎ 801/789-1181.

Mirror Lake Campground off Hwy. 150 is a perennially popular camping spot for Wasatch Range families. Less crowded options include **Bridger Lake**, 54 miles northeast of Kamas, and its neighbor on the Mirror Lake Highway, **China Meadows**.

DINOSAUR

Most visitors to Dinosaur inexplicably come for the day or even half-day, so campers can be almost assured a site except during the absolute busiest weekends of the year.

Backpackers are welcome to camp at areas at least a quarter-mile off roads or trails. Free permits are required and preparation (water, first aid) is mandatory. Sites are first-come, first-served, except for group campsites, which may be reserved by calling ☎ 801/789-2115.

Lovely **Split Mountain Campground**, four miles east of the dinosaur quarry, has four group campsites available by reservation, 15 tent sites and flush toilets. Ultra convenient for river runners, **Green River's** 88 tent sites are five miles east of the Dinosaur Quarry. Water and fireplaces are available.

Echo Park, 38 miles from park headquarters, is popular for campers and has water and views of Steamboat Rock.

Rainbow Park's scenic primitive sites are 26 miles from the quarry via Island Park Road. **Gates of Lodore**, a hefty 106 miles from headquarters via Maybell, CO and Hwy. 318, has 17 sites and pit toilets.

FLAMING GORGE

You'll find infinitely more variety in Flaming Gorge's campsites than in the local hotel and motel accommodations.

Antelope Flat has group and individual sites available. On-site facilities include drinking water and picnic tables. The large group site must be reserved. **Mustang Ridge** no longer is home to herds of wild horses, but it is a popular stopping place for campers who take advantage of the good fishing nearby.

The campsites clustered on the road to **Red Canyon Visitor Center** are desirable because of the views they offer and the tranquil setting.

A local claimed he could fly-fish from his tent in **Deep Creek**, 21 miles south of Manila off Hwy. 44. No fees are charged at this little hideaway.

Kingfisher Island may be reached by boat. It has eight tent sites, picnic tables, fresh water and toilets. **Lucerne Valley**, eight miles east of Manila, offers all services and a group site. Pronghorn antelope may be hovering outside your tent come morning.

Call ☎ 800/283-226 to reserve a space at any of the above sites.

As you'd expect, there are excellent camping sites available only by boat. Approximately 20 miles from the dam near Sheep Creek Bay boat ramp is a site called **Hideout**. Drinking water, toilets, picnic tables and grills are available. Reserve a fee site by calling ☎ 800/280-CAMP. Between the dam and Lucerne Marina are **Jarvies Canyon, Kingfisher Island** and **Gooseneck**, which offer sites on a first-come, first-served basis.

Dispersed camping is allowed in undeveloped areas of the national forest on the road to **Spirit Lake**, located beyond the Ute Fire lookout tower.

In splendid **Sheep Creek Canyon**, camping is only allowed October through May due to the threat of floods the rest of the year. Lush and dramatic, it is worth the wait.

On the Wyoming side of the reservoir are floating camps at **Big Bend**, four miles south of Buckboard Crossing, and **Flattop**, three miles south of the Squaw Hollow ramp.

Most of the campsites shut off their water by mid-October but still allow campers to use the facilities for no fee.

Hookups for RVs are available at the **Flaming Gorge KOA**, Box 157, Manila, UT 84046, ☎ 801/784-3184.

There are two campgrounds a quarter-mile away from the John Jarvie site in **Brown's Park**. **Bridge Hollow Campground** has potable water and is a fee site.

Southern Utah

There may be more deer, antelope, bighorn sheep, lizards, and rattlesnakes than human residents in this epic sandstone wonderland that includes Arches, Canyonlands, Capitol Reef, Bryce Canyon and Zion National Parks, the Glen Canyon Recreation Area, Lake Powell, several national monuments, remote primitive areas and state parks. Nearly 80% of Utah's land is administered by public agencies and just running through this list it's easy to see that southern Utah's public lands are extensive. Beside sheer size, these lands include some of the most unusual and improbable landscapes in the world.

Red sandstone buttes, blue mesas, purple rock pinnacles, narrow spires, and deep, plunging canyons line the muddy Colorado River and decorate the uplands of the Colorado Plateau as if it were a rock garden of the gods. If geology can be surreal, then this is it.

Lofty mountains with lakes and forested slopes in the Henry, Abajo (Blue) and La Sal mountains bring a blessedly cooler climate than the lower desert-like plateaus.

Mazes of slickrock trails that are easy to cross when dry, but slippery when wet, lead to deserted cliffs, towering vistas, and empty lands that provide a geology lesson in the forces of wind, water, and erosion. Even a man-made feature, Lake Powell, the centerpiece of the Glen Canyon Recreation Area, impresses with its scope; it is 186 miles long, the second largest man-made reservoir in the United States.

Few people live here, and relatively few have trodden these mysteriously vacant grounds, among the last places in all the United States to be explored.

All of southern Utah offers vast recreational opportunities. Just sightseeing is something of a quest amid this mostly arid topography. There are few paved roads, but hundreds of miles of gravel and dirt tracks more suitable to pack animals than vehicles. Hiking and biking trails wind through stunted juniper and pinyon forests, over slickrock and down into shady cottonwood riversides. Since most of southern Utah is public land, with small towns spaced far apart along scenic byways, adventurous possibilities are the norm, rather than the exception. Limits for recreation are bounded only by imagination.

Float a lazy river or bounce through roaring rapids. Ride a horse into areas where the hand of man has had little impact. Travel by mountain bike or four-wheel-drive to secluded campsites affording views of unsurpassed, strange beauty that are reminiscent of another planet. Examine remote archaeological ruins. Fish your own vacant stretch of river. Hike for weeks on end without ever seeing another soul. Bask in flaming pastel sunsets.

Geography & History

Land, water, and skies that rival the beauty of those anywhere in the world are clearly the major attractions here, the ancient lure for settlers and travellers such as the Anasazi Indians, who left only ruins and petroglyph inscriptions nearly a thousand years ago. They were followed by Paiutes and Navajos, who began settling in for the long haul when the Anasazi were disappearing.

Later, Spanish explorers scouted trade routes to California through the slickrock and canyons, and a one-armed Civil War veteran named John Wesley Powell paddled and mapped the Colorado River.

Among the most tenacious influences on the area were Mormon settlers, branching off from the Great Salt Lake area to spread their religion. A Mormon wagon train travelling from Cedar City, in southwestern Utah, set out for southeastern Utah in 1875, anticipating a six-week trip. Instead, they had to blast through rock and build roads; it took six months of torturous travel to reach Bluff. Once they reached their destination, they stayed.

The Mormon influence is still keenly felt today in just about all of southern Utah's small towns. Many of them are laid out around a central church in the grid pattern designed by Brigham Young.

These towns still impress as moral, one example being their rather arcane liquor laws. Most alcoholic beverages must still be purchased in state-operated shops. Mixed drinks are served in some licensed restaurants, but they cannot offer you a cocktail or wine list unless you ask for it. Bars serve only 3.2% beer. Most people drink in private clubs. The good news is that you can buy a temporary membership to these clubs for about the cost of a mixed drink.

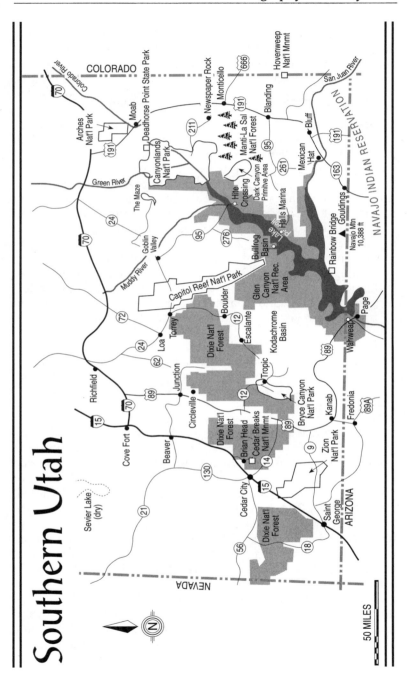

As for the grid system applied to city streets, which typically produces a confusing address such as 100 East 200 North, you just need to remember a few things. Streets run north-south and east-west from a mid-point, usually the site of a Mormon Temple. Blocks are numbered in increments of 100. Once you've located the mid-point, 100 East 200 North is one block east and two north.

The grid system notwithstanding, travel through here is considerably easier, though not a whole lot less labyrinthine than the routes of the pioneers. You will put many miles on your car if you try to traverse the whole area covered in this chapter, but along the way you will see some of the most impressive scenery in the country. You won't always find a sophisticated concentration of services, but you can usually reach a motel and restaurant if you allow for it in your plans. Gas stations are few and far between. Fill up whenever you can.

Adventure outfitters are plentiful and a skilled one will provide everything you need, including permits, specialized equipment, and food. A knowledgeable guide can provide perspective in this rugged, immense, and challenging land filled with delightful surprises around each curve in the road or bend in the river.

Getting Around

There are few air connections to this region. The closest major airports are in Salt Lake City, Las Vegas, or Grand Junction, Colorado. Driving is the best way to get around, but those who want to fly can check with **Alpine Air**, ☎ 801/373-1508 or 800/253-5678. Alternatively, go through the airline's Moab representative, **Tag-A-Long Tours**, ☎ 801/259-8946. The airline offers daily service between Moab's Canyonlands Field and Grand Junction or Salt Lake City. **Sky West/Delta Connection**, ☎ 800/453-9417, also offers service to Cedar City, St. George, and Page, Arizona. For information see below under area touring categories.

Driving in the region is particularly convoluted due to the unusual topography of canyon networks, the Colorado River, and the simple lack of roads across the central portion of southern Utah. The shortest distance between two points is rarely a straight line.

It is not even possible to travel by road through Canyonlands National Park to the three distinct sections of the enormous park;

to explore each area requires a circuitous routing along widely spaced entrance roads. A fourth section of the park, the River District, including Cataract Canyon and the confluence of the Green and Colorado rivers, is accessible only by the river or by strenuous hiking trails. It creates the boundaries of the other three sections, Island in the Sky to the north, the Needles to the east, and the Maze to the west. The entire Canyonlands Park encompasses some 527 square miles, making it the largest park in the state.

The suggested itinerary for this area follows a zig-zag course from the northeastern corner of southern Utah, starting in the **Moab** area and moving south through **Monticello, Blanding,** and **Bluff.** It skirts the edge of the Navajo Reservation and heads in a northwesterly direction. This route passes through **Natural Bridges National Monument** and across the northern extremity of **Lake Powell** and the **Glen Canyon National Recreation Area.** North of there is the only road access to the Maze Section of **Canyonlands National Park** and the only paved road through the large **Capitol Reef National Park.**

From Capitol Reef, the route dips southwesterly again, through the little-visited, fascinating, and challenging **Escalante River** canyons. This is followed by stops in **Bryce Canyon National Park, Cedar Breaks National Monument** and **Zion National Park** before winding back eastward, finishing in **Page,** Arizona, on the lower stretches of Lake Powell.

Information

The free promotional material offered by various Utah sources is among the best anywhere. There's a lot of it, though, so plan ahead and contact these sources far in advance of your trip. The Utah Highway Map (available from the Travel Council, below), for example, is available in French, Spanish, German, Japanese, or English, and it includes a directory to national and state parks, historic sites and museums, ski and summer resorts, and outdoor adventures. Other free hand-outs include detailed descriptions and maps of mountain biking, hiking and jeep trails.

Utah Travel Council, Council Hall, Capitol Hill, Salt Lake City, UT 84114-1396, ☎ 801/538-1030 or 800/200-1160, fax 801/538-1399, provides copious free information, including maps, hotel guides, and lists of airlines, guides and outfitters, scenic flights, bike tours, river trips, four-wheel-drive routes, and boating.

INFORMATION SOURCES

For information on State Parks contact one of the following:
Utah Division of Parks and Recreation, Main Office, 1636 West North Temple, Salt Lake City, UT 84116. ☎ 801/538-7221.
Utah Division of Parks and Recreation, Southeast Region, 89 East Center, Moab, UT 84532-2330. ☎ 801/259-8151.
Utah Division of Parks and Recreation, Southwest Region, PO Box 1079, Cedar City, UT 84720-1079. ☎ 801/586-4497.

Other useful information sources include the following:
Utah Guides & Outfitters Association, 153 East 7200 South, Midvale, UT 84047. ☎ 801/566-2662.
US Bureau of Land Management, State Office, 324 South State, Suite 301, PO Box 45155, Salt Lake City, UT 84145-0155. ☎ 801/539-4001.
US Forest Service, Intermountain Region Office, 2501 Wall Avenue, Ogden, UT 84401. ☎ 801/625-5306.
National Park Service, PO Box 25287, Denver, CO 80225-0287, ☎ 303/969-2000.
US Geological Survey, 2300 South 2222 West, West Valley City, UT 84117. 801/975-3742. (Provides topographical and geological maps.)

For camping reservations, ☎ 800/284-2267. Most campgrounds are first-come, first-served, but if you know where to camp you can try calling in advance.
Utah Campground Owners Association, 1370 West North Temple, Salt Lake City, UT 84116. ☎ 801/521-2682. (For private campground information, especially for those travelling in RVs.)

Southern Utah has four multi-agency information centers offering free state-wide travel information.
Escalante Interagency Office, 755 West Main, Escalante, UT 84726. ☎ 801/826-5499.
Hanksville Information Office, 406 South 100 West, Hanksville, UT 84734. ☎ 801/542-3461.
Moab Information Center, Corner of Center and Main Streets, Moab, UT 84532.
Monticello Multi-Agency Visitor Center, PO Box 490, 117 South Main, Monticello, UT 84535. ☎ 801/587-3235 or 800 574-4FUN, fax 801/587-2425.

Touring

Moab

Moab is by far the biggest town in southeastern Utah, and its population of 5,000 includes entrepreneurs at the hub of virtually the entire adventure travel industry for an enormous region.

Moab is located on US 191, just south of Arches National Park and UT 128, a scenic road that meanders alongside the Colorado River past Fisher Towers, Castle Rock, and the Priest and Nuns formation. If the towers and Castle Rock look familiar, it's probably because they've been the settings for numerous TV commercials. The 1,500-foot-tall slender red rock spires of Fisher Towers are distinctive, and you probably remember seeing cars photographed from above, improbably balanced atop Castle Rock. There is a picnic area and a three-mile hiking trail around the base of Fisher Towers. Other sites along the road afford contrasting views of the snow-capped La Sal Mountains, and turn-outs lead in a short distance to Colorado River beaches – good for picnics or fishing.

Moab, more so than other towns farther south, is the preferred base by many for exploring Utah's Canyonlands, which is a generic name for this whole region of dramatically sculpted landforms, high alpine mountains, and desert valleys, as well as the name of the national park. The area has certainly been discovered by many adventure-seeking souls (too many, if you ask certain old-time locals), as evidenced by a plethora of adventure outfitters based here. A staggering variety of trips by mountain bike, river raft, four-wheel-drive, hiking, horseback, and backcountry skiing are offered here.

The Green and Colorado rivers are easily accessible, as are the dramatic, dizzying vistas of Dead Horse State Park and the Canyon Rims Recreation Area. Arches National Park is just a few miles away, and the Island in the Sky and Needles District of Canyonlands National Park are close by.

The motels and restaurants are more plentiful around Moab than farther south, but the crowds are bigger here too, especially from May to September. Motel rooms or even campsites may be hard to come by on the spur of the moment during those months.

This long-time ranching community was transformed into a uranium boom town in the 1950s. As the glow faded from uranium mining, Moab was re-invented as a Hollywood film location for numerous features and commercials, and finally as a vacation destination. Today it is in full flower as a recreation mecca.

In town is an interesting and unlikely attraction dealing with the movie history of the area – **Hollywood Stuntman's Hall of Fame**, 100 North 100 East, Moab, UT 84532, ☎ 801/259-6100. Exhibits recall the many films that have been shot in the area and include videos of amazing stunts, familiar-looking costumes worn by stunt doubles for *The Flying Nun,* and Paladin's black cowboy duds from the classic Western series *Have Gun Will Travel.* You will also find items used in more recent Moab films, such as *Thelma and Louise* (they took their fabled dive just outside of Canyonlands National Park), and *City Slickers II.*

The **Dan O'Laurie Museum**, 118 East Center, Moab, UT 84532, ☎ 801/259-7985, displays prehistoric Indian pottery, sandals, baskets and tools, such as the elegantly simple corn-grinding *metate,* which is merely a rock. Other exhibits detail early Spanish explorers, the mining era, pioneer life in Moab, and mineral specimens from the area, including uranium ore and dinosaur fossils.

Understandably, Moab has a lot of rock shops. **Ottinger's Rock Shop**, 137 North Main, Moab, UT 84532, ☎ 801/259-7312, offers rocks for sale and also presents nightly slide shows highlighting area scenery.

South of town, **Arches Vineyard**, 2182 US 191, Moab, UT 84532, ☎ 801/259-5397, is Utah's only winery. Tours and tastings are offered.

The best place to get a handle on all the things to do around here, both in and out of town, is at the office of the **Grand County Tourism Council**, PO Box 550, 805 North Main Street, Moab, UT 84532, ☎ 801/259-1370 or 800/635-6622. The staff can provide information and even a few videos on historic walking tours in Moab, car or four-wheel-drive trips, hiking trails, mountain bike routes, movie locations around the Moab area, winter recreation ideas, and accommodation and restaurant details.

Also in Moab are the main administrative offices for Arches and Canyonlands national parks, as well as Natural Bridges National Monument. Contact **National Park Service**, 125 West 200 South, Moab, UT 84532, ☎ 801/259-7155.

The Bureau of Land Management maintains two Moab offices. Contact **BLM District Office**, 82 East Dogwood, Box 970, Moab, UT 84532, ☎ 801/259-6111, or **BLM Grand Resource Area Office**,

Sand Flats Road, Box M, Moab, UT 84532, ☎ 801/259-8193, which handles Colorado River and Westwater Canyon permits.

Arches National Park

The entrance to Arches National Park is three miles north of Moab on US 191. The park contains some of the strangest-looking, most implausible geography anywhere, ranging in elevation from 3,960 feet to 5,653 feet, and including enormous red rock pinnacles, fins and domes, plus the largest concentration of natural stone arches in the world. More than 1,600 arches have been found within the 73,368 acres of the park, and new ones are found all the time.

Near the park entrance is a visitor center featuring displays on the geological and human history of the park. You can also pick up brochures and maps here, the free backcountry permits required for hikers and backpackers, and additional free literature, including trail guides outlining hikes to some of the off-road arches. Native plants are marked on a short **nature trail** that starts here.

There is a paved road through the park that leads to the main sights of interest, a round-trip of 39 miles. Along the way, the road passes such sites as **South Park Avenue**, mammoth clusters of vertical sandstone slabs edging a dry wash that resemble Manhattan skyscrapers lining a broad avenue. The site was the film location for the opening scenes of *Indiana Jones, The Last Crusade.* Other parts of the park provided locations for *Thelma and Louise.*

Farther up the park road there's a short trail around **Balanced Rock**, an enormous stone set precariously on a rocky pedestal. Past Balanced Rock there's a turnoff to the **Windows Section**, which includes four giant arches – the North and South Windows, Turret Arch and Double Arch – all of which may be easily viewed from short walks.

There are also unpaved roads in the park, including one that branches from the main road, a few miles past the Windows turnoff, and leads to **Wolfe Ranch**, site of an old homestead and a trailhead for a three-mile round-trip hike to Delicate Arch. **Delicate Arch** is perhaps the best-known arch in the park, if only by virtue of its recurrent appearances on the covers of brochures and in television commercials. You have to cross a swinging footbridge and walk up a few steep slopes, gaining 500 feet in elevation, to reach it.

The **Fiery Furnace** area is farther up the main park road and includes unusual, tightly stacked, fin-shaped rocks 100 feet tall. A 2½-hour ranger-led tour is recommended for covering a confusing two-mile trail through the narrow, maze-like canyons. **Devils Garden** lies at the end of the main road and is the site of a picnic area and campground, as well as the trailhead for the large and impressive **Landscape Arch**, plus many others.

Hiking trails off the main road lead to view sites, and there are remote backpacking areas as well as four-wheel-drive roads inside the park boundaries. For additional information, contact **Arches National Park**, PO Box 907, Moab, UT 84532, ☎ 801/259-8161.

Canyonlands National Park
(Island In The Sky District)

The Island in the Sky District of Canyonlands National Park is accessed via the same roads from Moab that lead to Deadhorse Point (see above). Signs indicate where to go. It is the most easily accessed portion of the vast Canyonlands Park, with paved roads that lead to imposing overlooks, numerous hiking trails, and four-wheel-drive roads.

This section of the park has its own visitor center where you may obtain the free backcountry permit required for any backpacking or camping along the White Rim Four-Wheel-Drive Trail. Beyond the center, you cross the narrow neck of land that connects to the Island in the Sky, which is similar to Deadhorse Point, but larger (40 square miles). The visitor center offers no services beyond information about the park and there is no water on tap. For information, ☎ 801/259-7164.

Much of the hiking to secluded side canyons and arches is strenuous around here, and jeeping the **White Rim Trail** down to the Colorado River is only for well-experienced drivers. Short hikes are possible, though, and the one to **Mesa Arch** is only a half-mile round-trip. It leads to a staggering view from the edge of a 2,000-foot cliff. It starts 5½ miles from the visitor center. To get to the trailhead, turn left past the Mesa Arch trailhead, at the road junction. Continue driving for 2½ miles, then turn right and drive four miles to Grandview Picnic Area.

A good deal of the region can be viewed from **Grandview Point**, where you can see the Henry, La Sal and Abajo mountains, as well as miles of curling canyons rising above the Colorado River.

Numerous named rock formations are also visible, including the Needles, Lizard Rock, the Maze, and the Golden Stairs.

Two other trails start at the picnic area. **White Rim Overlook Trail** covers a 1½-mile round-trip to look out over Monument Basin. **Gooseberry Trail** is only for more serious hikers. It covers 2½ miles one-way and drops over 1,400 feet in elevation.

View points for **Upheaval Dome**, a crater-like hole three miles long and 1,200 feet deep, are accessed via the short, one-mile round-trip **Crater View Trail**. Go back down the road from Grandview Point and bear left at the main road junction. Continue to the end of the road and the trailhead. No one knows for sure what created the crater, although some geologists suspect it was formed by the crash of a giant meteorite. If you're really intrigued by this site you may want to tackle an eight-mile hike that encircles it.

Deadhorse Point State Park

This is considered by many to be Utah's most spectacular state park. Located nine miles north of Moab on US 191, then 23 miles south on UT 313, the park sits on an isolated, island-like mesa atop sheer sandstone cliffs, towering 2,000 feet above the serpentine Colorado River as it winds through multi-colored rock pinnacles. Steeples and broad buttes take on constantly shifting hues according to the time of day and the angle of the sunlight.

From the impressive park overlook you can see 5,000 square miles of Colorado Plateau country, including the La Sal and Abajo mountains. This site, with only one way on or off the mesa across a narrow strip of land, was used by early cowboys as a natural corral for horses, but one herd of steeds was left out in the sun too long and died of thirst, trapped high above the river, hence the park's name.

Deadhorse has a visitor center, campground and picnic area, as well as hiking trails. For information contact **Deadhorse Point State Park**, Box 609, Moab, UT 84532, ☎ 801/259-2614.

Deadhorse Point State Park

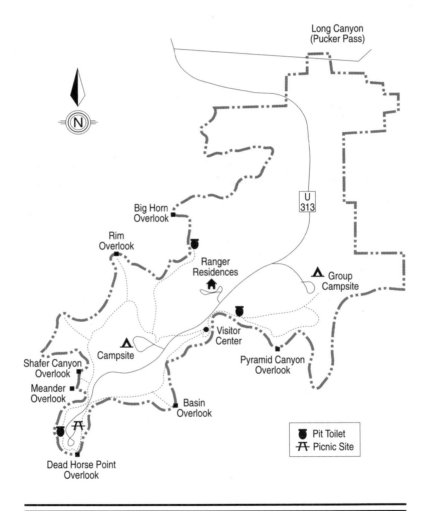

Long Canyon
(Pucker Pass)

N

U
313

Big Horn
Overlook

Rim
Overlook

Ranger
Residences

Group
Campsite

Visitor
Center

Shafer Canyon
Overlook

Campsite

Pyramid Canyon
Overlook

Meander
Overlook

Basin
Overlook

Dead Horse Point
Overlook

Pit Toilet
Picnic Site

South of Moab & Canyonlands
(Needles District)

On the way to the Needles District, on US 191, 15 miles south of Moab, there's a weird, kitschy tourist attraction called **Hole-in-the-Rock**. It's a 5,000-square-foot, 14-room house and gift shop built around rock pillars, all set within solid sandstone rock. The Flintstones-like edifice includes a bath tub built into rock and a 65-foot chimney drilled through solid rock.

Thirty-two miles south of Moab on US 191 is a marked turnoff to the west for the **Canyon Rims Recreation Area**. It's a 20-mile drive to the **Needles Overlook**, which offers impressive views from 1,000 feet of the Island in the Sky, Deadhorse Point, the Needles District, and the Abajo, La Sal and Henry mountains. It also shows the confluence of the Green and Colorado rivers, and Canyonlands' Maze District. Five or six miles before the Needles Overlook is a gravel road heading north for 17 miles to the **Anticline Overlook**, another ethereal cliff-top perch 1,600 feet above the Colorado River, which separates the overlook from Deadhorse Point.

Wildlife is common throughout the Canyon Rims area. Look across the sagebrush flats for pronghorn antelope, muledeer, and coyotes, or up in the sky for swallows and swifts.

There are several campgrounds within the recreation area, as well as hiking and four-wheel-drive trails. For information, contact the BLM office in Moab.

Twelve miles west of US 191 is **Newspaper Rock State Park**. Sandstone cliffs near the parking area are carved with an incredible assortment of petroglyphs ranging from the Anasazi era through modern Navajo times. They include Kokopelli figures (the ubiquitous Indian flautist whose image appears all over the Southwest), a large animal that may represent a mastodon, and animal fertility scenes. A short **nature trail** details regional flora. There is also a picnic area and campground, but no water.

The paved road (UT 211) continues past Newspaper Rock Park, through Indian Creek Canyon, to the Needles District.

A mile before the ranger station, just outside the park, is the **Needles Outpost**, Box 1107, Monticello, UT 84535, ☎ 801/259-2032. Open March to October, this is the last chance before entering the park to buy gas, food, and supplies. There is a general store, campground, and snack bar, as well as showers, firewood, maps, books, information and a 4,500-foot landing strip. The outpost also offers scenic flights, jeep tours, and jeep rentals.

The **Needles Ranger Station,** ☎ 801/259-6568, inside the park, is where you obtain required backcountry hiking and camping permits, as well as hiking and jeep trail guides. The paved road continues through the park to scenic overlooks and turnoffs for jeep roads and hiking trails.

About a half-mile past the ranger station is a quarter-mile hiking trail to **Roadside Ruin,** an Anasazi stone structure used to store grains.

About another quarter-mile on the main road is a turnoff to **Cave Spring Trail.** It's a one-mile drive to the trailhead for the half-mile loop trail. Nearby is a cave that was used as a campsite by cowboys for nearly 100 years until the area was declared a national park in 1964.

Two and a half miles past the ranger station is a turnoff for **Squaw Flats Campground** and a picnic site at Elephant Hill (three miles past the campground). There are several trailheads at the campground and picnic site, and a rugged four-wheel-drive road continues beyond Elephant Hill.

Five miles past the ranger station is the **Pothole Point Nature Trail,** a half-mile loop. Another mile farther on the main road is the start of the **Slickrock Trail,** a 2½-mile round-trip to scenic overlooks. The paved main road ends at the **Big Spring Canyon Overlook,** 6½ miles past the ranger station.

San Juan County

Be grateful these small southeastern Utah towns have gas stations, restaurants, and motels. There may not appear to be much in the way of visitor services available in this part of the state, but your choices are far greater today than they were a few years ago.

Monticello is on US 191, 54 miles south of Moab. It offers the closest town access to the **Abajo Mountains,** a rugged range reaching as high as 11,362 feet at Abajo Peak. There are no marked hiking trails in the Abajos and even backcountry four-wheel-drive roads may be difficult to follow.

One four-wheel-drive route, the **Blue Mountain Loop,** ascends to within a mile of Abajo Peak. It is possible to hike to the peak from there, but it is recommended that you stop first in Monticello to consult with the following useful information sources.

INFORMATION SOURCES

Manti-La Sal National Forest, 496 East US 666, PO Box 820, Monticello, UT 84535, ☎ 801/587-2041, can provide details about hiking, backroads, and camping in the Abajos.

BLM San Juan Resource Area, 435 North Main, PO Box 7, Monticello, UT 84535, ☎ 801/587-2141, administers the Grand Gulch, Dark Canyon, and several other primitive areas. It also covers the San Juan River.

National Park Service, 32 South 100 East, PO Box 40, Monticello, UT 84535, ☎ 801/587-2141, can provide information, books, and maps of Natural Bridges National Monument, Arches, and Canyonlands parks.

Monticello/San Juan County Multi-Agency Visitor Center, 117 South Main, PO Box 490, Monticello, UT 84535, ☎ 801/587-3235 or 800/574-4FUN, fax 801/587-2425, can provide all manner of regional travel information, including cross-country skiing and snowmobile trail guides (and much of the information available from the Forest Service, BLM, and National Park Service). It also offers current materials relating to accommodations and dining.

San Juan County, of which Blanding is the largest town, population 4,000, is on the edge of the Navajo Reservation. There is a high percentage of Indian residents and some good shops selling Native American jewelry, pottery, rugs, and other arts and craft work. The best one is **Blue Mountain Trading Company**, PO Box 263, Blanding, UT 84511, ☎ 801/678-2570. **Huck's Museum and Trading Post**, US Highway 191 South, Blanding, UT 84511, ☎ 801/678-2329, contains a substantial private collection of Indian artifacts in a log building on the south end of Blanding.

Blanding's premier attraction is **Edge of the Cedars State Park**, 660 West 400 North, PO Box 788, Blanding, UT 84511, ☎ 801/678-2238. The park contains an excellent museum displaying Anasazi pottery and other Anasazi artifacts, as well as exhibits detailing later Indian occupation and pioneer life. Outside are restored ruins, including a *kiva*, an enclosed living chamber, that you enter by climbing through a hole in the roof and down a ladder.

Bluff is a community of only 250 or so. There are several small motels, a couple of restaurants and trading posts, including one with a very good restaurant, Cow Canyon Restaurant.

About three miles east of Bluff is the **San Juan Footbridge**, a swinging bridge across the San Juan River that leads to a cliff dwelling known as **17 Room Ruin**.

Mexican Hat is a small town 22 miles north of the Utah-Arizona border on US 163, separated from the Navajo Nation by the San Juan River. It's named after a large rock north of town that looks like an inverted sombrero. A popular put-in and take-out point, as well as a convenient spot to stop for supplies on a river run, the town is well-known to river rats. It is mainly distinguished by its surroundings, not by its in-town amenities which, although colorful, are modest.

The Goosenecks of the San Juan River are nine miles northeast of Mexican Hat at the end of UT 316, west of UT 261. They comprise a series of tight switchbacks carved into a 1,500-foot-deep chasm, containing 380 million years of geological history. The phenomenon is called an entrenched meander, which means the river curves tightly back upon itself, spanning six miles of river frontage that are compressed within a distance of only 1½ miles. There is a famous overlook at the end of UT 316 in **Goosenecks State Park**, PO Box 788, Blanding, UT 84511, ☎ 801/678-2238, where there is a picnic area. Camping is allowed, but there is no water.

Moki Dugway is 11 miles northeast of Mexican Hat on UT 261. It is a three-mile graded dirt section of road that rises a precipitous 1,200 feet up the side of a sandstone cliff. Once a uranium ore hauling route, it now is known for the panoramic views it offers. Just south of Moki Dugway, off UT 261 10 miles northwest of Mexican Hat, is one end of the 18-mile-long **Valley of the Gods Loop Road** (see below, under Adventures, On Wheels). A deserted scenic road, it passes through desert lands decorated with stone outcrops that resemble a compressed Monument Valley. A four-wheel-drive vehicle is not strictly necessary for this road, except under wet conditions. Valley of the Gods returns to US 163 eight miles northeast of Mexican Hat.

Muley Point is at the end of a four-mile dirt road, southwest of Moki Dugway. It provides an ethereal overlook of the canyons surrounding the San Juan River and views south to Monument Valley.

Cedar Mesa is the name of the primitive area accessed from atop Moki Dugway. The mesa top contains numerous Anasazi and Pueblo Indian sites, and the canyons leading to the mesa contain cliff dwellings and granaries.

Monument Valley

Monument Valley Navajo Tribal Park, PO Box 93, Monument Valley, UT 84536, ☎ 801/727-3287, is a famous 30,000-acre Navajo reserve straddling the Arizona-Utah border east of US 163, 23 miles north of Kayenta and 25 miles south of Mexican Hat. You have to enter the park through Utah, on a three-mile entry road east of US 163, but the main scenic attractions are back across the border in Arizona. The entry road near the highway end supports a row of stands offering frybread, Navajo tacos, mutton sandwiches, silver jewelry, and rugs. At the end of the road there is a visitor center with bathrooms, gift and book store, campground, tour guides and traditionally dressed models who will pose for photographers at a small cost.

The closest services are at **Goulding's Lodge**. The lodge, a mile west of US 163 across the highway from the park entrance, includes a motel, restaurant, gift shop, museum, tour services, landing strip, grocery store, and gas station.

The next closest services are in Kayenta or Mexican Hat. If you're shopping for antique Indian arts and crafts try the **Oljeto Trading Post**, nine miles northwest of Goulding's. Follow the paved road running past the Goulding's complex for some unusual finds.

Monument Valley's year-round visitor center is adjacent to a campground, open in summer only. From this area you can look out over red buttes, mesas, and pinnacles rising off the valley floor in distinctive individual majesty, like a proud tribe turned to stone. Monument Valley is particularly known as one of the favorite locations of Hollywood director John Ford, who filmed several John Wayne movies here. Other stars, such as Henry Fonda, appeared in Ford's classics *Fort Apache* and *My Darling Clementine*, made here. *The Searchers, The Trial of Billy Jack,* and *The Legend of the Lone Ranger* are among other features filmed in Monument Valley. There is a 17-mile loop road through the valley that is open to private vehicles, but no backcountry exploration is permitted without a Navajo guide. That deserted-looking backroad that beckons is probably a Navajo family's driveway.

There are numerous view site turnoffs within the park and ample opportunity to stop and admire craft items offered in open-sided, thatch roof sheds or simply displayed on a blanket.

The **scenic drive**, a rather confusing and virtually unmarked sandy track filled with numerous opportunities for wrong turns, passes named sites, some with special spiritual significance to the Navajo people, as well as **John Ford Point**, honoring the movie maker. Other activity on the valley floor, aside from car, bus, and jeep tour traffic, includes Navajo herdsmen trailing sheep through gullies and canyons studded with juniper, pinyon, and wind-blown, dusty sage, overshadowed by the mammoth, vertical rocks.

Even though you are not able to wander very far on your own, the views from the valley bottom drive are impressive, but a lot of people want to see more, hence the booming local industry in guided tours. An encampment of operators outside the visitor center offer a variety of scheduled or customized tour services throughout the day and night. Special photography tours depart before dawn or in the late afternoon to capture long valley shadows. Full moon evening tours are scheduled and wildlife tours depart at certain hours depending on the animals being sought. You can generally book a scheduled tour on the spot for the same day, although the valley does get crowded in the summer and tours are in great demand.

The elegant, expansive valley seems to stretch forever in time, the eons marked by the dominating monoliths, volcanic steeples, isolated buttes, and mesas. The Mittens, Merrick Butte, Elephant Butte, Three Sisters, Camel Butte, Sentinel Mesa, Totem Pole, and Yei Bei Chei, are just some of the massive, human-humbling angular stone sentinels that form the archetypal landscape instantly recognizable as the Southwest.

The fascinating details incorporated in that image, found in the nooks and crannies of Monument Valley, encourage the allotment of a day or more for surveying prehistoric Indian ruins, pictographs, hidden arches, and sandstone pinnacles standing atop the desert landscape. If you only see one Southwestern sunset, this is the place to plant yourself on a rock escarpment and watch the shadows lengthen across the desert flats, the slanting rays of late day sun coloring the rocky sandstone, enlightening a subtle range of pinkish hues, darkening into shades of red. A feverish glow radiates under a dimming blue sky, finally giving up the last daylight in bright bands of mauve, pink, purple, and red near the horizon, colors transposed from the rocks, now in silhouette.

Monument Valley is popular in summertime and there may be crowds around the visitor center, campground, and Goulding's Lodge. The busiest part of the scenic drive is the first mile or so, near the center. After the sharp descent into the valley bottom there are different ways to go, so the traffic disperses. Still, you are not likely to have a transcendent private experience in here unless you arrange for some sort of guided tour into the hinterlands of the tribal park. The park's popularity and the lack of extensive accommodations in the area means you should not count on a last-minute reservation at Goulding's between May 15 and September 15. During this period it also gets extremely hot here (in the 100° range). Even if you're just going out for an hour or two on the scenic drive, carry water and food.

Springtime is beautiful in the desert, with wildflowers in bloom; fall is usually comfortably warm.

· A small, good book on the area is *A Traveler's Guide to Monument Valley*, by Stuart Aitchison, Voyageur Press, 1993.

Natural Bridges National Monument

There are two roads leading to Natural Bridges National Monument from southeastern Utah: UT 95, west from Blanding, or UT 261, north from Mexican Hat. Beyond the turnoff for Natural Bridges, UT 95 continues in a northwesterly direction to Hite Crossing at Lake Powell, and Hanksville. UT 276 branches off in a southwesterly direction from UT 95 and goes to Hall's Crossing Marina, where there is a ferry across Lake Powell to Bullfrog Basin Marina. It then continues north to re-connect with UT 95 northwest of Hite Crossing.

Sites of special interest north of Mexican Hat on UT 261 are listed above, under San Juan Touring.

Travelling west from Blanding, UT 95 passes close to numerous canyons and Indian ruins. **Butler Wash Overlook** is 15 miles west of Blanding. The site is reached by a half-mile trail marked with rock cairns and contains 23 Anasazi structures, including a square *kiva* estimated to be more than 800 years old.

Two and a half miles west of Butler Wash on UT 95 is a parking area providing scenic overlooks at the top of **Comb Ridge**, an 80-mile-long ridge characterized by 800-foot-tall cliffs that drop into Comb Wash.

Northwest of Comb Wash is **Arch Canyon**, a site full of unmarked hiking trails that lead to several other scenic canyons, with scattered Anasazi ruins throughout the area. Four miles north of the junction with UT 95, on County Road 263, is an overlook into Arch Canyon.

Cave Canyon Towers are the ruins of seven unstabilized Anasazi towers built around a spring-fed pool. Other ruins and petroglyphs are nearby. The site is set off a rough, unmarked jeep road, a quarter-mile east of the junction of UT 95 and County Road 263, then a half-mile south.

The residents of **Mule Canyon Ruin** were probably associated with the Anasazi who lived at Cave Canyon Towers. The site is two miles northwest of the Cave Canyon ruins. It has been stabilized and includes a *kiva*, a circular tower, and a dozen rooms, all linked by tunnels. The site is accessed by a highway turn-out on UT 95, 26 miles west of Blanding.

The entrance to **Natural Bridges National Monument**, Box 1, Natural Bridges, Lake Powell, UT 84533, ☎ 801/259-5174, is three miles west of UT 261 on UT 95, then five miles farther northwest on UT 275. The site contains three enormous stone bridges created by flowing water.

A solar-powered visitor center and campground is near the entrance to the park. A slide show and exhibits in the center describe the geological pressures that produced the bridges and the surrounding canyon country, as well as Indian history of the area, and local plant and animal life. The rangers can provide information on the park, the local area, and the large solar electrical system.

Overlooks of the canyon country, bridges, and Indian ruins are situated along the eight-mile **Bridge View Drive** park road, which is open year-round. Short trails lead from parking areas to each bridge, or a nine-mile loop trail along the river connects all three of the bridges. No backcountry permits are required, but camping is only permitted in the campground near the visitor center.

The first viewing spot for **Sipapu Bridge** is two miles from the center. The rock bridge spans 268 feet and is 220 feet high. A mile farther is another viewpoint halfway down a steep one-mile round-trip trail that leads to the bottom of Sipapu.

Horse Collar Ruins, an 800-year-old Anasazi site, may be seen from a viewpoint another quarter-mile up the road, or you can get to the ruins from the canyon-bottom trail.

The viewpoint and trailhead for **Kachina Bridge** are two miles farther up the road. This one is 210 feet tall and spans 204 feet. A trail to the canyon bottom is 1½ miles round-trip. Anasazi pictographs can be seen along the way.

Owachomo Bridge can be viewed from a stop another two miles farther on Bridge View Drive, where a trailhead to Owachomo is also located. This is the easiest of the natural bridges to view. It's only a half-mile round-trip to the base of the 106-foot-high by180-foot-wide bridge.

DARK CANYON WILDERNESS & PRIMITIVE AREA

Dark Canyon Primitive Area and the adjacent Dark Canyon Wilderness are accessed 15 miles north of Natural Bridges National Monument. No motorized vehicles are permitted in these areas, but there is a dirt road that branches north from UT 275 (about a mile past the junction with UT 95), and from there it's six miles to Bears Ears Pass. Two miles north of Bears Ears Pass the road branches left. From there it is another four miles to a trailhead for Upper Woodenshoe Canyon, part of the wilderness area.

Another access is south of Hite Marina, farther west on UT 95, where dirt roads lead to the Sundance Trail. An alternative way to reach Dark Canyon, 14 miles north of Hite Marina, is via boat on Lake Powell.

The lower wilderness area of the 45,000-acre preserve is administered by the Manti-La Sal National Forest office in Monticello. The upper primitive area portion is administered by the **BLM** office at Kane Gulch (see below) or the BLM's Monticello office (435 North Main, PO Box 7, Monticello, UT 84535, ☎ 801/587-2141).

The large canyon system, which can only be investigated by hikers or horseback riders, contains broad and narrow canyons. Diverse varieties of vegetation can be found at elevations ranging from more than 8,000 feet in the forested north, to 3,700 feet along the desert-like shore of Lake Powell.

Wildlife, including bighorn sheep, deer, coyotes, and the occasional black bear or mountain lion, are drawn to flowing water at the south end of the canyon. Anasazi ruins are also found within the canyon system.

GRAND GULCH PRIMITIVE AREA

Grand Gulch Primitive Area is a 50-mile-long canyon system containing significant Anasazi ruins (including cliff dwellings), mesa-top structures, and numerous examples of rock art. It begins five miles south of Natural Bridges at 6,400 feet elevation. Fifty miles later the twisted canyons, cliffs as high as 600 feet, and spires reach the San Juan River, elevation 3,700 feet.

The area is filled with a greater variety of wildlife and vegetation than Dark Canyon. Combined with the Anasazi sites clustered in the upper reaches of the area, Grand Gulch is a gigantic outdoor natural and cultural history museum.

The area is popular with hikers and horseback riders, many of whom are content to visit short sections on three- to four-day excursions. It may be getting too popular. Restrictions to access could be in force by the time you read this, so check with the authorities first.

A ranger station is located at **Kane Gulch**, four miles south of UT 95, on UT 261. Its hours are somewhat unpredictable. Information on the area is available from the BLM office in Monticello.

Glen Canyon National Recreation Area

Hall's Crossing/Bullfrog/Bullfrog Basin/
Hite Crossing/Lake Powell

Continuing westward from the area around Natural Bridges there are three choices at the southerly UT 95-UT 276 junction (eight miles west of UT 275, the Natural Bridges Road).

UT 276 veers in a southwesterly direction for 45 miles to Hall's Crossing Marina, where there is a ferry that crosses Lake Powell to Bullfrog Basin Marina. From there, it covers another 46 miles north, along the eastern side of the Henry Mountains, to rejoin UT 95, north of Hite Crossing.

For those travelling in a four-wheel-drive vehicle there is the option of a 65-mile dirt road from Bullfrog that follows the western flank of the Henry Mountains, along the Waterpocket Fold, to Capitol Reef National Park.

The other option is to continue on UT 95 for 60 miles, through Hite Crossing, crossing over three bridges at the northern end of Lake Powell, to the northerly junction of UT 95 and UT 276. From the junction it is 26 miles to Hanksville, an access point for the Maze District of Canyonlands National Park, Goblin Valley State Park, and Capitol Reef National Park.

Lake Powell, a 186-mile-long man-made lake, is the centerpiece of the **Glen Canyon National Recreation Area**, a 1.2-million-acre wilderness of untracked canyons and rugged terrain. With 1,960 miles of shoreline, the lake provides more water frontage than the west coast of the United States. Most of the lake is in Utah, but the greatest concentration of services is based out of the area around Page, Arizona, where the lower five miles of lake are located. These services are covered below, under the touring sections for Page/Lake Powell.

The services available at **Hall's Crossing** are a couple of stores, private and public campgrounds, and a ranger station. You can rent trailers, called housekeeping units, park an RV or camp in a tent, stock up on food and supplies, fill your tank with gas, get a shower and do your laundry. **Hall's Crossing Marina**, UT 261, PO Box 5101, Hall's Crossing, Lake Powell, UT 84533, ☎ 801/684-2261 or 800/528-6154, fax 801/684-2319, includes a ranger station and a store offering essential supplies, including boating equipment. The marina also offers waterskiing, houseboat rentals, fishing tours, and tours to Rainbow Bridge. Those travelling by boat can dock here and get gas.

The **John Atlantic Burr Ferry** can carry eight passenger cars, two buses, and as many as 150 passengers on the 20-minute crossing to Bullfrog Marina. The passage can save as many as 130 miles of driving. It departs hourly from 8 AM to 7 PM, mid-May to October, on even-numbered hours from Hall's Crossing and odd-numbered hours from Bullfrog. From April 15 to May 14, and October 1 to November 1, the ferry runs only from 8 AM to 5 PM. From November 2 to April 14 it runs only from 8 AM to 3 PM. Every so often the ferry is closed for repairs or is unable to run due to bad weather. A sign is supposed to be posted at the road junction of UT 276 and UT 95.

Bullfrog Resort & Marina, Box 4052, Bullfrog, Lake Powell, UT 84533, ☎ 801/684-2233 or 800/528-6154, fax 801/684-2312, offers more boating and tour services than Hall's Crossing Marina. It is larger and includes full-service gas stations that offer repair service for cars or boats. There is also another public campground, a ranger station, a marina and a visitor center. **Defiance House Lodge**, which houses the Anasazi Restaurant, is also here. The lodge runs boat tours (from April to October) to Rainbow Bridge and Defiance House, a restored Anasazi site 12 miles north. Several trailer and RV parks are also operating at Bullfrog, with shower and laundry facilities plus a variety of housekeeping units.

Twenty miles west of Natural Bridges on UT 95 is **Fry Canyon**, where there is a modest grocery store, gas station, motel, snack bar and campground (which may or may not be open). Although these provide the only services until Hite Marina (another 25 miles farther up UT 95), don't count on anyone being around here to help you out.

Hite Marina, Box 501, Lake Powell, UT 84533, ☎ 801/684-2278 or 800/528-6154, is below Cataract Canyon and the farthest north of all the Lake Powell marinas. Services include several primitive campgrounds, a few small grocery/convenience stores and gas stations for cars or boats. Docking space is available, as are boat rentals for fishing, waterskiing or houseboating. Trailer housekeeping units are also available.

Goblin Valley, Hanksville & Canyonlands' Maze District

HANKSVILLE

Little **Hanksville**, population 400, at the junction of UT 95 and UT 24, claims whatever fame it can from the area east of town known as Robber's Roost, which was once a hideout for Butch Cassidy and his outlaw gang and is now home to 350 free-roaming buffalo. The town is most popular with visitors as a staging area for backcountry trips into the Maze District, Goblin Valley State Park, and Capitol Reef National Park.

The only certified attraction in Hanksville is probably the wooden paddle-wheel that was once used to crush ore at the nearby Woolverton Mill. You'll find it at the regional BLM office, a half-mile south of UT 24 on 100 West (First Street). There are also several 19th-century structures in town, including an old stone church. There are a few motels, a bed & breakfast, a campground, plus several modest restaurants.

The remote and extremely rugged **Henry Mountains** are south of town. Running along the eastern slope of the Waterpocket Fold and Capitol Reef National Park, they are flanked by tortuous canyons and discouraging desert. Terrain ranges from desert plateaus to the 11,522-foot North Summit Ridge of Mount Ellen, complete with gnarled bristlecone pine and spruce forests. The range contains one of the only free-roaming buffalo herds in the United States, as well as mule deer, bighorn sheep, and mountain lions. Backcountry travel can be difficult, but there are several campgrounds and numerous hiking and four-wheel-drive roads that may or may not be passable at any given time.

For information contact the **Hanksville Information Center**, 406 South 100 West, Box 99, Hanksville, UT 84734, ☎ 801/542-3461. The office provides free material for the entire state as well as the immediate area.

CANYONLANDS' MAZE DISTRICT

The **Maze District** of Canyonlands National Park is accessed off UT 24, 21 miles north of Hanksville. A dirt road east from there covers nearly 60 miles through the Glen Canyon National Recreation Area to the park. The only bare bones services available in the entire area are found at the **Hans Flat Ranger Station**, ☎ 801/259-6513, outside the Maze in the Glen Canyon National Recreation Area (25 miles from the turnoff on UT 24). The ranger station is the best source of up-to-date backcountry information for surrounding areas of both the Glen Canyon National Recreation Area and the Maze District. Other details are available from the **National Park Service** (125 West 200 South, Moab, UT 84532, ☎ 801/259-7155).

This western district of Canyonlands is the most rugged and least crowded area of the 527-square-mile national park, comprising 30 square miles of Anasazi ruins, Indian rock art, unlikely stone towers, slender, gravity-defying rock fins, sheer cliff walls, and other seemingly chaotic elements of strangely beautiful, challenging topography. Many hold perfectly descriptive names such as Golden Stairs, Doll House, and Land of Standing Rocks.

The area is only for serious outdoor people. Make sure you enter with a full tank of gas, sufficient water, food, and any other supplies you may need. There are no services available other than information and emergency water at the ranger station. The soft sand or hard-packed clay roadbeds are virtually impassable in wet weather.

Within the Maze District trails through severe desert lands and confusing canyon networks are mostly unmarked; travellers need current topographic maps and confidence in their navigational skills. Backcountry permits are required for hikers and campers in the Maze. Primitive campgrounds are available, some near spring water or river water sources that need to be purified before consumption. No permits are required for backcountry travel or camping in the Glen Canyon National Recreation Area.

It is highly recommended that you consult with the park ranger regarding road and trail conditions, as well as available water sources. Also, file your travel plans with the ranger; if something does go wrong, the likelihood of being found is slim if the authorities don't know where to look for you. There are good reasons why the Maze is one of the least-used national parks. It is extremely tricky in there, terribly hot in the summer, always isolated, and far from help. It is also magnificently primitive and stunningly beautiful. By all means check it out, and use caution.

Horseshoe Canyon, a site filled with incredible life-size, pre-Anasazi cave paintings, is only slightly more accessible than the Maze. A four-wheel-drive is required to get close to the site, followed by some foot-scampering. For details, see below, under On Foot.

GOBLIN VALLEY STAT E PARK

The turnoff to **Goblin Valley State Park**, PO Box 637, Green River, UT 84525, ☎ 801/564-3633, is a half-mile farther north on UT 24 from the road to the Maze District. From that turn to the west, it's another 12 miles to the bizarre sandstone goblins, of which there are hundreds. These rocks have been naturally sculpted into whimsical or spectral forms, depending on your perspective, complete with eroded eyes and other bodily orifices, among a delirious scramble of rock fins, pinnacles, and small arches.

There are several short hiking trails in the six-square-mile park that lead to particularly evocative areas and scenic overlooks. There are also jeeping, biking, and longer hiking trails that may be accessed from this area, including southeastern areas of the San Rafael Swell, 12 miles north of Goblin Valley. These are covered below, under Adventures.

The **San Rafael Swell**, administered by the BLM, is a colorfully layered rock dome, laced by canyons and craggy outcrops, 80 miles long and 30 miles wide. It protrudes 2,000 feet above the desert floor on its eastern flank, the San Rafael Reef. It is expected that this area will become Utah's next national park. In the meantime, contact the **BLM San Rafael Resource Area Office**, Drawer AB, Price, Utah 84501, ☎ 801/637-4584, for information about backcountry driving, jeeping, biking, and hiking.

Capitol Reef National Park

Capitol Reef National Park, Torrey, UT 84775, ☎ 801/425-3791, is a geological oddity of upthrust rock with towering cliffs and plunging desert canyons highlighted by improbably lush flower-laden meadows during spring and early summer. Second in size among Utah's national parks (behind Canyonlands),

Capitol Reef's 378 square miles range from elevations around 3,800 feet to nearly 9,000 feet. The park stretches in a narrow band of layered, pinched rocks, water pools created by the slanted tiers, desert canyons, arches, and finely eroded spires, for nearly 100 miles – almost to Lake Powell.

The heart of the park is the **Waterpocket Fold**, a 100-mile-long uplift combining numerous layers of folded rock elevated high above the desert floor. The eccentric, compressed folds that catch water are the waterpockets, and these are surrounded by every variety of eroded rock sculpture found anywhere in Utah's Canyonlands.

Capitol Reef is the northern part of Waterpocket Fold, perhaps the area with the most intensely strange and evocative cliffs and rock forms. Some of the arched mounds as tall as 1,000 feet, eroded out of sandstone 1,000 feet thick, reminded pioneer travellers of the dome of the Capitol Building in Washington, DC. They had some time to think about the second part of the name – the massive stone reef impeded their progress and left them stranded like a sea vessel wallowing in coral-guarded shallows.

The most accessible attractions of the park are in this area, fairly close to the only paved road crossing the park. Then there is the immense backcountry, laced with rugged hiking, biking, horseback riding, and jeeping trails, remote campgrounds and statuesque, bright multi-colored rock forms decorated with Indian ruins and primitive rock art. It is a little-visited and truly remote natural wonderland, with fertile areas along the rivers and streams, and stark but intriguing rocky deserts everywhere else.

A visitor center is 37 miles west of Hanksville, or 11 miles east of Torrey, on UT 24. The road follows the course carved by the Fremont River, which slices through the reef. The center offers a slide show and interpretive exhibits related to the geological and cultural history of the area, including Indian artifacts and Mormon history displays, plus details on the flora and fauna of the park. Information about hiking trails and four-wheel-drive roads through the park may be obtained here, along with reports on current conditions and the required free camping permits.

There are no food services or accommodations available in the park, but there is a campground two miles south of the visitor center. It is surrounded by **fruit orchards**, which are maintained by the Park Service, and visitors are allowed to pick apricots, cherries, apples, pears, or peaches during the June-to-October harvest season. You can eat all you want for free while wandering around the orchards. If you want to take some fruit along for the ride, or back to your campsite or motel, a nominal fee is charged.

The old **Mormon Fruita Schoolhouse** is a mile east of the visitor center on UT 24, and a half-mile farther east are pre-Anasazi petroglyphs carved into a cliff on the north side of the road. An old settler's cabin, made of chiseled pieces of sandstone, is six miles east of the center. A roadside waterfall is one mile farther east.

Two and a half miles west of the center is a short gravel road leading a quarter-mile south to **Panorama Point**, which offers a broad view of Capitol Reef and Boulder Mountain, actually a high plateau to the south.

A mile farther south are short, easy trails leading to the **Goosenecks Overlook**, elevation 6,400 feet, which looks down on Sulphur Creek, and **Sunset Point**, offering more expansive views of distant topography.

The park's **Scenic Road** heads south from UT 24 for 12½ miles, below river-carved cliffs along the reef, and into the canyons of Grand Wash. More petroglyphs are found 10 miles south, in **Capitol Gorge**, another canyon.

Other roads into the northern depths of the park from UT 24 are recommended for four-wheel-drive, although a few may be accessible to passenger vehicles. Contact the ranger station for road condition reports. Also, inquire about portions of the **Notom Road**, which goes south for 60 miles along the east side of the reef, or the **Burr Trail**, which heads 40 miles west across the reef from Notom Road to Boulder, or see below under On Wheels, Four-Wheel-Drive Trips.

Torrey to Bryce Canyon

Torrey, 11 miles west of Capitol Reef National Park on UT 24, is the closest town to the park offering accommodations and dining. There are several motels and modest restaurants. Other than that, there's not much happening here.

Bicknell and **Loa** are smaller towns northwest of Torrey on UT 24, also offering accommodations and dining possibilities. Loa actually has a tourist site, a **cheese factory**, which offers free samples. One reason for heading west on UT 24 from Torrey might be to stop in at the Teasdale Ranger Station, which administers the northern and eastern parts of the Dixie National Forest. The office is two miles west of Torrey on UT 24, then one mile south.

INFORMATION SOURCES

Teasdale Ranger Station, Dixie National Forest, PO Box 99, Teasdale, UT 84773, ☎ 801/425-3435.
Capitol Reef Reservations, PO Box 36, Teasdale, UT 84773, ☎ 801/245-3578 or 800/507-2624.
Wayne County Travel Council, PO Box 7, Teasdale, UT 84773, ☎ 800/858-7951.

Among the attractions in this area are the scenic drive possibilities along **UT 12**, a paved two-lane road heading south from Torrey to Boulder. For the next 122 miles to Red Canyon, this is a designated Scenic Byway, and the scenery is perhaps the most diverse in the state. It's a memorably pretty drive through aspen and evergreen forests, over a 9,200-foot-high pass on the Aquarius Plateau, also known as Boulder Mountain – the highest plateau in the United States. The route offers classic overlooks of Capitol Reef, Waterpocket Fold, the Henry Mountains, and the Circle Cliffs. There are several tree-shaded campgrounds along this route and opportunities for mountain hiking and fishing on nearly 100 alpine lakes. The lake country offers a sharp contrast to the nearby desert lands, as well as the imposing rocks of Capitol Reef and the canyons of the Escalante River farther south, continuing through the epic rock gardens of Bryce and Red canyons.

For information and maps of trails and fishing spots, contact the appropriate Forest Service office, Teasdale Ranger Station (see above) or, for the southern and western part of the Dixie National Forest, **Escalante Ranger District**, PO Box 246, Escalante, UT 84726. The Escalante office is on West Main.

Boulder, population 150, is 35 miles south of Torrey on UT 12. It's another very small town and was the last town in the United States to have a road built to it. Until 1939 mail was delivered by pack train. Today it has a few stores and gas stations, and even a new (1994) guest ranch – Boulder Mountain Ranch (see below under Accommodations) – to supplement a three-room do-it-yourself motel. The latter operates an honor system: You can take a room if the door's open, then leave your money when you check out; a maid comes by to clean once a day and collect the modest fees.

Boulder is the western terminus of the 40-mile **Burr Trail Road**, which crosses the Waterpocket Fold in the southern part of Capitol Reef National Park. The eastern end of the Burr Trail Road is at the junction with the Notom-Bullfrog Road, which runs north to south along the eastern boundary of the park. At the road junction,

Capitol Reef lies 30 miles to the north, and Bullfrog Marina at Lake Powell lies 30 miles south. Only the first 20 or so miles of the Burr Trail Road are paved from Boulder. Sharp dirt switchbacks cross the fold. In good weather, many people routinely drive this scenic road without four-wheel-drive vehicles. A number of trails and backroads fan off from here for hiking, biking, or jeeping.

Anasazi Indian Village State Park, PO Box 1329, Boulder, UT 84716, ☎ 801/335-7308, is three miles south of Boulder on UT 12. It contains the ruins of an Anasazi community, circa 1050-1200 A.D., thought to have housed as many as 200 residents. You can walk through the various ruins, or take a look at a replica six-room Anasazi dwelling, which illustrates a variety of construction methods. A small museum features excavated artifacts from the site, a slide show, and other informative displays, including a small model of the village as it probably looked in its heyday, and a replica of a granary and petroglyph panel.

In the 30 miles from Boulder to Escalante, UT 12 descends into the Escalante Canyon system, featuring hundreds of miles of wilderness hiking trails through slender slot canyons, to the Escalante River, which drains into the Colorado River. The Escalante was the last river to be found and surveyed in the contiguous 48 states.

Calf Creek Recreation Area, ☎ 801/826-4466, is nine miles south of Boulder, or 15 miles east of Escalante on UT 12. Calf Creek is a tributary of the Escalante River, which cuts a fertile swath through the surrounding layers of colorful sculpted rock. It has a small shaded campground and a picnic area.

A level 2½-mile trail along the canyon bottom from the campground leads to a 126-foot waterfall, **Lower Calf Creek Falls**. The falls tumble into a crystalline pool surrounded by oasis-like hanging gardens thriving amid the harsh, rocky splendor of the desert canyon. The trail closely follows the creek flowing through the box canyon, once used as a corral for cattle and, before that, by the Anasazi and earlier Indians who may have lived in caves along the canyon. Their primitive rock art is still visible today. Information about the area is available from the BLM office in Escalante (see below).

Escalante Petrified Forest State Park, PO Box 350, Escalante, UT 84726, ☎ 801/826-4466, is 1½ miles northwest of the town of Escalante, off UT 12. It has a shaded campground and self-guiding trails past colorful, gem-like slabs of petrified wood, dinosaur bones, and the ruins of a pre-Anasazi Indian village. **Wide Hollow Reservoir** is next to the campground, offering fishing and boating.

The town of **Escalante** has only 600 residents, but it is, nonetheless, the largest town for 60 miles in any direction. This is where you'll find current information about exploring the remote and extensive backcountry that is the real attraction in these parts. Modest accommodations and dining are available, along with several gift and outdoors shops, and small grocery stores.

INFORMATION SOURCES

There is a **Dixie National Forest office** in Escalante at 270 West Main. Other helpful offices in town include one for the **BLM,** Escalante Resource Area, PO Box 246, Escalante, UT 84726, ☎ 801/826-4291, and next door, a mile west of town on UT 12, one for the **National Park Service**, PO Box 511, Escalante, UT 84726, ☎ 801/826-4315. The Forest Service can provide hiking, driving and fishing maps and information on current conditions in the forests north of town. The BLM or Park Service has information and hiking maps to the Escalante River drainage canyons and into the Glen Canyon National Recreation Area. Either office can provide the necessary backcountry permit required for primitive camping.

There is also an **Escalante Interagency Office**, 755 West Main, PO Box 246, Escalante, UT 84726, ☎ 801/826-5499, which offers information on travel throughout the region, including maps and details about backcountry hiking, biking, jeeping, fishing and camping areas administered by the several federal agencies in town.

An additional source for area information is the **Escalante Chamber of Commerce**, PO Box 326, Escalante, UT 84726, ☎ 801/826-4810.

Beyond Escalante, UT 12 winds through the undistinguished small Western towns of Henrieville and Cannonville, where there is a turnoff to **Kodachrome Basin State Park**, PO Box 238, Cannonville, UT 84718, ☎ 801/679-8562. The park is seven miles south of UT 12 on a paved road. It is known for its colorful, photogenic cliffs, arches and petrified geyser holes, also known as sand pipes. These unusual formations are standing shafts of rock left exposed by the erosion of surrounding rocks, some the size of a person, others nearly 200 feet tall. One large standing rock, named after Fred Flintstone, really does look like the cartoon character, and other shapes are equally evocative. There is a picnic area and a campground, as well as a small concession stand for cold drinks, where you can arrange for horseback or wagon rides through portions of the large park.

Well-marked, easy hiking trails, including a short **nature trail**, lead to brightly colored rocks, arches, and the protruding sand pipes.

Angel's Palace Trail covers an easy one-mile loop from the group campground. **Eagle's View Trail** offers great views, but you have to climb up 1,000 feet from the campground. It ends two miles later in Henrieville.

Two sometimes marginal dirt roads head south from the park to US 89, providing a short-cut to Kanab or the southern end of Lake Powell. In dry weather these routes are generally okay without a four-wheel-drive. In any weather, road signs may be lacking, so a certain amount of innate navigational skill may be helpful. It also helps if you take your time; ostensible short cuts such as these may well save miles but not time. For details, see below, under Adventures, On Wheels.

UT 12 winds north from Cannonville through **Tropic**, another small rural town featuring some old historic architecture, as well as a couple of motels, B&Bs, and restaurants, a virtual metropolis for these parts. You can actually buy an ice cream cone here. One of the restaurants, at the **Bryce Pioneer Village**, is beside a log cabin built by Ebenezer Bryce, the namesake of Bryce Canyon.

You can hike from UT 12, north of town, on the three-mile round-trip **Mossy Cave Trail** into Bryce Canyon National Park. The trailhead is off UT 12, near the Water Canyon Bridge, four miles east of the turnoff to the park visitor center at the junction of UT 12 and UT 63. The trail provides the first glimpses of the vertical rock forms prevalent in Bryce Canyon and leads to an alcove with hanging gardens and refreshing water seeps.

Driving north from Tropic through Tropic Canyon, UT 12 passes into the northern area of **Bryce Canyon National Park**, Bryce Canyon, UT 84717, ☎ 801/834-5322, distinguished by evocative, multi-colored, free-standing rock spires and towers beneath the rim of the Paunsaugunt Plateau.

The enchanting mazes of hoodoos, pinnacles, and crenelated cliffs have been formed over 60 million years into whimsical sculptural shapes that look like palaces and chess pieces, mythical beasts and humans, all of which range through a bursting, ever-changing palette of tones according to the time of day and the angle of the sun.

The park is open year-round, but there may be snow in winter at the park's cool 6,600-9,100-foot elevations. Park roads are plowed but, unlike the crowded summers, few visitors show up. Winter is a special, extra-colorful time to visit, with bright snow and crusts of ice glimmering off the dazzling stone sentinels that inhabit the park.

Clocking mileage from Tropic, you have to drive a total of nine miles through the park from east to west on UT 12, and then turn south for three miles on UT 63 to reach the visitor center and the park's scenic drive. Just before you reach the park entrance, you will pass through a sprawling commercial enterprise you may mistake for the park itself, or perhaps a frontier Disneyland. This would be **Ruby's Inn**, a virtual municipality and legitimate destination in its own right, containing an enormous motel, the largest gift shop in Utah, several restaurants, a host of guided activities ranging from horseback to helicopter rides, and a rare-for-Utah state licensed liquor store. For information on Ruby's Inn see below, under Accommodations.

The **Bryce Canyon Visitor Center** features exhibits and a slide show explaining the natural and cultural history of the park, focusing on park geology, flora and fauna, as well as Indians and pioneering explorers and homesteaders. Park rangers lead numerous interpretive programs, campfire talks and hikes from May to September. Staff at the center can provide maps, handouts, and information on hiking and camping inside the park, and outside in the Dixie National Forest. Ruby's Inn is also a good source for area information.

The park is small by Utah standards, covering only 35,000 acres, and you can take in some marvelous views of the area from the scenic drive. Even so, as with the rest of southern Utah, you really need to get out of the car and walk a bit to soak up the flavor of the place. Sixty miles of trails, many of them fairly short and easy, lead directly to geological features that are barely visible from the scenic drive.

A number of trails are detailed below, under Bryce Canyon National Park On Foot. Overnight camping is only permitted on the Under-the-Rim Trail or Riggs Spring Loop Trail. Required backcountry permits are available from the visitor center.

The 17-mile **scenic drive** actually begins two miles before the center at **Fairyland Point**, overlooking hoodoos and contorted formations of Boat Mesa and the Chinese Wall in Fairyland Canyon. From Fairyland Point you can look out over the north rim of Bryce Canyon to Powell Point – named for John Wesley Powell, who first charted the Colorado River – and beyond for many, many miles. This is also a starting point for the **Rim Trail**, which covers 5½ miles around the top of Bryce Amphitheater to Bryce Point. The Rim Trail also connects to several other trails.

Sunrise and **Sunset Points** are a mile south of the center and are connected by a paved half-mile stretch of the Rim Trail. In the morning and evening the point overlooks offer highlighted views of the majestic Queen's Garden, the amphitheater and far beyond. A trail into the amphitheater starts at each point.

You can walk for a half-mile on the Rim Trail from Sunset Point, or drive a mile farther south on the scenic drive to **Inspiration Point**, which overlooks statuesque forms with a military bearing known as the Silent City.

Four miles from the visitor center, off the scenic drive, is **Bryce Point**, offering more overlooks to the north from the south end of Bryce Amphitheater. This is one end of the Rim Trail, and the starting point for several others, including **Peekaboo Loop Trail**, which leads to views of Alley Oop, Three Wise Men, and Fairy Castle among other famous sites. It is the only park trail open to horseback riders.

Paria View is off a side road to Bryce Point, offering rim views of the Pink Cliffs, Yellow Creek and beyond.

Farview Point is nine miles south of the center on the scenic drive. It features extensive views spanning several hundred miles, including the layer-cake levels of surrounding plateaus, the distant Aquarius Plateau and the chalky White Cliffs.

Natural Bridge is close to the scenic road, two miles past Farview Point. Another mile farther is **Agua Canyon Overlook**, surveying the rosy Pink Cliffs and jumbled hoodoos, and two miles farther is **Ponderosa Canyon Overlook.**

The drive then passes through evergreen and aspen glades before the road ends at an elevation of more than 9,000 feet near **Yovimpa Point** and **Rainbow Point**. They are only a short distance apart, but offer very different perspectives of the Colorado Plateau and rock formations below.

Bristlecone Loop Trail follows a one-mile loop from Rainbow Point past ancient, gnarled pine trees that are thought to be among the oldest living things on earth. Other longer trails start around here, too.

A **Walk-on Guide Service,** ☎ 801/679-8734, is offered in Bryce Canyon by a man named Ronnie. He hops aboard your car and explains folklore, history, and geology inside the park or out, and adds real cowboy stories told by a real cowboy. Presumably he scrapes his boots before the start of the tour.

Just west of Bryce Canyon on UT 12 is **Red Canyon**, essentially part of the same geological formations as the national park, but with far fewer people wandering around. There is a campground, hiking trails, and four-wheel-drive roads through pine forests and erosional features that easily rival nearby Bryce Canyon. This is a very special place that is often ignored by passing motorists.

A visitor center is on UT 12, 10 miles west of UT 63. For information, contact **Powell Ranger District**, 225 East Center Street, PO Box 80, Panguitch, UT 84726, ☎ 801/676-8815.

Another popular recreation area is located south of UT 12 along East Fork of the Sevier Scenic Backway. The road passes through a designated "watchable wildlife area," where you may possibly see mule deer, elk, and pronghorn antelope, as well as smaller animals and birds. Numerous backroads fan off from here for hiking, biking, or four-wheel-drive excursions. Seven miles from Red Canyon/UT 12, the road reaches **Tropic Reservoir**, with facilities for camping, boating, and fishing.

Scenic Tours & Shuttles, PO Box 25, Bryce, UT 84764, ☎ 801/834-5200 or 800/432-5383, fax 801/834-5200, can provide van transportation throughout the Bryce Canyon region and all of southwestern Utah. It offers wildlife tours, sunrise and sunset tours, hiking shuttles, plus one- or two-hour tours. In addition, guided all-terrain vehicle tours are offered for an hour or a half-day. Pre-ride instruction on safety and helmet use is included. Car rentals can also be arranged.

Cedar Breaks National Monument

From Bryce Canyon and Red Canyon there are two ways to reach Cedar Breaks National Monument, an often overlooked, rugged canyon filled with colorful cliffs and spires surrounded by aspen and evergreen forests. Either way, you have to drive 12 miles from the junction of UT 12 and UT 63 to US 89. You can then turn south on US 89 and drive 20 miles to Long Valley Junction (a small crossroads town with a few motels and restaurants), and head west on UT 14 for 22 miles to UT 148, which is the southern entrance to the park. Alternatively, drive north for seven miles on US 89 from UT 12, to Panguitch, then 28 miles southwest on UT 143 to Cedar Breaks' north entrance.

There are a few motels and restaurants in **Hatch**, north of Long Valley Junction on US 89. Eight miles west of the junction of US 89 and UT 14 is a turnoff to **Strawberry Point**, nine miles south of UT 14 on a dirt road. At the end of the road is a short trail to a scenic overlook at 9,000 feet, encompassing the Markagunt Plateau and Zion National Park.

Also on the way to Cedar Breaks, heading west from Long Valley Junction on UT 14, are recreational areas around Duck Creek Village, Duck Lake and Navajo Lake.

Panguitch, long useful mainly for the services it provides in modest motels, restaurants, and gas stations, is really starting to come around these days. There are a couple of decent restaurants, a curious taxidermy museum and even a fashionable cappucino-espresso bar. There are also some historic brick structures in town. There's an information center in the city park. For area-wide information, including Bryce and Zion national parks and Scenic Byway 12, contact the extremely helpful **Garfield County Travel Council**, PO Box 200, Panguitch, UT 84759, ☎ 801/676-2311 or 800/444-6689. There's also a Forest Service office in town.

If you wind up spending a night in Panguitch or close by, you'll note that there's not a whole lot to do (no bars!). However, if it happens to be a Tuesday through Saturday night between June 20 and the end of August, you might chance upon a live theatrical production at the **Panguitch Playhouse**, PO Box 596, Panguitch, UT 84759, ☎ 801/676-8513. The Panguitch Players perform "a sometimes hilarious live stage show," featuring "refined and moral entertainment," at the Historic Panguitch Social Hall (50 East Center Street).

Heading south from Panguitch on UT 143 is **Panguitch Lake**, a small resort area. Four miles south of Panguitch Lake on UT 143 is a turnoff to the east, leading in two miles onto a dirt road to **Mammoth Creek Springs**, a clear-flowing, lush, vegetated garden spot.

Ten miles past the springs turnoff on UT 143 is **Mammoth Cave**, the remnant of an ancient lava flow. You can walk and crawl through two levels of tunnels.

Cedar Breaks National Monument, 82 North 100 East, Room 3, PO Box 749, Cedar City, UT 84720, ☎ 801/586-9451, contains a massive amphitheater 2,500 feet deep and three miles wide, filled with whimsical rock forms, spires and pinnacles in a full artist's palette of bright colors. It looks a lot like Bryce Canyon but – at 2,000 feet higher, ranging from 8,000 feet to 10,600 feet – the feeling is one of more ethereal serenity. And the crowds here are considerably thinner than at better-known Bryce.

The high altitude means a short season here. Due to snow closures, the five-mile **scenic rim drive** (UT 148) is generally open to cars only from mid-May to mid-October, although it is open to snowmobilers and cross-country skiers in winter.

A visitor center, a mile north of the park's south entrance on the scenic drive, is also open only in the summer. It has a few small exhibits describing flora and fauna, as well as rocks in the park and surrounding areas. Interpretive programs and hikes are led by park rangers. There are four overlooks on the scenic drive and several hiking trails along the rim, but no trails descend into the amphitheater from inside the park.

Brian Head, elevation 9,850 feet, is on UT 143, 2½ miles north of Cedar Breaks National Monument, or 14 miles south of Parowan, a rock-ribbed Mormon community and the oldest town in this part of Utah. Since the Cedar Breaks road from the south is often closed in winter, the Parowan route from the north may be the only way to reach Brian Head at that time of year.

Brian Head is the site of a year-round resort complex, featuring downhill and cross-country skiing in winter, and mountain biking in summer. In addition, the resort area has around 3,000 rooms in condos, hotels, and motels, so the level of amenities is somewhat more sophisticated and diverse than is found throughout most of the area covered in this chapter. You can find hot tubs and swimming pools, decent food, and even wine lists. Several choices for accommodations and dining are covered below, under Cedar Breaks National Monument Accommodations & Restaurants.

You can drive to the top of **Brian Head Peak**, elevation 11,307 feet, in a passenger car. Drive south two miles on UT 143, then three miles northeast on a dirt road to reach the mountain top for expansive scenic views.

For area information, contact **Brian Head Chamber of Commerce**, Brian Head, UT 84719, ☎ 801/677-2810.

Zion Overlook is 16 miles east of Cedar City, eight miles west of the south entrance to Cedar Breaks National Monument on UT 14. When you pull off the road you can see a big slice of southwestern Utah, all the way south to Zion National Park.

Cedar City & St. George

Cedar City really is a city, at least compared to everything else so far in southern Utah. It has a population of around 11,000 and is even close to a real interstate highway, I-15, 50 miles northeast of St. George (southwestern Utah's other commercial metropolis). Cedar City is 18 miles west of Cedar Breaks National Monument on UT 14. There are plenty of places to stay and eat in town.

The city is justifiably renowned for its **Utah Shakespearean Festival**, 351 West Center Street, Cedar City, UT 84720, ☎ 801/586-7878 or 800/PLAYTIX, (see below, under Eco-Tours & Cultural Excursions).

The **Iron Mission State Historical Park and Pioneer Museum**, 585 North Main, PO Box 1079, Cedar City, UT 84720, ☎ 801/586-9290, contains items relating to the history of the area, from ancient and modern Indian artifacts to pioneer-era farm equipment and horse-drawn vehicles. There's even a stagecoach complete with bullet holes supposedly deposited by Utah's most famous outlaw, Butch Cassidy.

INFORMATION SOURCES

Cedar City Chamber of Commerce, 286 North Main, PO Box 220, Cedar City, UT 84720, ☎ 801/586-5124, maintains a visitor center to provide information about the city and surrounding areas. One of their free brochures details a 14-site historical tour of the town. The most interesting place on the tour is probably the **Rock Church** at Center and 100 East, ☎ 801/586-8475. It was made out of many different types of local rocks during the Depression, when local Mormons couldn't afford anything else.

All Southern Utah Free Reservation Center, 97 North Main, PO Box 1222, Cedar City, UT 84721, ☎ 801/586-1275, might be worth a try for booking accommodations and activities around here.

The local office of the Dixie National Forest can help with information about backroad adventures on the Markagunt Plateau. Contact **Cedar City Ranger District**, 82 North 100 East, PO Box 627, Cedar City, UT 84720, ☎ 801/586-2421.

The airport in town is served by **Skywest/Delta Connection**, with service primarily to Salt Lake City, Las Vegas and St. George. For information, ☎ 801/586-3033 or 800/453-9417.

Rental car agencies at the airport include **Avis**, ☎ 801/586-3033, and **National**, ☎ 801/586-7059. In-town car rental agencies include **Hertz**, ☎ 801/586-6096, and **Speedy**, ☎ 801/586-7368.

Travelling west of Cedar City on UT 56 leads quickly away from civilization and back into the sage-laden, sandy terrain of the **Escalante Desert**. After 19 miles, there's a turnoff to the south, which leads in three miles to the remains of **Old Iron Town**, a ghost town that once thrived on iron smelting. There's not much left today, but you can see some foundations and ovens and, if you want to stop for a picnic, there's a table.

Continuing west for another 20 miles, then turning south onto UT 18 leads back into the farthest western portion of the Dixie National Forest. After 12 miles you can turn west to **Enterprise Reservoir** to fish, or continue south on UT 18, up the flank of Big Mountain.

Six miles south of the Enterprise exit on UT 18 is a turnoff to **Mountain Meadows Massacre Site and Memorial**. There's a small monument a mile west of the main road. In 1857, local Mormons and Indians killed 120 members of a wagon train that was passing through on the way to California. It took 20 years to bring one of the major culprits to justice, but eventually he was executed here, at the massacre site.

Seven miles farther south on UT 18 is the small town of Central, where a turn to the east leads in seven miles to **Pine Valley**, site of one of the oldest Mormon churches in the state. Pine Valley is high in the forested, cool mountains again, on the edge of the **Pine Valley Recreation Area** and **Pine Valley Mountain Wilderness Area**. There's not much happening in the way of business here, other than the **Pine Valley Lodge** (see below, under Cedar City Accommodations), which does offer cabin rentals and horseback riding. There are several campgrounds and many trails for hiking, as well as streams and a reservoir for trout fishing. You can also hire a backcountry guide at the lodge. The wilderness area is accessible only on foot or by horseback.

Back on UT 18, heading south for six miles will bring you to **Veyo**. This town is notable mainly for the **Veyo Pool Resort**, which features a natural hot springs swimming pool. Ten miles southwest of Veyo on UT 91 is **Gunlock State Park**, the centerpiece of which is Gunlock Reservoir, noted for boating and waterskiing, as well as bass fishing.

Fifteen miles farther southeast on UT 18 and east on UT 300 is **Snow Canyon State Park**, PO Box 140, Santa Clara, UT 84765, ☎ 801/628-2255. The park has crenelated red rock escarpments, contrasting black lava beds, volcanic cones, sand dunes, desert flora, rattlesnakes, lizards and three lava caves that can be explored on foot. There is a campground, hiking trails, and horseback riding.

The newest attraction amid the beauty of Snow Canyon, seen in movies such as *Butch Cassidy and the Sundance Kid* and *The Electric Horseman*, is a privately owned, $25 million performing arts center called **Tuacahn**. It is the site of an outdoor theatrical show called *Utah!* (see below, under Eco-tours and Cultural Excursions). The Indian word "Tuacahn" means "canyon of the gods" and it is an appropriate one for this stunning site.

The village of **Santa Clara**, four miles west of St. George on UT 91, is the site of the **Jacob Hamblin Home**, ☎ 801/673-2161, a pioneer homestead open to tours, and the true historical home of the leading character in the *Utah!* production at Tuacahn.

St. George is five miles southeast of Snow Canyon on UT 18, or 50 miles south of Cedar City on I-15. It's the largest city in southern

Utah and the state's fastest growing one, with a population of around 30,000. It's booming primarily from a migration of retirees and winter residents (snowbirds) who come to "the other Palm Springs" for the salubrious, warm and sunny climate, not to mention a glut of golf courses and factory outlet stores. No doubt part of the appeal of St. George to new residents is in its Mormon inclinations. You're a lot less likely to be bothered by drunk drivers or drive-by shootings in Utah than elsewhere, and yet St. George is only an hour from the Nevada state line and just a couple of hours from Las Vegas, with all its decidedly un-Mormon-like ideas of fun.

One of the earliest snowbirds was Brigham Young, who built a house here in 1873, at 89 West 20 North, ☎ 801/673-2517. Guided tours of the **Brigham Young House** show the many original furnishings. It's part of a 23-site historic **St. George Walking Tour** sponsored by the **Daughters of the Utah Pioneers Museum**, 145 North 100 East, St. George, UT 84770, ☎ 801/628-7274. The museum contains pioneer portraits and artifacts, and is also part of the nine-block walking tour.

The most obvious landmark in town is the **St. George Temple** at 400 East 200 South. Built in 1877, it's Utah's oldest Mormon church, and you are only allowed to admire it from the outside – just like all Mormon temples – unless you're a bonafide Mormon. Guided tours of the grounds are available and non-Mormon visitors are allowed in a small visitor center, ☎ 801/673-5181, featuring historical displays and background on the Mormon religion. Anyone can take a guided tour of the **Mormon Tabernacle**, at Main and Tabernacle, ☎ 801/628-4072.

Another interesting cultural attraction is the **St. George Art Museum**, 175 East 200 North, ☎ 801/634-5800, featuring unverified works said to have been painted by Degas, Rembrandt, and Van Gogh. Yet another cultural site is a 15-foot-high, 127-foot-long tiled mural depicting local history. The mosaic is on an outer wall at the **Dixie College Fine Arts Building**, 700 East 100 South.

INFORMATION SOURCES

Southwestern Utah's Color Country, PO Box 1550, St. George, UT 84770-1550, ☎ 800/233-UTAH, fax 801/673-3540. This is a main source for regional information about all of southwestern Utah and can probably provide just about everything you might get from any of the other sources.

St. George Chamber of Commerce, 97 East St. George Boulevard, St. George, UT 84770, ☎ 801/628-0505. This 1876 building was once a county courthouse and is worth a stop even if you don't want any brochures.

Washington County Travel & Convention Bureau, 425 South 700 East, St. George, UT 84770, ☎ 801/634-5745, offers visitor info.

Southern Utah Tourist Information and Services, 135 North 900 East, Suite #2, St. George, UT 84770, ☎ 801/628-7710 or 800/765-7710, fax 801/628-3634, can also provide brochures.

Pine Valley Ranger District Office, 196 East Tabernacle, St. George, UT 84770, ☎ 801/673-3431, can provide information on outdoor activities for the areas north of St. George in the Dixie National Forest, Pine Valley Recreation Area, and Pine Valley Mountains Wilderness Area.

The local **BLM** office is at 225 West Bluff Street, St. George, UT 84770, ☎ 801/673-4654, or 801/628-4491.

St. George Municipal Airport is served by **Skywest/Delta Connection**, with service primarily to Salt Lake City, Las Vegas, Phoenix and Cedar City. For information, ☎ 800/453-9417. Rental car agencies at the airport include **Avis**, ☎ 801/673-3686, or **National**, ☎ 801/673-5098. There are several other car rental agencies in town, including **Dollar**, ☎ 801/628-6549, and **Budget**, ☎ 801/673-6825.

Zion National Park

Zion National Park, Springdale, UT 84767, ☎ 801/772-3256, lies northeast of St. George and northwest of Lake Powell in a stunning canyon filled with massive sandstone cliffs and protruding rock formations ranging in elevation from 3,600 to 8,700 feet. Colorful mesas tower above convoluted canyons and lush valleys enlivened by waterfalls and rivers. Hiking trails are both plentiful and rewarding. Horseback trips are available.

Visiting the whole park takes a bit of trucking around. The main entrance is north of Springdale, 60 miles due south of Cedar City. Alternatively, it is 42 miles northwest of St. George, west of I-15, off UT 9. There's also an east entrance to Zion from Mt. Carmel Highway (UT 9), west of the town of Mt. Carmel Junction. It goes through some of the most remote terrain in the park. A third access road to Zion is 35 miles northwest of St. George, 16 miles south of Cedar City, off I-15, on the 5½-mile Kolob Canyons Road. In this northwestern corner of the park a small visitor center is situated just inside the park boundary. There are a few small exhibits plus maps and information on Kolob area trails. Backcountry permits required for overnight trips are available at the center.

Beyond the Kolob Visitor Center, **Kolob Canyons Road** continues past numerous scenic stops characterized by colorful cliffs and mountainous terrain, through the Finger Canyons of the Kolob. The road ends at **Kolob Canyons Viewpoint**, which overlooks many of the major geographic features of the park. Several hiking trails start along the road, including a trail to **Kolob Arch**, which may be even longer than Landscape Arch in Arches National Park, depending on who's doing the measuring.

Yet another road passes through a portion of Zion Park – the **Kolob Terrace Road**. To reach it from Kolob Canyons Road, return to I-15 and head south for 15 miles to UT 17. This meets UT 9 six miles west of the town of Virgin. Here, the road starts to the north. It's paved only through the park and after 20 miles, just before Lava Point, it turns to dirt and gravel the rest of the way to UT 14, five miles east of Cedar City.

The steep road, usually closed in winter, passes a number of scenic views of canyons and watercourses. It also provides access to some of the more remote backcountry hiking trails in the park, including the 13-mile, multi-day **West Rim Trail**, which most people hike the other way, from Zion Canyon to the Kolob. Other challenging trails lead to Kolob Arch. Contact park rangers for information on these rugged backcountry trails.

Lava Point is 21 miles northeast of Virgin. Its 7,890-foot elevation provides stunning views of the Zion Canyon Narrows, as well as sites much farther away, such as Cedar Breaks and the Pink Cliffs. There is a primitive campground and north of Lava Point, beyond the park boundary, is the **Kolob Reservoir**, for boating and fishing.

Springdale is a little town near Zion's south entrance. All visitors' services, including groceries, dining, accommodations, and RV parks, are available here. A side trip south from town leads to the ghost town of **Grafton**, where parts of *Butch Cassidy and the Sundance Kid* were filmed and a cemetery marker memorializes a family killed by Indians in 1866.

Outskirts south of Springdale are good for hiking, biking and four-wheel driving far from the crowds of Zion. Contact the BLM office in St. George for information.

Just outside Zion National Park, the third offering in what is being billed as "The Trio Grande" (along with the Utah Shakespearean Festival and the *Utah!* show at Tuacahn), is yet another man-made feature presented at the new **Zion Cinemax Theater**. Here, you can see a 40-minute film called *Treasure of the Gods*, presented on a screen 60 feet tall and 80 feet wide. Viewers get an overview of the natural wonders of all the Southwest, not just Utah, including dizzying footage shot in Zion and Bryce

Canyon, as well as Arizona's Canyon de Chelly and Monument Valley, and Colorado's Mesa Verde. I can't even remember the story, which seemed incidental to the spectacular footage of rock climbers and long distance runners amid powerful scenery, but it did include Anasazi Indians, Spanish treasure seekers, and a flash flood through a slot canyon. The film did its job, though. It sure made me feel antsy about getting out of a movie theater and into the park lands that are still, primarily, what this state is all about. The theater is at 145 Zion Park Boulevard, Springdale, UT 84767, ☎ 801/772-2400.

Zion National Park

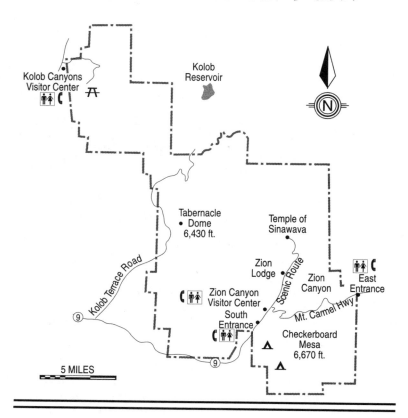

Zion Scenic Drive is a six-mile route that follows the North Fork of the Virgin River through 2,400-foot-deep **Zion Canyon**. It starts north of Springdale, a half-mile north of the year-round visitor center, which is filled with exhibits relating to park geology and geography, abundant park wildlife, Anasazi Indian artifacts and pioneer Mormon exploration. This is where you can pick up information on hiking trails and the permit you'll need for camping in the backcountry. In addition, many ranger-led interpretive programs and hikes are offered. A schedule is posted here.

At intervals along the scenic drive, parking areas are provided near spots with especially scenic views (Court of the Patriarchs, Mountain of the Sun, Great White Throne, and Weeping Rock). Hiking trails branch off from the scenic drive which ends at the **Temple of Sinawava**, a natural amphitheater of bright cliffs, distinguished by two tall spires in the middle.

Halfway up the scenic drive is the venerable **Zion Lodge**, built in 1925. It has a stunning setting, with the river running by and tall cliffs and rock outcrops soaring above. The lodge offers year-round accommodations, a dining room, snack bar, horseback rides, vehicle tours, and shuttles for hikers.

Kanab to Page, Arizona, Glen Canyon & Lake Powell

Travelling east 24 miles from Zion National Park on the Zion-Mt. Carmel Highway leads through the southeastern portion of the park. This area is a maze of twisting canyons, hoodoos, slickrock and the aptly-named **Checkerboard Mesa**. The road passes through a long tunnel and after 10 miles joins with US 89 at **Mt. Carmel Junction**, where there are a few shops, restaurants and motels.

Three and a half miles south of the junction is a turnoff on US 89 to **Coral Pink Sand Dunes State Park**, PO Box 95, Kanab, UT 84741, ☎ 801/874-2408. The paved road leads 11 miles southwest to the park, where half the desert terrain is sand dunes – some several hundred feet high, some tinted a definite pinkish color most noticeable early in the morning or late in the afternoon. Hiking trails criss-cross the park, there is a campground, and there are special four-wheel-drive areas that are popular with dune buggy enthusiasts. There is a fenced-off three-acre area set aside for jumping, diving, rolling and playing in the sand. Other restrictions apply in an effort to protect the fragile desert environment. Contact the park for information.

Also on the way heading south on US 89, 5½ miles north of Kanab, is **Moqui Cave**, a tantalizingly tacky gift shop in a cave, specializing in locally extracted rocks and minerals. There's also a museum displaying Indian arrowheads and pottery, one of the largest fluorescent mineral displays in the USA, the largest collection of dinosaur tracks in southern Utah, and a display of foreign monies.

Kanab, 17 miles south of Mt. Carmel Junction on US 89, is filled with modest motels and restaurants, pioneer architecture and historic links with Hollywood movie and TV productions. One of the few vestiges of Hollywood's apparently played-out love affair with the area is **Lopeman's Frontier Movie Town**, 297 West Center Street, ☎ 801/644-5337, open April to November. It's a fake Western town displaying movie sets, false front shops, and fake shoot-outs. If you want to see the real Hollywood locations, ask here for directions to the sites of the opening scenes for the 50s TV series *The Lone Ranger* and *Rin Tin Tin,* or visit the **Johnson Canyon Movie Set**, PO Box 332, Kanab, UT 84774, ☎ 801/644-3187, nine miles east of Kanab on US 89, then five miles north, up Johnson Canyon. The decrepit site looks like a typical ghost town until you start wandering around with a tour guide. He shows you photos from numerous feature films and TV shows that were made here, and slowly the scene takes on a different aspect. Over there is Doc's office in *Gunsmoke*. A few doors down is Miss Kitty's Long Branch Saloon. Recognizable movie stills depict Charlton Heston and Forrest Tucker in 1953's *Pony Express,* Gregory Peck, Telly Savalas and Omar Sharif in 1969's *Mackenna's Gold. Have Gun Will Travel* and *Wagon Train* are also included among Hollywood productions filmed here.

The stars who acted in movies filmed in Kane County (though not necessarily Johnson Canyon) include Richard Burton, Sammy Davis Jr., Clint Eastwood, Henry Fonda, Jodie Foster, Preston Foster, James Garner, Ava Gardner, Jack Nicholson, Gregory Peck, Ronald Reagan, Frank Sinatra, James Stewart, John Wayne, and Raquel Welch.

Back in Kanab, yet another link with Hollywood is **Denny's Wigwam**, 78 East Center Street, ☎ 801/644-2452 or 800/854-8549. Denny is a large man who once doubled in Western films for Dean Martin and still radiates a theatrical charm. He hosts the show here, which includes a ton of Western bric-a-brac identified as a Western museum, covered wagons, a blacksmith shop, a John Wayne Room, group Western cookouts, a cavernous gift shop crammed with cowboy and Indian stuff, a Western wear emporium (hats, boots, clothing), and an old-fashioned ice cream parlor. He wears the sort of colorful cowboy duds you would expect to see on a 1950s-era Western movie star, tells funny stories, drops names shamelessly from the movie days, and poses for pictures with tourists, who seem to eat it all up in grand portions.

There are some possibilities for backcountry travel in the area; hiking trails and four-wheel-drive roads meander through the desert. And Kanab, though not the most sophisticated town, does offer inexpensive motels and restaurants. It is actually perfectly situated as a base. Explore Zion and Bryce, the North Rim of the Grand Canyon (you can drive straight south from Kanab to reach the North Rim), and Lake Powell, all within a few hours of here, in different directions. For information, contact **Kane County Information Center**, 41 South 100 East, Kanab, UT 84741, ☎ 801/644-5033, or 800/644-KANE, or the local office of the **BLM**, 318 North 100 East, Kanab, UT 84741, ☎ 801/644-2672.

To complete the tour of southern Utah, you must cross the state line and head to Page, Arizona. This is the main gateway to Lake Powell and is 75 miles east on US 89.

Travelling east from Kanab on US 89, the scenery becomes more desolate and desert-like. Nine miles east of town is the southern end of the **Skutumptah Canyon Road**, at Johnson Canyon, which is paved at this end and goes north through the Vermillion Cliffs, White Cliffs and Pink Cliffs. It leads to Kodachrome Basin State Park after 49 miles.

Forty-three miles east of Kanab is the BLM's **Pariah Canyon Ranger Station**, which administers the Pariah Canyon Vermillion Cliffs Wilderness Area, a remote area of little-visited canyons and watercourses spanning the Utah-Arizona border. There is a truly adventurous 40-mile hiking trip possible here, but only for the well-experienced, self-sufficient hiker. For information, see below under Kanab to Page Hiking.

On US 89, 75 miles east of Kanab, is **Page**, Arizona, the largest town on the shore of Lake Powell. It developed in 1957 as the construction base for the 710-foot-high Glen Canyon Dam, which created the 250-square-mile lake, most of which is in Utah. The dam was completed in 1964. Page has since grown as a major service town, offering motels, campgrounds, RV parks, restaurants, gas stations, and shops. All-important boat rentals are available at **Wahweap Marina**, a few miles north of town.

Most people don't spend a lot of time in Page, but coming and going through here, there are a few interesting attractions. These include the free tour of **Glen Canyon Dam**, ☎ 520/645-2511.

INFORMATION SOURCES

Tthe **Carl Hayden Visitor Center**, ☎ 520/608-6404, features a movie about Lake Powell, exhibits on the construction of the dam, and a Navajo rug display.

The **National Park Service**, PO Box 1507, Page, AZ 86040, operates an information booth in the visitor center adjacent to the dam. This is where you can get details on camping, hiking, and boating activities within Glen Canyon National Recreation Area.

Page/Lake Powell Chamber of Commerce, 716 Rim View Drive, PO Box 727, Page, AZ, ☎ 520/645-2741, offers information on town and lake activities. It also makes tour reservations.

Sky West/Delta Connection, ☎ 520/645-9200 or 800/453-9417, offers scheduled service connecting Page with Salt Lake City, Flagstaff, Phoenix and Las Vegas.

Avis, ☎ 520/645-2024, rents cars at the airport. **Budget**, ☎ 520/645-3977, has an office in town.

The **John Wesley Powell Memorial Museum**, at Lake Powell Boulevard and North Navajo Drive, ☎ 520/645-9496, displays an historical exhibit on the Colorado River and the people who have run it over the years. Other displays tell the movie-making story of the area, as well as more distant geological and social history.

Lake Powell's nearly 2,000 miles of shoreline extend throughout hundreds of branching fingers of sheer-walled canyons that range in color from pale tan to flaming orange. Networks of waterways intertwine through the canyons, offering ever-changing waters for a variety of watersports. Scuba diving to submerged Indian ruins in the lake is just one option. Part of the adventure that lures three million travellers each year is the varying water level; you can never be sure to see the same coves, caves, or inlets again. You can travel in your own boat or rent one at a marina. Stepping ashore you can find hiking trails into remote backcountry, including the Escalante River Canyon, Dark Canyon or the Grand Gulch Primitive Area.

Wahweap Lodge and Marina, Box 1597, Page, AZ 86040, ☎ 520/645-2433, is six miles north of Page and includes the Rainbow Room restaurant and an RV park.

Guided tours available include half-day or full-day boat excursions to Rainbow Bridge National Monument. For information, see below under Lake Powell Boating. Also offered are dinner and sunset tours on Wahweap Bay aboard the *Canyon King* – a stern-wheel paddleboat. All manner of boat and water accessory services can be found here; houseboats in various sizes, motor boats, jet skis, waterskis, and fishing gear. You can stock up on provisions for your houseboat or picnic at the nearby campground operated by the Park Service.

Wahweap operates a free bus service for guests from mid-May through mid-October, between the lodge and selected Page destinations, including the airport, the shopping center, river float tour offices, the John Wesley Powell Museum and the Carl Hayden Visitor Center at Glen Canyon Dam.

Dangling Rope Marina, ☎ 520/645-2969, is situated 40 miles uplake from Wahweap and is accessible only by water. Facilities include a ranger station, grocery store, and marine gas station.

Adventures

Adventures in southern Utah's isolated backcountry can provide enlivening challenges, excitement, and fun. This may be one of the most hauntingly beautiful places you'll ever see, but it is still quite rugged. Lack of preparation can swiftly turnan outing into a disaste. A topographic map is a must for backcountry excursions. Always carry sufficient water for everyone (a gallon daily, per person), and it is highly recommended that you consult with Forest Service or BLM offices for updates on conditions and predicted weather changes. Roads and trails that are passable when dry may not be when wet. Canyon bottoms and washes may flood in sudden thunderstorms. River conditions change all the time. Extremely hot and dry weather can compromise your enjoyment in the shadeless backcountry. For state-wide weather reports call the National Weather Service, ☎ 801/524-5133. For road conditions, ☎ 801/964-6000 or 800/492-2400.

For those preferring to engage the demands of the backcountry with a skilled guide, a number of reputable outfitters are included below. For additional information contact **Utah Guides & Outfitters**, 153 East 7200 South, Midvale, UT 84047, ☎ 801/566-2662.

On Foot

There are thousands of miles of hiking and backpacking trails in southern Utah. Hikes range from leisurely walks along nature trails to strenuous rocky scrambles. Many bike trails and jeep roads are also good for hiking.

Remember the following:

❑ Always take the necessary precautions. Pay attention to weather changes.
❑ Watch children; make sure they don't wander off.
❑ Never hike alone.
❑ Certain backcountry restrictions are enforced in national parks. Check first.
❑ Fires are not usually allowed in the backcountry, so a backpacking cook stove is necessary.
❑ Where backcountry camping is permitted, campsites must be at least a half-mile from roads, trails, or other improved facilities.
❑ Backcountry permits are required. These are available free from the administering agency.
❑ All garbage must be carried out or deposited in provided receptacles.
❑ Pets are not allowed on hiking trails, river trips, or in the backcountry. In areas that do allow pets, they must be on a leash at all times.
❑ Stay on designated trails. Steep slopes and cliff edges can be dangerous, and damaging to fragile soils. All plants, animals and artifacts are protected. It is against the law to disturb them.
❑ Fishing is allowed with the proper license.

The Hiker's Guide to Utah, Dave Hall, Falcon Press, 1991, is a detailed and useful volume.

In addition to hiking and backpacking, Utah offers one of the world's grandest stages for rock climbing adventures. For information from experts about some of the possibilities, contact **Exum Mountain Adventures Rock and Alpine Climbing**, 1427 East Ironwood Avenue, Salt Lake City, UT 84121, ☎ 801/273-1850. Additional rock climbing information is available from park rangers, forest service and BLM sources listed throughout the text.

MOAB

Enticing trails start right in town, or close by. Look here for hikes with packstock or, for the skilled adventurer with adequate gear and a climbing partner, rock and ice climbing. Popular climbing areas are in the vicinity of **Fisher Towers, Arches National Park, Potash Road,** and **Indian Creek.**

The following are among the best hiking and backpacking areas.

Mill Creek Canyon starts on Powerhouse Lane, at the end of Mill Creek Drive. It's a short hike skirting the edge of the creek to several shaded swimming holes, or you can keep going beyond a fork in the trail for a more challenging hike.

Hidden Valley Trail starts south of town, off US 191 to Angel Rock Road. Continue to a right turn onto Rimrock Lane. The trailhead is in a parking lot. It's a two-mile hike with a series of switchbacks to the Moab Rim. At the top is a satisfying view of Moab and Spanish Valley.

Corona Arch Trail starts 10 miles west of Moab, off UT 279 (Potash Road), near the railroad tracks in a parking lot. It's 1½ miles one-way to views of Corona and Bow Tie arches.

Negro Bill Canyon starts off UT 128 (River Road), three miles past the junction with US 191. The parking lot is marked. Two miles up the trail is Morning Glory Arch; its 243-foot span makes it the sixth largest natural stone arch in the country. It's possible to continue hiking beyond the arch and all the way back to Moab (about 15 miles), but there is no maintained trail and a topographic map might come in handy.

The **La Sal Mountains** (Utah's second highest mountain range) cover an area 15 miles long and six miles wide. Ranging as high as 12,721 feet at Mount Peale, the La Sals are laced with nearly 100 miles of hiking trails.

The mountain terrain is extremely different from the sandy river country of giant rocks and canyons. The aspen- and spruce-forested La Sals are filled with streams, lakes, and wildlife, including black bears. For information on trails, contact the US Forest Service in Moab.

Moab Outabouts, PO Box 314, Moab, UT 84532, ☎ 801/259-2209, runs guided hiking and backpacking trips in the Moab/La Sals/Canyonlands area.

ARCHES NATIONAL PARK

You can hike through the backcountry here or follow well-marked, established trails to numerous sites, including Delicate Arch (three miles round-trip), and the Devils Garden. The **Devils Garden Trail** leads to the greatest concentration of off-road arches in the park. If you go only as far as Landscape Arch, 106 feet high and spanning 306 feet, it is a two-mile round-trip hike. A four-mile round-trip will lead you to Double O Arch. Complete trail and backcountry information is available at the park's visitor center (PO Box 907, Moab, UT 84532, ☎ 801/259-8161).

ISLAND IN THE SKY DISTRICT

Neck Spring Trail starts on the other side of the road from the Shafer Canyon Overlook, a half-mile past the visitor center. It's a five-mile loop descending 300 feet to several springs.

Lathrop Trail starts a mile past the center and offers a challenging hike down to the Colorado River, descending 2,100 feet in nine miles. It is the only marked foot trail in this area that leads from the mesa top to the river. A primitive campground is on the edge of the river. Bring plenty of water; There's not much shade.

Mesa Arch Trail is much easier than Lathrop, covering only a half-mile for the entire round-trip to Mesa Arch. The trailhead is on the left, 5½ miles from the center.

Hands-on learning trips focusing on challenging real-life situations are offered by **Outward Bound**, 384 Field Point Road, Greenwich, CT 06830, ☎ 203/661-0797 or 800/243-8520, fax 203/661-0903. Southern Utah wilderness trips run six to 29 days and are devised to build teamwork, trust, and concern for others. Itineraries include rock climbing, whitewater rafting, hiking, and kayaking.

NEEDLES DISTRICT

More than 50 miles of maintained trails wind through the Needles District. You can hike for an hour or many days in the backcountry.

There may or may not be water available and any that you come upon would need to be treated. It's probably best to carry water, and don't forget insect repellent and sunscreen in the summertime.

A trail near the Squaw Flat Campground leads to **Peekaboo Trail**, a 10-mile round-trip past Indian ruins, including steep slickrock segments. The halfway point of this trail is **Peekaboo Campground**, where petroglyphs can be seen on the surrounding rock walls. Other marked trails veer off through Squaw Canyon or Lost Canyon, and loop back to the Squaw Flats Campground. **Elephant Hill Trail**, at the picnic area three miles past Squaw Flat Campground, leads to some of the park's most testing and beautiful terrain. **Chesler Park Trail** (off Elephant Hill Trail) is a six-mile round-trip through the slender, multi-colored rock spires that gave the Needles District its name. From Chesler Park, a meadow surrounded by towering sandstone needles, a five-mile trail loops around the entire park district.

The rather difficult **Lower Red Lake Canyon Trail** also begins from the Elephant Hill Trail and drops 1,000 feet in 10 miles to the Colorado River. Remember that it's another 10 miles back up. Don't consider this hike under the hot, mid-summer sun unless you're a reptile. Bring plenty of water.

The **Confluence Overlook Trail** starts at the end of the paved park road at Big Spring Canyon Overlook. It is an 11-mile round-trip leading to a 1,000-foot-high viewpoint of the Colorado River. There are excellent views of side canyons and the Needles along the way.

Wild Horizons Expeditions, West Fork Road, Darby, MT 59829, ☎ 406/821-3747, offers guided naturalist/conservationist backpacking trips in Canyonlands National Park for a maximum of eight hikers. All must be willing to shoulder 40-pound backpacks for six to seven miles each day. Scheduled trips run from March to September and emphasize safe, low-impact hiking and camping. Customized and family trips are available.

MONUMENT VALLEY

Where backcountry activities on Navajoland are allowed, permits and fees are required. Information is available from **Navajo Parks & Recreation Department,** PO Box 308, Window Rock, AZ 86515, ☎ 520/871-4941, ext. 6647. The office is next to the zoo. Permits are available by mail or in person and there is a walk-in permit station at the Cameron Visitor Center, south of Cameron Trading Post on US 89 at the junction with AZ 64.

Rock climbing and off-trail hiking are prohibited on the Navajo Reservation. In many places, loose, fragile rock and unfamiliar terrain may make climbing and hiking hazardous.

Hiking without a licensed Navajo guide is not permitted in Monument Valley. Guided hiking tours in Monument Valley, Mystery Valley and Hunts Mesa are offered by **Fred's Adventure Tours,** PO Box 310308, Mexican Hat, UT 94531, ☎ 801/739-4294, and **Black's Hiking and Van Tours,** PO Box 393, Mexican Hat, UT 84531, ☎ 801/739-4226. Otherwise, inquire of the local tour operators around the visitor center for hiking guide services by the hour or extended overnight backpack trips. A number of these operators are listed below, under jeeping.

NATURAL BRIDGES NATIONAL MONUMENT

A nine-mile trail loops past the three natural bridges, the Horse Collar Ruins, and along the base of the White and Armstrong canyons. It can be accessed from any of the bridge trailheads. Backcountry hiking is not permitted in the national monument itself.

DARK CANYON & GRAND GULCH

Seeing Dark Canyon entails remote backcountry hiking far from any human intrusion or possible help. A number of shorter trails comprise a 40-mile-long trail that passes through Woodenshoe, Peavine, Hammond, and Upper Dark Canyons, among others, leading to Anasazi pictographs and refreshing desert water holes.

Although the actual hiking may not be difficult and no permit is required, it is recommended that you consult with BLM or National Forest information sources in Monticello for access road and trail conditions.

Hiking in Grand Gulch is similar to Dark Canyon; it's rugged going and you're on your own. You can camp anywhere, but there are no developed sites and water sources may not be available. Trailheads on the east side of the Upper Grand Gulch area are at **Kane Gulch** and **Bullet Canyon**. A 25-mile trail connects the trailheads.

Collins Spring Trail is the western access to Collins Canyon and the Lower Grand Gulch area. It's a 40-mile hike from Kane Gulch to Collins Spring. No hiking permit is required but, again, check with the appropriate offices for current conditions. They can also provide hiking maps, and it's not a bad idea to let them know your travel plans.

Less visited, but no less absorbing, are hikes in the vicinity of **Fish Creek** and **Owl Creek** (east of Grand Gulch and UT 261, a mile south of Kane Gulch). There are Anasazi ruins throughout these canyons, plus arches and spring-fed rock pools. Twelve-mile-long **Slickhorn Canyon** contains numerous Anasazi ruins south of Grand Gulch to the San Juan River. Trail access is west of UT 261, 10 miles south of Kane Gulch. For current information and trail maps, contact the BLM ranger station in Kane Gulch (see above, under Touring Natural Bridges National Monument) or the **BLM** office in Monticello (435 North Main, PO Box 7, Monticello, UT 84535, ☎ 801/587-2141).

A liberating alternative for backpackers is hiking with pack stock. **Pack Creek Ranch**, PO Box 1270, Moab, UT 84532, ☎ 801/259 5505, fax 801/259-8879, offers an opportunity to travel into some of Utah's most remote and intimidating terrain with a horse to carry your gear. Four-day trips are scheduled for a maximum of 12 hikers in April, May, September, and October. They include exploring, camping, and five to eight miles of hiking daily in one of the three following areas.

In **Lower Grand Gulch**, participants camp near Indian ruins and explore cliff dwellings, rock art, side canyons, and old trails before meeting a boat on the San Juan River for a final day of rafting.

In **Upper Grand Gulch** trips, participants hike through deep, winding canyons, with an opportunity to explore ancient Indian ruins and Indian rock art panels.

Guided trips into **Dark Canyon** focus on Anasazi ruins and rock art, as well as splashing around in improbable, oasis-like, desert water holes.

Guided hiking trips of a half-day to six days in southeastern Utah are offered by **Tours of the Big Country**, PO Box 309, Bluff, UT 84512, ☎ 801/672-2281.

Hikers wishing to explore Dark Canyon can make arrangements for drop-off and pick-up services at Hite Marina.

The **Four Corners School of Outdoor Education**, PO Box 78, East Route, Monticello, UT 84535, ☎ 801/587-2156, offers a six-night hiking tour with llamas in mid-September, called "Stories From Navajo Bridge & Rainbow Mountain." The trip covers a 30-mile hike around and through side canyons on rough trails with significant changes in elevation. Llamas carry the gear. As you circle the base of Navajo Mountain and explore side canyons stretching to Rainbow Bridge, an archaeologist-naturalist guide team directs discussions emphasizing the natural and cultural history of Navajo Mountain, an area that has figured into Navajo mythology and legend for thousands of years.

HENRY MOUNTAINS

There are numerous old mining trails and jeep roads suitable for hiking in the Henrys, but most trails are unmarked and unmaintained. The BLM office in Hanksville (see above, under Touring Hanksville) can provide information. An excellent source for hikers in the Henrys and other remote parts of canyon country is *Canyon Hiking Guide to the Colorado Plateau*, by Michael R. Kelsey, Wasatch Book Distribution, PO Box 1108, 66 West 400 South, Salt Lake City, UT 84110, ☎ 801/575-6735.

There is a partial trail from Lonesome Beaver Campground to Mount Ellen's peak. It's an eight-mile round-trip with an elevation gain of 3,300 feet.

GLEN CANYON, THE MAZE DISTRICT & GOBLIN VALLEY STATE PARK

The many miles of trails and rugged jeep roads through the **Maze District** are largely unmarked and there are no services close by. Free backcountry permits are required for travel through here. These are available from the Hans Flat Ranger Station or from the National Park Service office in Moab (see above, under Touring).

Backcountry permits are not required for the **Glen Canyon National Recreation Area**, which adjoins the Maze. Any travel in this area is going to be challenging though, so check with the ranger station regarding conditions before venturing out. Several hiking routes are accessed only after driving 35 miles from the ranger station, deep into the backcountry. For ideas, see below, under Maze District Jeeping.

Horseshoe Canyon, west of the Maze District and site of the Great Gallery, is a little easier to get around, though not by much. You can drive close to the trail leading to the Great Gallery, but you'll need a four-wheel-drive. To get there, bear left (north) at the Hans Flat Ranger Station and continue for seven miles. The trailhead is two miles south of the main road; there should be a sign to the trail on the west rim of the canyon. Follow the trail down 500 feet in one mile to the bottom of the canyon. The Great Gallery is to the right, about two miles away. There are a couple of primitive campsites in the canyon. Backcountry permits are required for camping, so while you're at the ranger station, pick the ranger's brain about current conditions.

There are several hiking trails in **Goblin Valley State Park**, all accessed off gravel roads through the park. Most offer two- to three-mile round-trips, and there are several miles of slot canyons to explore on foot in Little Wild Horse and Bell canyons, just outside the park boundaries to the west.

CAPITOL REEF NATIONAL PARK

The few roads through the park only take you to a small fraction of the most scenic areas. There are a number of short hiking trails suitable for day trips within easy reach of the park's visitor center, or numerous longer backcountry trails are suitable for backpackers. Park rangers stationed at the center can inform hikers of road and trail conditions and provide information about restricted areas and regulations for rock climbers.

Most of the hiking in this park is fairly difficult. Some of the slickrock slopes and many of the trails are steep. Trail markings may be hard to follow. As for restrictions, no pets are allowed, backpackers may not camp within a half-mile of roads or trails, and no fires are permitted. You'll need a cook stove to prepare food, and your own water; water sources are unreliable.

Summer is hot and buggy; preferred hiking seasons are spring and fall. Wisdom dictates avoiding low spots in washes which may flood rapidly in the event of a sudden downpour. Respect the weather – flash floods can carry a car, so imagine what one could do to you.

A number of trails intersect throughout the park, allowing for long or short hikes. Good hiking trails include the following:

Grand Wash Trail is an easy, level route along a dry river bottom that slices completely through Capitol Reef. You can access Grand Wash from UT 24 or from the end of Grand Wash Road – a 4½-mile drive from the visitor center – off the southwesterly Scenic Road. From there it's a two-mile hike down the wash to the Fremont River.

Instead of hiking down, **Cassidy Arch Trail** climbs a challenging 1,000 feet in less than two miles. You can turn off this trail after a mile onto **Frying Pan Trail**, which reaches Cohab Canyon in three strenuous miles, with lots of ups and downs over slickrock and canyons. Cohab was named for Mormon polygamists who once hid from the law there. **Cohab Canyon Trail** then takes over and drops a mile down to the Fruita Campground.

You can access Cohab Canyon and the above trails from the parking area for **Hickman Natural Bridge Trail**, two miles east of the center. The Cohab Canyon trailhead is across the road, or you can follow a different well-marked one-mile trail from the parking lot to the 133-foot-long, 75-foot-high natural bridge. On the way there's a classic view of Capitol Dome framed by the natural bridge.

The Rim Overlook Trail veers off the Hickman Natural Bridge Trail and covers two miles, one-way, to a 1,000-foot-high bird's-eye perch over the Fremont Valley. Portions of the craggy park and mountains lie far beyond.

Three miles west of the visitor center is the trailhead for **Chimney Rock Trail**, a strenuous 3½-mile loop leading to scenic views of the Reef. Access to Chimney Rock Canyon starts at the same place and follows the canyon for nine miles to the Fremont River at UT 24, four miles east of the center. Avoid this route in wet weather. Flash floods are a possibility and heavy rains will raise the water level in the river, which is normally low enough to cross on foot.

Capitol Gorge lies at the end of the Scenic Road, 11 miles from the center. You can walk four miles through the slender gorge on the **Pioneer Trail**, which was the old state highway until 30 years ago, to Notom Road. Another option is to climb two miles, more than 1,000 feet up the nearby **Golden Throne Trail** for a fine view of the park from the bottom of the colorfully striated Golden Throne formation. This is one of the park's most prominent features, sitting at an elevation of 6,500 feet atop the reef.

Many hikers follow the Pioneer Trail for only a mile, past some badly eroded petroglyphs and the Pioneer Register where old-time travellers scratched their names and thoughts into the rock. Turnaround point for the short route is a level mile down the gorge, at the natural tanks, otherwise known as waterpockets.

Other hiking areas in the southern portion of the park may be accessed off Notom Road. These include the **Lower Muley Twist Canyon**, accessed off Burr Trail Road, two miles west of Notom Road. The canyon twists tortuously along the top of the Waterpocket Fold then down 900 feet to Hall's Creek after 12 miles.

Several trails also veer off from **Upper Muley Twist Canyon**. The upper canyon starts west of Lower Muley Twist Canyon, a mile past the peak of the switchbacks over the fold on Burr Trail Road. If you have a jeep, you can drive a few miles up the canyon, then hike in six miles to the head of the canyon or climb a mile up the **Strike Valley Overlook Trail** at the end of the road for a scenic view.

Hiking in the northern section of the park can lead you to rarely visited canyons, the reverential monoliths of Cathedral Valley, and desert badlands. See below, under Capitol Reef National Park Mountain Biking for some ideas, or contact the ranger station for trail guides, reports on current conditions, the necessary backcountry permits, and topographic maps (which are a must when travelling through this rugged backcountry).

ESCALANTE

There are numerous hiking possibilities in the canyon country around the Escalante River, from easy, short hikes to rivers for swimming, to overnight excursions past Indian ruins near incredible alcoves and amphitheaters. You can hike to caves and grottoes with hanging gardens, or all the way to Lake Powell, 85 miles from Escalante. It's a remote area, though, and backcountry permits are required. Contact the BLM or National Park Service offices in Escalante (see above, under Touring Escalante), for permits and current information, including trailhead and hiking route maps.

Be prepared to get wet. Most routes include shallow river crossings, though sometimes the water is higher, and there is always a flash flood danger, particularly in summer. Spring and fall offer cooler weather and less chance of flooding. You can usually find water to drink, but you do need to purify it first. Bring insect repellent and sunscreen.

There are many spots where you can camp; just don't pick a low spot that might flood. Any hiking plans should include a copy of *Hiking the Escalante,* by Rudi Lambrechtse (Wasatch Publishers). It details numerous backcountry hiking routes and is as indispensable as the topographic maps you need to navigate this challenging wilderness of arches, buttes, and canyon networks.

The highest point of **The Great Western Trail**, which links Canada with Mexico by a scenic hiking route that crosses the United States, is atop Boulder Mountain, in Utah. There are four access points to the trail along UT 12. These are Sunflower Flat Road, Pleasant Creek Road, Deer Creek Road, and North Slope Road.

Additional trails are accessed right in Escalante or from the UT 12 bridge, 15 miles east of town. A good hike that does not require extreme preparation connects those two spots. Head east down the river from town through the main canyon. In seven miles you reach Death Hollow, where you should find some swimming holes. You can take a side trip up Death Hollow, or continue east another five miles to Sand Creek, with more swimming holes upstream. Alternatively, continue east past Escalante Natural Bridge and in another two miles you'll come to the UT 12 bridge.

A longer hike starts at the UT 12 bridge and covers 25 miles to Harris Wash. From there it's another 12 miles west through Harris Wash to Hole-in-the-Rock Road. This hike takes you through numerous slot canyons and surprisingly fertile meadows, splashes through quite a few streams and past arches, hanging gardens and dry washes – in short, the full array of Escalante Canyon country scenery. You need good maps for this trek.

A 65-mile, multi-day hike to Lake Powell starts at the **Harris Wash Trail**, off Hole-in-the-Rock Road south of Escalante, and requires a shuttle. You hike east through Harris Wash to the Escalante River, then down the river past Fence Canyon, Twenty-Five Mile Wash, Moody Creek, the huge and impressive Stevens Arch and into Coyote Gulch, a mile from Lake Powell. To get back to the Hole-in-the-Rock Road, hike west up Coyote Gulch.

In eight miles you turn southwest on Hurricane Wash and it's seven miles from there to the road, 45 miles south of Escalante.

Other canyon hiking possibilities are from numerous trailheads off Hole-in-the-Rock Road leading east to the Escalante River, or from the Burr Trail Road east of Boulder, and south into the Escalante River canyons.

There are three canyons near the southern tip of Hole-in-the-Rock Road that you can follow for relatively short hikes to Lake Powell. Contact the BLM or National Park Service for details of hiking **Fortymile Gulch**, a 12-mile round-trip, **Willow Gulch**, a seven-mile round-trip, or **Fiftymile Creek**, a seven-mile round-trip.

In addition, there are numerous mountain country hiking trails north of Escalante off the 38-mile-long **Hell's Backbone Road**. Contact the BLM office in Escalante for details.

Wild Horizons Expeditions (West Fork Road, Darby, MT 59829, ☎ 406/821-3747) offers ecologically oriented, guided backpacking trips of six to eight days through Escalante Canyon, March to September.

Escalante Canyon Outfitters, PO Box 1330, Boulder, UT 84716, ☎ 801/335-7311, offers guided hiking and backpacking trips, plus horsepacking trips, and five-day, base camp hiking trips where you walk while a horse carries your gear. Wine anyone?

Escalante Outfitters & Bunkhouse, 310 West Main Street, PO Box 158, Escalante, UT 84726, ☎ 801/826-4266, is a small well-stocked outdoors shop with several small log cabins for guests. The cabins are rustic and cheap, and the shop also offers guided tours, including hiking and backpacking trips.

Boulder Outdoor Survival School, PO Box 3226, Flagstaff, AZ 86003, ☎ 520/779-6000, runs educational programs in the pristine outdoor setting of the Escalante River area, eschewing high tech bells and whistles to focus on back-to-basics outdoor skills training, primitive skills, survival training, and walkabouts.

BRYCE CANYON

Hiking trails here can be taken in large or small doses. Overnight trips are only allowed on the Under-the-Rim Trail and Riggs Spring Loop Trail. Fires and wood gathering are not allowed in the park. Except for the Rim Trail, every trail goes down into the canyon, so the hiking is fairly strenuous coming back up.

Fairyland Loop Trail covers a fairly strenuous eight-mile loop, gaining 750 feet in elevation, starting at either Fairyland Point or

Sunrise Point. One of the hundreds of fantastical rock forms along the way is the monolithic Gulliver's Castle. Others include the Chinese Wall, Tower Bridge and Fairyland. An alternative to the entire loop is to hike down to the rock spires in the amphitheater and back up to where you started.

Queen's Garden Trail is a two-mile round-trip from Sunrise Point, down into hoodoos deep in the amphitheater, including evocative forms such as Queen Victoria and Queen's Castle. This is the easiest trail beneath the rim. Connecting trails from this route meet with the Navajo Loop, Rim and Peekaboo Loop Trails.

Navajo Loop Trail descends a steep 500 feet in a half-mile from Sunrise Point into the midst of a battalion of hoodoos known as the Silent City, and also connects with several other park trails in the bottom of the amphitheater. Along the way it passes forms known as the Turtle, Organ Grinder's Monkey, and Thor's Hammer.

Peekaboo Loop Trail is a strenuous hike that can be accessed from several different places, taking you through some of the park's best scenery, including the Alligator, Fairy Castle, Cathedral, and Wall of Windows. If you start at Bryce Point, or from Sunrise Point and the Queen's Garden Trail, you will have a seven-mile round-trip. From Sunset Point and the Navajo Loop Trail it's a mile shorter. The elevation change is 827 feet.

Under-the-Rim Trail is the most ambitious hike in the park, covering 23 miles, round-trip, on a multi-day route. It passes below the Pink Cliffs and stretches from Bryce Point to Rainbow and Yovimpa points. You can tackle shorter segments of the trail from the scenic drive, such as the four-mile round-trip from Bryce Point to the mushroom-like Hat Shop formations.

Riggs Spring Loop Trail covers a nine-mile loop from Yovimpa Point or Rainbow Point and provides some of the best park views of the Pink Cliffs. It is strenuous, though, and has an elevation change of 1,625 feet.

Seventeen miles north of Bryce Canyon junction (UT 12 and UT 63), at **Pine Lake**, is the start of a moderate 16-mile round-trip hike to Powell Point, one of southwestern Utah's prettiest overlooks from 2,000 feet. A shorter, eight-mile round-trip is also possible. For details, see below under Biking.

Just west of Bryce Canyon on UT 12 is the similar-looking **Red Canyon** area of the Dixie National Forest. There are trails in here that look exactly like Bryce Canyon. The main difference is that fewer people hike through Red Canyon.

Pink Ledges Trail offers a short, quarter-mile hike from the visitor center on UT 12, 10 miles west of UT 63, through startling pink and red rock formations.

Buckhorn Trail begins near Red Canyon Campground and leads you a mile up to the canyon rim.

For information, phone the **Red Canyon Visitor Center**, ☎ 801/676-8815, or contact the **Forest Service** office in Escalante (PO Box 246, Escalante, UT 84726). There is a trailhead kiosk situated east of the center which is the start of five trails that are open to hikers, bicyclists and horse riders. The area is open year-round, and these trails are good for cross-country skiing or snowshoeing in winter.

MountainFit, 663 Battery Street, Fifth Floor, San Francisco, CA 94111, ☎ 415/397-6216 or 800/926-5700, fax 415/397-6217, offers week-long, all-inclusive hiking tours in southwestern Utah. The tours stress pampered, healthy living for up to 14 adventurous participants who do not want to rough it too much. They include yoga each morning, jacuzzis, massages at night, spa cuisine, and accommodations in luxurious mountain lodges.

CEDAR BREAKS NATIONAL MONUMENT

There are several trailheads on the Cedar Breaks rim drive. **Wasatch Rampart Trail** covers a four-mile round-trip from the visitor center. It curves along the south rim of the amphitheater, through a sweet-smelling forest of ancient, thousand-year-old bristlecones at Spectra Point, followed by grassy meadows, then on to another rim overlook at trail's end.

Alpine Pond Loop covers a two-mile loop from Chessman Ridge Overlook, or from a trailhead a mile farther north. It dips below the rim and through a spruce and aspen forest to Alpine Pond, where you can fish if you have a Utah fishing license.

Bristlecone Pine Trail is a short trail from Chessman Point to a rim overlook.

Rattlesnake Creek Trail starts outside the park's north entrance and descends 3,500 feet in nine miles to Ashdown Creek, which you can hike upstream into the Cedar Breaks Amphitheater. You can also hike away from the park and head downstream through the Ashdown Gorge Wilderness Area.

CEDAR CITY & ST. GEORGE

There are miles of hiking trails in the Pine Valley Recreation Area, east of the town of Pine Valley. Contact the Pine Valley Ranger District (see above, under Touring Cedar City & St. George) for information and trail maps.

Brown's Point Trail (which starts at the Pines Campground), and **Whipple Trail** (which starts at North Juniper Campground), lead in four miles and six miles respectively to **Summit Trail** in the adjacent 50,000-acre Pine Valley Mountain Wilderness Area. Summit Trail covers 35 miles one way, eventually climbing to the top of Signal Peak.

There are also many hiking trails in **Snow Canyon State Park**, 12 miles northwest of St. George. **Hidden Pinyon Trail** starts near the

Shivwits Campground and covers an easy 1½-mile round-trip to a canyon overlook.

West Canyon Trail is a seven-mile round-trip starting close to the stables, a mile south of the campground. Several other trails branch off from this trail for backpacking excursions and overnight camping.

Lava Tubes Trail starts a mile north of the campground and covers one-mile on a round-trip to the park's lava caves.

ZION NATIONAL PARK

In general, spring and fall are the best times to hike through Zion. Summers are hot and also the most crowded time in the park, unless you travel the backroad trails off Kolob Canyons Road or Kolob Terrace Road. Winters are pretty when it snows, but trails may be obscured and it gets mighty cool at night. Higher elevation trails are closed by snow in winter. A list of 165 miles of park trails is available from any of the visitor centers.

Maintained trails off **Zion Scenic Drive** lead to great spots you can't see from the road. In addition, there are all sorts of backcountry trails suitable for rock climbers and mountaineers with the proper equipment and route-finding skills. Always check with park rangers first for current backcountry conditions and overnight camping permits.

There are several hiking trails that start from the Kolob Canyons Road in the northwest corner of the park. **Taylor Creek Trail** starts two miles from the Kolob Canyons Visitor Center and covers three miles one-way through the Middle Fork of Taylor Creek to Double Arch Alcove. Be prepared to get wet crossing the creek.

La Verkin Creek Trail starts four miles past the Kolob Canyons Visitor Center at Lee Pass. It leads seven miles, one-way, to Kolob Arch. The trail initially drops 800 feet to Timber Creek, then crosses La Verkin Creek before reaching the 310-foot rock span, which is 330 feet tall. The arch really glows in the early morning light, the reason why photographers prefer to make this an overnight trip.

Rugged and steep trails off the Kolob Terrace Road include the West Rim Trail and Hop Valley Trail, both of which start near Lava Point, 20 miles northeast of Virgin. **West Rim Trail** covers 13 miles, all the way back to Zion Canyon. **Hop Valley Trail** covers 14 miles round-trip to Kolob Arch.

Consult with a park ranger regarding trail conditions and backcountry permits before striking out on these challenging treks. Main Zion hiking trails take you away from the bustling crowds that overwhelm the park's scenic drive and overlooks in summertime, while leading to wonderful areas redolent in Indian history and eons of geological activity. The most frequent visitors here have always been wild creatures, not humans.

Travelling north on the six-mile scenic drive, trails are as follows:

Watchman Trail is named for a 2,600-foot-tall sandstone rock that greets visitors near the park entrance. The trail starts in either Watchman or South campground and covers a 2½-mile round-trip, climbing 370 feet to views of Zion Canyon and Springdale.

Sand Bench Trail is often shared with horseback riders. It's an easy two-mile loop, gaining 500 feet in elevation from a trailhead near the stunning Court of the Patriarchs Viewpoint, providing excellent views of Lower Zion Canyon.

Emerald Pools Trails are three trails to waterfalls, rock pools, and views of the forested slopes of Zion Canyon. Two trails start near Zion Lodge on a paved trail leading a half-mile to Lower Pool. Middle Pool is a quarter-mile farther. A third trail starts at Grotto Picnic Area and also reaches the pools. Beyond the Middle Pool, a very steep half-mile trail, with chain handholds embedded in the rock wall, leads to Upper Emerald Pool, the prettiest of all, with a sandy beach beneath stratospheric cliffs.

West Rim Trail is a fairly major undertaking, covering 13 miles round-trip and gaining 3,700 feet in elevation from Grotto Picnic Area to West Rim Lookout, or 13 miles one-way to Lava Point. The route provides ethereal canyon views and is conveniently paved to the end of Walter's Wiggles, a lengthy series of tight switchbacks that take you to the top of Scout Lookout (1,000 feet in elevation). At Scout Lookout you can hike a half-mile, gripping another chain hand-grip, to the top of Angels Landing – a stone tower 1,500 feet above the Virgin River. From Scout Lookout, it's 3½ miles to West Rim Lookout, then another 6½ miles to Lava Point.

Weeping Rock Trail starts at Weeping Rock parking area and is an easy, half-mile round-trip hike, gaining 100 feet in elevation. It goes past drizzling, hanging gardens to a fine view of the Great White Throne, a multi-colored, 2,400-foot-tall stone outcrop.

East Rim Trail covers a steep 7½-mile round-trip, gaining 2,150 feet in elevation to Observation Point. There are great views along the way, as well as access to the backcountry on the Hidden Canyon and Echo Canyon trails, which veer off the main route. This trail is not recommended for those with fear of heights.

Gateway to the **Narrows Trail** starts at the end of the scenic drive, near the Temple of Sinawava – an immense rock amphitheater with two prominent stone towers in the middle – and covers a paved two-mile round-trip into a slender canyon 2,000 feet high, yet only 20 feet wide at the Virgin River Narrows.

Orderville Canyon Trail goes a few miles farther into the Narrows, but hiking into this area leads to extremely rugged backcountry without trails. Plan to get wet; you'll be hiking in the river and it could be above your waist, or higher. A backcountry permit is required for any travel in the Narrows and, although a "Narrow Canyon Danger Level" is posted daily at the visitor center, it is still a smart idea to talk to a ranger about current conditions. The trail is closed when flash flooding is a danger, and from late October through June due to cold temperatures and high river levels.

Canyon Overlook Trail starts at the east side of the long tunnel on the Zion-Mt. Carmel Highway (UT 9). It's a one-mile round-trip through desert-like terrain, offering views of prominent features on the east side of Zion Canyon and a wonderful view of lower Zion Canyon.

Zion Excursions, PO Box 521436, Salt Lake City, UT 84152-1436, ☎ 801/581-9817 or 800/293-5444, fax 801/582-3308, operates from the 8,000-acre Zions Ponderosa Ranch, which shares seven miles with the eastern border of Zion National Park. There are log cabins and private campsites at the ranch. They also offer rentals of all-terrain vehicles, mountain bikes, tents and sleeping bags.

All the trips start at the ranch, which provides direct routes into Zion Narrows, Observation Point, Echo Canyon, and Cable Mountain, among other sites. Complete excursions include use of the private camping area, shuttle transfers (from the campground to all trailheads, and from trail end to campsite), horseback riding, trail-side lunches and post-hike refreshments, Dutch-oven dinner, and access to many miles of mountain biking trails. You can arrange visits to the ranch for a half-day, full day, or for multiple days.

A tour company based in California offers guided hiking trips in this area. For information, contact **Southern Utah Hiking Adventures**, PO Box 21276, Oakland, CA 94260, ☎ 510/654-5802 or 800/882-4238, fax 510/654-5802.

KANAB TO PAGE, ARIZONA

For hikers seeking something more forgiving to sink their toes into than a rocky hiking trail, the terrain at **Coral Pink Sand Dunes State Park**, west of Kanab, could be the ticket. Just watch out for dune buggies; drivers of all-terrain vehicles also enjoy tracking through a designated 1,000 acres of the dunes.

A possible week-long hiking trip is the **Pariah River Canyon**, a BLM wilderness area, starting 43 miles west of Kanab, south of US 89, and ending 40 miles later at Lee's Ferry, Arizona. The route starts in a 2,000-foot-deep gorge, winds through narrows, past arches and entails a fair bit of river wading before ending at the Colorado River. To negotiate this area you must be able to read a map; the route is not well marked. The trail is closed in threatening weather, particularly if there's a danger of thunderstorms, which can flood the narrows near the north end of the trail. Because of this danger, required permits are available no more than 24 hours in advance, and all hikers must start at the north end of the canyon, in Utah. The BLM ranger office on US 89, east of the Pariah River, provides permits, weather forecasts, and hiking maps. Information is also available from the **BLM** office in Kanab (318 North 100 East, Kanab, Utah 84741, ☎ 801/644-2672). Several other shorter and easier trails also lead to the Paria River.

POWELL & GLEN CANYON NATIONAL RECREATION AREA

Nobody says much about hiking around Lake Powell. Most of the hiking near the lake is rugged and over difficult unmarked trails. It is also spectacularly remote and uncompromised in the backcountry where you can find numerous arches, hidden canyons, and prehistoric sites. Areas to consider are near **Rainbow Bridge National Monument**, which is equally far from any of the major marinas, or the **Escalante River Canyons**, **Grand Gulch Primitive Area**, and **Dark Canyon Wilderness**, which are most easily accessed through the northern marinas at Hite, Hall's Crossing, or Bullfrog. Contact park rangers at Lake Powell marinas for information, or phone the National Park Service at ☎ 520/645-2511.

Of course, you can hike just about anywhere from a boat, but there are a couple of decent hikes accessible by car, too.

Wiregrass Canyon offers a three-mile backcountry hike to the lake, not far from the Glen Canyon Dam. Drive 10 miles north of the dam on US 89 to Big Water, then east on UT 277 to UT 12. It's 4½ miles south on Warm Creek Road to a sign that says "Wiregrass Canyon Backcountry." You can park here. About a mile from the parking lot is a little stone arch.

The **Lower Escalante Canyons** (see above) are accessible around mid-lake on the north side, providing both easy and challenging terrain, from stream beds you can walk through, to slickrock configurations you must negotiate otherwise. Drive here through Escalante and Hole-in-the-Rock Road (see below under Jeeping), or access by boat. No permit is required for day hikes, but overnight trips require a free backcountry permit available from the ranger station in Escalante (☎ 801/826-5499 or 801/826-4315).

Flint Trail heads north from Hite Marina into the Orange Cliffs area. Numerous slickrock hiking options are possible, as well as backcountry camping overlooking Canyonlands National Park. This is also a popular mountain biking area.

A popular and relatively easy seven-mile hike is to **Rainbow Lodge Ruins**. The trail starts a mile past Rainbow Bridge National Monument on the San Juan Arm of Lake Powell, and leads southeast through Horse Canyon to the site of a once fashionable lodge that counted John Wayne and Teddy Roosevelt among its guests. Several other trails veer off to nearby arches and rock formations. From the same spot, east of Rainbow Bridge, you can hike 13 miles northeast to Navajo Mountain.

These hikes are on Navajoland and hikers need permission from **Navajo Nation Recreational Resource Department**, Box 308, Window Rock, AZ 86515.

Destiny Adventures, 52 6th Avenue, Page, AZ 86040, ☎ 520/645-9496, operates daily hiking tours in the vicinity of Lake Powell, and rock climbing tours. You can register at the sports shop (outdoor gear, clothing and gifts) on 6th Avenue, or at the John Wesley Powell Museum.

On Horseback

MOAB, CANYONLANDS & SAN JUAN COUNTY

Pack Creek Ranch (PO Box 1270, Moab, UT 84532, ☎ 801/259-5505, fax 801/259-8879) offers the ultimate getaway on overnight horseback trips to a base camp in the La Sal Mountains. Participants follow old cowboy trails, drink cold, clear, natural spring water, inhale the scent of pine forests, and take in stunning views of Utah's canyon country. Sleeping bag, tent, Dutch-oven cooking, horses and tack are supplied. Campfire stories, some of them true, are told about the Southwest. The family running this outfit has been in this area for a long time, knows it well, and includes members who figure prominently in local folklore.

Sunset Trail Rides, PO Box 302, Moab, UT 84532, ☎ 801/259-4362, offers trail rides by the hour in the La Sals and red rock country, or a two-hour evening ride with a campfire dinner included. The rides leave from a ranch nine miles south of Moab on US 191.

Ed Black Horse Tours, Mexican Hat, UT 84531, ☎ 801/739-4285, focuses mainly on the Monument Valley area, and also offers customized canyon country horseback trips.

San Juan Horseback Tours, Mexican Hat, UT 84531, ☎ 801/683 2283, offers horseback trips in San Juan County.

Horseback trips into parts of Navajoland within Utah are offered by the following outfitters:

Bigman's Horseback Tours, PO Box 1557, Kayenta, AZ 86033, ☎ 520/677-3219, runs a variety of trips in the areas around Mitchell Butte, Mystery Valley, Rain God Mesa, and Big Chief, all south of Monument Valley.

Monument Valley Horseback Trailrides, PO Box 155, Mexican Hat, UT 84531-0155, ☎ 801/739-4285 or 800/551-4039, has customized horseback trips for four to 25 riders in Monument Valley, Mystery Valley, Hunts Mesa, and Horse Canyon.

With Navajo guides you explore these areas for an hour, a day or up to five days on camping trips, riding through ancient Anasazi and Navajo lands. Longer trips lead you to remote places visited by few non-Indians where you will see broken pottery shards littering the ground beneath boulders packed with petroglyphs, while coyotes howl at night in the moon shadows of the monoliths.

This is a Navajo-run company. Two or more guides accompany each trip. Overnight packages include food, sleeping bags, and tents (if you bring your own gear there is a dramatic difference in price). A truck meets the group nightly with supplies and food. Trips are offered year-round.

Triple Heart Ranch Tours, Mexican Springs Trading Post, Mexican Springs, NM 87320, ☎ 505/733-2377, offers horseback trips in the vicinity of Monument Valley.

Don Donnelly Stables, 6100 Kings Ranch Road, Gold Canyon, AZ 85219, ☎ 520/982-7822 or 800/346-4403, runs trips exploring the beauty of Arizona and Utah from the comfort of a well-made Western saddle, including a Monument Valley ride offered in spring and fall. The trip starts with airport pick-up in Gallup and features comfortable camps set up with spacious tents, cots, toilets, hot showers, a dinner tent, gourmet chef, and evening entertainment. Indians and ranchers sometimes drop by to share stories around the campfire. Gear and equipment are transported by truck.

Rainbow Trails & Tours, PO Box 7218, Shonto, AZ 86045, ☎ 520/672-2397, offers horseback trips to Rainbow Bridge National Monument.

CAPITOL REEF NATIONAL PARK

Hondoo **Rivers & Trails**, 95 East Main, PO Box 98, Torrey, UT 84775, ☎ 801/425-3519 or 800/332-2696, fax 801/425-3548, runs a number of pack trips into the deep backcountry of the Colorado Plateau. A five-day fall foliage ride is offered in late September through Capitol Reef National Park, and the Escalante and Circle Cliffs wilderness areas. Other five-day trips into Capitol Reef are scheduled June through September.

Five- or eight-day rides in May explore the San Rafael Swell. A six-day trip in June coincides with the peak wildflower blooming season in the Wasatch Plateau, and another six-day trip through the Henry Mountains in July follows the trail of free-roaming herds of buffalo. Trips are for a maximum of 10 riders and use good to rugged trails suitable for riders of all abilities, with options of challenging terrain for the more experienced. Excursions begin and end in Torrey.

Outlaw Trails, Inc., 29 Raindance Ranch, Box 129, Hanksville, UT 84734, ☎ 801/542-3421, fax 801/542-3450, offers multi-day horseback trips in Glen Canyon National Recreation Area, Canyonlands National Park Maze District, Capitol Reef National Park, and surrounding areas.

Rim Rock Rustic Inn, US 24, PO Box 64, Torrey, UT 84775, ☎ 801/425-3843 or 800/243-0786, fax 801/425-3855, offers guided horseback trips in Capitol Reef National Park. The rides are operated by **Pleasant Creek Trail Rides**, PO Box 102, Bicknell, UT 84715, ☎ 801/425-3315 or 800/892-4597. Hour-long rides are available at the resort. Day-long to week-long rides can also be arranged.

HORSEBACK OUTFITTERS

Escalante Canyon Outfitters (PO Box 1330, Boulder, UT 84716, ☎ 801/335-7311) offers guided horseback trips in the Escalante River canyons.

Scenic Safaris, PO Box 278, Cannonville, UT 84718, ☎ 801/679-8536 or 801/679-8787, runs guided trail rides of a half-hour, one hour, or a half-day in Kodachrome Basin State Park, to the Panorama and Secret Passage Trail, Grand Parade Trail, Angel's Palace Trail, and Big Bear Geyser Trail. Overnight pack trips are also offered in and around Kodachrome Basin, as well as throughout other areas of southern Utah, including Bryce and Zion national parks. Stagecoach rides on the Panorama Trail are also offered at their Kodachrome Basin Trailhead Station from April through October. The small shop provides local information, food and supplies for all visitors.

Bryce-Zion-Grand Canyon North Rim Trail Rides, PO Box 128, Tropic, UT 84776, ☎ 801/834-5219 (Bryce); ☎ 801/772-3967 (Zion); ☎ 602/638-2992 (Grand Canyon); or ☎ 801/679-8665 (off-season). This company leads trail rides in Bryce Canyon and Zion national parks from Bryce Lodge and Zion Lodge. In Bryce, a two-hour ride reaches the floor of the canyon on the Peek-a-boo Loop Trail, and a half-day ride gives a complete tour of the canyon. The Zion rides include a one-hour trip from the Zion Lodge to the Virgin River, or a three-hour (half-day) trip on Sand Bench Trail.

Color Country Outfitters and Guide Service, PO Box 58, Tropic, UT, 84776, ☎ 801/679-8761, has guided horseback rides and overnight trips into the Bryce, Zion and Capitol Reef areas.

Mecham's Outfitters & Guide Service, PO Box 71, Tropic, UT 84776, ☎ 801/679-8823.

Ruby's Inn offers a variety of trail rides through Bryce Canyon National Park, as well as backcountry horseback trips. For information, see below, under Torrey to Bryce Canyon Accommodations, or contact the following:

Scenic Rim Trail Rides, Best Western Ruby's Inn, c/o Trail Rides on UT 63 (mailing address PO Box 58, Tropic, UT 84776), ☎ 801/679-5341 or 801/679-8761, fax 801/679-8778. Rides leave from Ruby's through the ponderosa forests on the high plateau of the Bryce Canyon rim. Rides are offered for one, 1½, 3½ (half-day), or seven hours (full day). Overnight trips are also available on request.

Ruby's Outlaw Trail Rides, PO Box 1, Bryce, UT 84764, ☎ 801/834-5341 or 800/679-5859, offers horseback rides departing from Ruby's Inn daily for an hour, 1½ hours, two hours, a half-day or a full day (including a box lunch). Overnight trail rides depart on Monday, Wednesday or Friday, May through September, and include guiding, meals and tent accommodations at a cowboy camp in a high mountain meadow.

Ruby's Guide Service to the Paunsaugunt, PO Box 1, Bryce, UT 84764, ☎ 800/468-8660.

Red Canyon Trail Rides, at Bryce Canyon Pines Motel (☎ 801/834-5441; see below, under Accommodations), offers hour-long, two-hour, half-day or full-day rides from May through September in Red Canyon, Bryce Canyon's lesser-visited but no less intriguing borderland.

Black's Outfitters & Guide Service, PO Box 37, Panguitch, UT 84759, ☎ 801/676-8232, offers trips in the vicinity of striking Red Canyon.

Eagle Basin Outfitters & Guide Service, PO Box 947, Parowan, UT 84761, ☎ 801/477-8837, runs guided horseback trips in the Markagunt Plateau area near Brian Head.

Rick Marchal Pack Saddle Trips, Box 918, Hurricane, UT 84737, ☎ 801/635-4950, offers horseback trips in the Pine Valley Mountains Wilderness and surrounding areas.

Zion Sky Ranch, 10 miles west of Mount Carmel Junction, on UT 9, near the east entrance to Zion National Park, offers trail riding to canyon rim views on a private ranch.

Pine Valley Lodge operates guided horseback trips in the Pine Valley Mountains Wilderness Area. For information see below, under Cedar City & St. George Accommodations.

Snow Canyon Riding Stables, UT 300, Snow Canyon State Park, PO Box 58, Ivins, UT 84738, ☎ 801/628-6677 or 800/628-1158, offers trail rides and overnight pack trips based out of the park, 12 miles northwest of St. George, off UT 18.

Allen's Jacobs Lake Trail Rides, 548 East 300 South, Kanab, UT 84741, ☎ 801/644-8150, operates guided horseback tours for an hour, two hours, a half-day, a full day, two days or five days in southern Utah and northern Arizona.

CATTLE DRIVES & ROUND-UPS

Dalton Gang Outfitters, PO Box 8, Monticello, UT 84535, ☎ 801/587-2416, operate a 200,000-acre ranch. They consider it to be a real cowboy outfit in the brushy, rocky deserts and canyons of the Blue Mountains, bordering Canyonlands National Park and the Colorado River.

A maximum of six guests can ride horses from dawn to dusk, eat Dutch-oven meals, and camp out under the stars or in cabins without electricity (some with bathrooms or running water). Cattle work is done much the way it was 100 years ago and varies according to the time of year. It includes branding, round-ups, and trailing cattle and horses off the winter range in spring. In the fall you can haul hay, put out salt, round up yearlings for market, and drive cattle off the mountain. In winter you can cut ice and trail cattle to new ranges.

Pace Ranch, PO Box 98, Torrey, UT 84775, ☎ 801/425-3519 or 800/332-2696, fax 801/425-3548, is the headquarters for Hondoo Rivers & Trails (see above). The ranch moves 700 head of cattle from winter to summer pasture and back again, in spring or fall. It's a six-day, 25-mile trip through Capitol Reef National Park, passing through sculpted canyons featuring red rock spires and remote desert terrain.

LLAMA TREKS

Canyonlands Llamas, Box 1911, Moab, UT 84532, ☎ 801/259-5739, offers day trips and overnight pack trips with llamas.

Red Rock 'N Llamas, PO Box 1304, Boulder, UT 84716, ☎ 801/335 7325, offers guided, outfitted hiking trips with llamas packing all the gear and supplies through Capitol Reef National Park, along the Escalante River, or into the Glen Canyon National Recreation Area – in short, some of the most remote terrain anywhere. Scheduled trips of three to five days operate from March to October, with easy to moderately difficult day hikes from base camps into Hall's Creek Narrows, the Escalante River, Box Death Hollow, or Choprock Narrows. Day and customized trips are available.

On Wheels

A popular and relatively quick way to reach remote spots is by using the many, many miles of four-wheel-drive roads that criss-cross Utah's public lands. These are some of the most scenically rewarding and remote routes in the United States, and driving on some of these so-called roads can be hazardous. A certain level of off-road driving experience and skill is recommended.

A number of other scenic backroads are suitable for ordinary cars and, for those with the legs and lungs to make it, there are lesser tracks for bikes all over the area, ranging from short, easy loops to multi-day, cross-country routes in extremely remote terrain. For bike riders who don't mind the companionship of gas combustion engines, jeep roads are generally pretty good bike routes, too. They also hold appeal for cross-country skiers and snowmobilers in winter, when they remain generally unplowed and inaccessible to automobiles.

Some of the more accessible driving, jeeping and biking routes in various areas are listed below. Route-finding can be a tricky affair; if you plan to travel in the backcountry you need to be prepared and self sufficient. Accurate maps are a must and, since many of these excursions will take you far from the beaten path, it's wise to consider possibilities such as mechanical breakdowns in advance.

There are also restrictions to consider. On Forest Service and BLM land, off-highway vehicles are permitted only in designated areas, of which there are many. Consult with the administering agency for details, including brochures and maps for off-highway vehicle use. There are also many four-wheel-drive areas within or near state parks. Off-highway vehicles are not allowed in national parks, wilderness areas or on lake shores. For information about highway road conditions in Utah, ☎ 801/964-6000 or 800/492-2400.

A brochure titled *Southern Utah's Byways and Backways* details a number of driving routes. It is available from Visitor Information Centers in Moab, Monticello, Hanksville, Escalante, or St. George.

Canyonlands Marketing Cooperative, PO Box 698, Moab, UT 84532, ☎ 801/259-8431, offers several useful books as part of a Canyon Country Off-Road Vehicles Trail Series. They include such titles as *Arches and the La Sals Areas, Canyon Rims and Needles Areas, Island Area,* and *The Maze Area.* In addition, they offer *Canyon Country Mountain Biking and Canyon Country Slickrock Hiking and Biking,* as well as topographical maps of Arches and Canyonlands national parks, Glen Canyon National Recreation Area and Grand Gulch Primitive Area.

The best overall source for biking information throughout the state is **Bicycle Utah**, PO Box 738, Park City, UT 84060, ☎ 801/649-5806. This is a non-profit organization promoting on- and off-road cycling statewide.

Local bike shops are another good source to use. For additional information about the incredibly popular mountain biking opportunities in the Moab/Canyonlands area, contact the **Grand County Tourism Council** (PO Box 550, 805 North Main Street, Moab, UT 84532, ☎ 801/259-8825 or 800/635-6622), or US Forest Service, BLM, or National Park Service offices in Moab.

DRIVING TRIPS

Moab

You need not hug death-defying, cliff-side jeep roads to see the beautiful country around Moab. There are many short scenic drives that can be accomplished by careful drivers in ordinary vehicles.

Just north of Moab, **Scenic Byway 279** (Potash Road) runs west off US 191. It follows the Colorado River for 12 paved miles, past Indian ruins and rock art sites.

The Potash Road Petroglyphs are a series of rock art panels lining sheer cliffs for two miles on the north side of the road, eight miles west of Moab. The panels contain human, animal, and geometric designs estimated to span periods from 7,000 B.C. to 1,300 A.D. There are several road turnouts to the petroglyphs. The Potash Road turns to dirt at the Potash Plant (that gave the road its name) continuing on to the Shafer and White Rim Trails. This last stretch is recommended for four-wheel-drives only.

Kane Creek Canyon follows the other side of the Colorado River, south of the Potash Road, and reveals a tremendous variety of canyon country scenery. The road passes numerous petroglyphs, then turns into gravel after four miles and winds its way for another six miles into remote, otherworldly sandstone cliffs. Four-wheel-drive vehicles can continue across Kane Springs Creek to Hurrah Pass.

La Sal Mountain Loop Road covers 60 miles starting and ending in Moab, varying in elevation from 4,000 feet to 8,000 feet. It is open from May to October and you can drive the route starting at either end. Numerous jeep roads branch off from the main road.

If you drive north of Moab, the trip starts on **US 191** north to UT 128 and passes Matrimony Springs on the way to the mouth of Negro Bill Canyon, a popular hiking and biking area, the Big Bend Recreation Area and White Ranch, where a number of movies have been filmed. The loop turns south on Castle Valley Road and climbs into the foothills of the La Sals. Five miles south is a good view of Castle Rock and the Priest and Nuns formation. In another six miles you pass the remains of a mining town at Castleton.

A mile past **Castleton**, head off the main road to visit Pinhook Battlefield, where you can see the graves of eight settlers who were killed by Indians in 1881, or the area of Miner's Basin, where the remains of an 1890s gold-mining camp sit at 10,000 feet elevation. Four-wheel-drive vehicles are recommended for both these trips.

About 11 miles farther on the main road, another turnoff leads to Warner Lake, a five-mile trip on a good gravel road to a campground, mountain lake, and hiking trails at 9,200 feet. A few miles farther is a turnoff at Mill Creek Bridge to Lake Oowah, site of another small lake and campground. Another mile or so farther is a fairly rugged dirt road leading to Gold Basin and Geyser Pass, at 10,600 feet.

The main loop road passes through prime habitat for deer and elk as it winds down the mountains. Farther on, it passes Ken's Lake, a reservoir supplying Moab's water and also a good spot for fishing, swimming, or windsurfing, before returning to US 191 south of Moab.

JEEPING/FOUR-WHEEL-DRIVE TRIPS

Moab

The **Moab Rim Trail** starts off Kane Creek Boulevard, 2½ miles from the intersection with Main Street. The trail climbs for 1½ miles to the top of a plateau offering stunning views of Moab, Arches, and the La Sals. Hikers who follow this route can continue southeast to connect with the **Hidden Valley Trail**, which leads five miles back to US 191. If driving, the jeep road continues to meander up steep slopes and down through several sandy washes, with separate short side roads leading to viewpoints, before ending near the top of the Hidden Valley Trail.

Pritchett Canyon Road is not for the faint-hearted, but it does provide good canyon views of several arches and the Behind The Rocks area – a maze of enormous rock fins without maintained trails. For directions see below, under Moab Mountain Biking.

Within **Arches National Park**, there is a dirt road turnoff from the main road, a mile before the Devil's Garden area. The road covers 8½ scenic miles through Salt Valley, to Klondike Bluffs and Tower Arch.

Lockhart Basin Road is a 57-mile paved and gravel road that starts south of Moab off US 191, and connects with UT 211 a few miles east of the Needles District Visitor Center.

Tag-Along Expeditions, 425 North Main Street, Moab, UT 84532, ☎ 801/259-8946 or 800/453-3292, fax 801/259-8990, is a major tour operator in canyon country, offering a variety of guided trips, including a three-day overland jeep adventure in Canyonlands National Park. During the day, botanists and Canyonlands specialists guide you through remote areas of the Needles District, with chances to hike to Indian ruins and rarely visited red rock grottoes.

Also scheduled are four-wheel-drive charters for three or more passengers, half-day and full-day Canyonlands trips to Island in the Sky or Angel Arch, and four-wheel-drive trips combined with jet boat tours.

Lin Ottinger's Tours, 600 North Main, Moab, UT 84532, ☎ 801/259-7312, runs jeep trips to the most scenic view points and some of the best places for Indian petroglyphs, led by local rock specialists.

Great Jeep 'n Guide, 550 North Main, Moab, UT 84532, ☎ 801/259 4567, runs guided four-wheel-drive trips, as well as sunset safaris. On the safari, you follow one of their jeeps in your own four-wheel-drive vehicle. The route is a scenic tour around Moab and includes a trail-side dinner of Navajo tacos on frybread.

Four-wheel-drive rentals (with or without bike racks) are available from **Certified Rentals**, 500 South Main Street, Moab, UT 84532, ☎ 801/259-6107.

North Main Service, 284 North Main, Moab, UT 84532, ☎ 801/259 5242, rents four-wheel-drives.

Farabee Rentals, 234, South Main, Moab, UT 84532, ☎ 801/259-7494, fax 801/259-2997, rents four-wheel-drive vehicles and offers trip planning assistance.

Island In The Sky District

Shafer Trail Road begins just past the visitor center in the Island in the Sky section of Canyonlands National Park. It was originally a cattle track, and was widened to accommodate vehicles used by uranium prospectors. It's not so bad going down the 1,200 feet in four miles, but it can be difficult coming back up. The road does connect with the White Rim Four-Wheel-Drive Road and the Potash Road (UT 279), so you aren't forced to drive up.

White Rim Four-Wheel-Drive Road gives the best variety of viewpoints over the awesome scenery found on various levels of Island in the Sky, including the high plateaus, the White Rim, and the Colorado River. Access is from the Shafer Trail Road or from the Potash Road.

This is a difficult 100-mile road for experienced drivers in four-wheel-drive vehicles only. Many travellers take a few days for this classic trip, with overnight camping at primitive campgrounds along the route. Backcountry permits and reservations are required for the campgrounds. These may be obtained in person or by mail, for free, at the visitor center or from the Moab office of the National Park Service.

Remember, there are no services or water sources anywhere along this route so plan ahead.

North American River Expeditions & Canyonlands Tours, 543 North Main, Moab UT 84532, ☎ 801/259-5865 or 800/342-5938, fax 801/259-2296, offers jeep trips through the Island in the Sky and the Needles Districts of Canyonlands National Park.

Needles District & San Juan County

Interlaced canyon networks, arches, spires, pinnacles, Indian ruins and rock art petroglyphs are all found along four-wheel-drive trails in the Needles District backcountry.

Relatively easy four-wheel-drive roads go into Lavender Canyon and Davis Canyon, east of the park border, off UT 211. Round-trip distances on the roads are 26 miles and 20 miles, respectively.

Colorado Overlook Four-Wheel-Drive Road starts at the Needles ranger station and covers a 14-mile round-trip highlighted by slickrock terrain and a stunning river view.

Salt Creek Canyon Four-Wheel-Drive Road starts close to the Cave Springs Trail (see above, under Touring South of Moab/Canyonlands/Needles District) and covers 30 miles round-trip. It takes in fascinating canyon territory and numerous arches. A side road goes from here to the often-photographed, 150-foot-tall Angel Arch.

Horse Canyon Four-Wheel-Drive Road veers to the left at the mouth of Salt Creek Canyon and covers a 13-mile round-trip through similar scenery.

Elephant Hill Four-Wheel-Drive Loop Road starts at the Elephant Hill picnic area (see above, under Touring South of Moab & Canyonlands' Needles District) and includes a challenging, steep climb up Elephant Hill over the 10-mile round-trip. This is a demanding route with cramped slots barely wide enough for a car to squeeze through, rock stairs, and a spot where you must back up to the edge of a cliff to make a three-point turn. Several hiking trailheads can be reached from the road, plus other four-wheel-drive roads such as Silver Stairs, Cyclone Canyon, and Devil's Chute.

Elk Ridge Road is a dirt road that starts eight miles west of Newspaper Rock State Park on UT 211 and goes 48 miles south to Natural Bridges Road and UT 95. It passes overlooks of the Canyonlands National Park, Dark Canyon Wilderness Area, the Henry and La Sal mountains, and Monument Valley.

South of the Needles District, off US 191 in Monticello, the **Blue Mountain Loop** begins by heading west on 200 South and climbs to within a mile of Abajo Peak (elevation 11,362 feet) at its mid-point. The road covers 22 miles before ending three miles north of Blanding on US 191.

From the center of Blanding, a 38-mile jeep road heads west, traversing Bears Ears Pass in the Abajos (elevation 9,058 feet) on the way to Natural Bridges National Monument.

Farabee 4x4 Rentals, Highway 666, Monticello, UT 84535, ☎ 801/587-2597, or South US 191, Blanding, UT 84511, ☎ 801/678-2955, rents jeeps.

Navajoland

The Navajo Tribe asks that visitors restrict travel to designated trails and established routes. Travel by four-wheel-drive vehicles, dune buggies, jeeps, and motorcycles is prohibited on backcountry roads.

Four-wheel-drive vehicle tours in Monument Valley and other areas generally inaccessible otherwise are offered by the following tour companies:

Goulding's Tours, PO Box 1, Monument Valley, UT 84536, ☎ 801/727-3231, fax 801/727-3344, offers half-day or full-day tours with Navajo drivers well-versed in local culture, geology, and history. Tours are scheduled March 15 through October and are available on request during winter months.

Golden Sands Tours, PO Box 458, Kayenta, AZ 86033, ☎ 520/697-3684, operates jeep tours of Hunts Mesa, Hoskinnii Mesa, and Monument Valley.

Tours of the Big Country, PO Box 309, Bluff, UT 84512, ☎ 801/672-2281, offers naturalist-guided vehicle tours of Monument Valley, based out of the Recapture Lodge.

Crawley's Monument Valley Tours, PO Box 187, Kayenta, AZ 86033, ☎ 520/697-3463, conducts vehicle tours of Monument Valley, Mystery Valley and Hunts Mesa.

Totem Pole Guided Tours, PO Box 306, Monument Valley, UT 84536, ☎ 801/727-3230, runs vehicle tours of Monument Valley, Mystery Valley, Hunts Mesa, Poncho House, Paiute Farms, and Hoskinnii Mesa.

Navajo Guided Tours, PO Box 456, Monument Valley, UT 84536-0375, has vehicle tours of Monument Valley and Mystery Valley.

Also try **Black's Hiking & Van Tours**, PO Box 393, Mexican Hat, UT 84531, ☎ 801/739-4226, and **Fred's Adventure Tours**, PO Box 308, Mexican Hat, UT 84531, ☎ 601/739-4294.

Jackson's Guided Tours, PO Box 375, Monument Valley, UT 84536-0375, runs vehicle tours of Monument Valley, Mystery Valley and Poncho House.

Bennett Guided Tours, PO Box 360285, Monument Valley, UT 84536, ☎ 801/727-3283, offers vehicle tours of Monument Valley and Mystery Valley.

Jeep Tours/Roland C. Dixon, PO Box 131, Kayenta, AZ 86033, ☎ 800/377-9370, offers jeep tours of Monument Valley.

Henry Mountains

There are numerous rough dirt roads crossing the Henrys, but conditions vary from bad to worse. Check with the BLM office in Hanksville (☎ 801/542-3461) for current road conditions.

Bull Mountain Road starts on UT 95, three miles north of the north end of UT 276 (north of Lake Powell), and loops westward through the Henrys for 68 miles, ending on UT 276, five miles south of UT 95 (eight miles south of the starting point).

Henry Mountains Bison Herd resides in a mountainous desert range with peaks as high as 11,000 feet. The site, south of Hanksville in the Henry's, contains one of the largest free-roaming buffalo herds in the United States, numbering around 350 animals. They were left in a different spot 50 years ago, migrated to this area a year later, and have been pretty much left alone since then. The road leading to the herd covers nearly 100 miles of steep dirt roads and sandy washes, and should be avoided when the ground is wet. It starts south of Hanksville, off 100 East, and finishes 27 miles west of Hanksville, on UT 24. Although viewing the animals is possible any time of year, they favor higher elevations in spring and summer, lower elevations on the west side of the Henry's in fall and winter. It's wise to consult with the BLM office in Hanksville regarding road conditions and to get a map of the circuitous route.

Glen Canyon & The Maze District

Jeeps and four-wheel-drive vehicles are really the only motor vehicles that can negotiate the long, sandy, or hard-packed clay washboard roads in the Maze and the surrounding Glen Canyon National Recreation Area.

Contact the Hans Flat Ranger Station or the National Park Service office in Moab (both listed under Touring) for road conditions.

Always fill your tank with gas before entering these areas. If possible, carry extra gas, water, food, and emergency gear.

Horseshoe Canyon may be slightly more accessible than the Maze. To reach the very bad jeep road that leads to the oversize petroglyphs of the Great Gallery, you bear left (north) and drive 21 miles past the Hans Flat Ranger Station to the east rim of the canyon. It's a two-mile hike down the steep canyon to the Great Gallery.

The 35-mile road leading to the Maze Overlook starts at the ranger station. You can see or hike down to the melted-looking rocks called the Chocolate Drops from the overlook, and there are several hiking trails that start here. One such trail descends into the canyon below, where you can see larger-than-life ancient Indian rock paintings at Harvest Scene.

Capitol Reef National Park

A rough jeep road begins on the other side of Pleasant Creek, eight miles south of the visitor center on the scenic drive, then three miles south on Pleasant Creek Road.

The **Notom-Bullfrog Road** covers 60 miles along the eastern border of the Waterpocket Fold, between UT 24 and Bullfrog Marina, on Lake Powell. It's not strictly a four-wheel-drive road, but one is certainly recommended for excursions in wet weather.

Burr Trail Road bisects Notom Road 30 miles north of Bullfrog and 30 miles south of UT 24. It covers 40 miles, crossing the fold in a series of tight switchbacks between Notom Road and the town of Boulder, west of the Capitol Reef National Park, on UT Scenic Byway 12. The segment through the park is unpaved, but normally accessible in a passenger car. It may be hazardous when wet. From the western park boundary to Boulder the road is paved.

Many other four-wheel-drive roads criss-cross the park, and the ones north of UT 24 lead to impressive sites such as Temple of the Sun and Temple of the Moon in Cathedral Valley. These are pretty rotten roads; particularly so in wet weather. Get advice on conditions in these remote areas from the park rangers at the visitor center before heading north on Hartnet Road, near the eastern edge of the park off UT 24, or farther east off UT 24, on the Caineville/Cathedral Valley Road.

About 20 miles north on the Cathedral Valley Road, **Thousand Lake Mountain Road** starts to the west through Upper Cathedral Valley and loops back to the east, covering 35 miles and ending back on Cathedral Valley Road.

One road that may not be so bad covers 25 miles into Cathedral Valley from the west, through Loa and Fremont. It crosses Thousand Lake Mountain, then drops down into the valley.

Jeep rentals, guided day tours of Cathedral Valley and Hell's Backbone, multi-day backcountry jeep trips and rock art seminars are offered by **Hondoo Rivers & Trails**, in Torrey (PO Box 98, Torrey, UT 84775, ☎ 801/425-3519 or 800/332-2696, fax 801/425-3548).

Escalante

There are numerous four-wheel-drive roads in this area. Various sources in town, including the BLM or National Park Service offices, can provide detailed information.

The **Burr Trail Road**, which is accessible to passenger cars in good weather, slices eastward across the Waterpocket Fold from Boulder, with a rough 30-mile jeep road leading south across Horse Canyon, Wolverine Canyon, Little Death Hollow, and Silver Falls Creek, where it loops back north to the Burr Trail Road.

Hell's Backbone Road follows the old pack train route between Escalante and Boulder for 38 miles through the mountainous terrain of the Aquarius Plateau (Boulder Mountain). It is theoretically accessible to passenger cars in good weather, though not when the road is wet, and the area does get heavy snow which usually keeps the road closed until May. (It's great for cross-country skiing and snowmobiling in winter.) In any weather, it's a dramatic ridge-line route, with sheer drops on both sides. Many four-wheel-drive roads, biking and hiking trails branch off from the main road to streams and fishing holes, including **Posey Lake Road**, which goes 40 miles north from Escalante, through Dixie National Forest. Access to Hell's Backbone is through Escalante, or west of UT 12, three miles west of Boulder.

Hole-in-the-Rock Road follows a rugged 56-mile trail cut by Mormon settlers in 1878. It took them six weeks to build a road through Hole-in-the-Rock, overlooking what was then the Colorado River (today it's Lake Powell). They had to lower wagons and livestock through the hole and the historic journey, from Escalante to Bluff, took six months to complete. Today, you can drive from Escalante to near the edge of Lake Powell in a four-wheel-drive. In dry weather, passenger cars can make it most of the way. The road heads south five miles east of Escalante, off UT 12, and crosses Harris Wash to Devil's Garden in 12 miles. The garden contains lots of improbable balanced rock forms. Farther on, after 36 miles, is Dance Hall Rock, a stone amphitheater near where the original Mormon settlers camped for several weeks while road construction continued up ahead. The last few miles of Hole-in-the-Rock Road are pretty rugged. At the road's end you can walk to the actual hole in the rock, through which you can see Lake Powell. You can't drive down the last half-mile to the lake, but you can hike it.

A shortcut to Lake Powell is the Smokey Mountain Road, a 78-mile dirt and gravel road, south from Escalante. On the way are great views of the lake, Navajo Mountain, Bryce Canyon, Table Cliffs, and Boulder Mountain. Sometimes you can see the smoke that gave this area its name. It comes from a smoldering underground coal mine fire that has been burning for more than 100 years. This is a good bike route, too, but not one that should be attempted by bike or four-wheel-drive in wet weather. The southern end of the road is on US 89, at Big Water, 20 miles north of Page.

Bryce Canyon & Kodachrome Basin

Tropic Reservoir, three miles west of the junction of UT 12 and UT 63, then south into Red Canyon, is the start of an extensive four-wheel-drive area known as the **East Fork Trail System.** For information contact the Powell Ranger District in Panguitch (see above, under Touring Torrey to Bryce Canyon National Park). The longest road in the trail system, East Fork of the Sevier River Road, goes south for 60 miles from the UT 12 intersection, three miles west of Bryce Canyon.

About 35 miles south of Escalante, a lengthy dirt road and a partially paved one (probably both best attempted in a four-wheel-drive vehicle), extend past Kodachrome Basin State Park to the south, emerging on US 89 between Kanab and Page, Arizona. The 49-mile, partly-paved, **Skutumptah Canyon Road** ends nine miles west of Kanab in Johnson Canyon. The 40-mile Cottonwood Canyon Road meets the highway 40 miles farther east, closer to Page.

Several multi-day hiking trails are accessed off these roads in Hackberry or the Upper Paria River canyons. Contact Kodachrome Basin park rangers for current conditions and information.

Ten miles south of the park, off the Cottonwood Canyon Road, is a one-mile turnoff to Grosvenor Arch, a giant-size double arch named for an official at the National Geographic Society.

All-terrain vehicle rides are offered a mile north of the Bryce Canyon National Park entrance on UT 63. The trips are over the

Great Western Trail (see above, under On Foot). For information, ☎ 801/679-8676.

Cedar City, St. George & Zion National Park

Five miles east of Cedar City is the north end of the **Kolob Terrace Road**, a partly-paved 50-mile stretch that passes through a little visited part of Zion National Park. The narrow, steep road passes the Lava Point Fire Lookout and Tabernacle Dome on the Kolob Terrace Highlands, before terminating in Virgin, west of the main park entrance on UT 9, six miles east of I-15.

There are quite a few backcountry roads in the **Dixie National Forest** southwest of Cedar City and north of St. George. Contact the Pine Valley Ranger District office in St. George for information (see above, under Touring Cedar City & St. George). Four-wheel-drive routes wind through areas south of Hurricane and Springdale to the Arizona border. Contact the BLM office in St. George (see above, under Touring Cedar City & St. George) for information on the **Sand Mountains** area.

Dixie Jeep Tours, 747 East St. George Boulevard, St. George, ☎ 801/674-7155, operates backcountry four-wheel-drive tours.

Coral Pink Sand Dunes State Park, south of Mt. Carmel Junction, off US 89, is popular with dune-buggy fans. Guided tours in all-terrain vehicles are offered from April to November by the **United States Trail Riding Association**, PO Box 35, Mt. Carmel, UT 84755, ☎ 801/648-5358.

Hunt's Rentals, ☎ 801/644-2370, in Kanab, rents four-wheel-drive trucks.

Angel Canyon Jeep Tours, 53 West Center, Kanab, UT, ☎ 801/644-2001, offers four-wheel-drive tours in southern Utah and northern Arizona.

Color Country Tours, ☎ 520/643-7509, is actually located across the state line in Fredonia, Arizona, but they will pick you up in Kanab for a guided four-wheel-drive visit to Jurassic-era dinosaur tracks, ancient ceremonial Indian caves, secret slot canyons, Western movie locations, Bryce, Zion or the Grand Canyon.

Page, Arizona & Lake Powell

Most people come to Lake Powell for the water, not the jeeping possibilities, which are limited by the fact that the area east of Page is largely Navajoland and is not generally open to unsupervised visitation. The safest bet is to take a guided jeep tour with **Lake**

Powell Jeep Tours, 108 Lake Powell Boulevard, Page, AZ 86040, ☎ 602/645-5501.

MOUNTAIN BIKING

Fat tires and red rock terrain have an affinity, or so it would appear from the profusion of mountain biking enthusiasts who are almost magnetically drawn to southern Utah. Although some of the popular trails may look like a frat party at times, it's more than likely you can pedal your way into privacy if that's what you want.

Utah's slickrock desert and canyon country is legendary mountain biking terrain, with forested mountains and sagebrush range. Sometimes you can tour slickrock in the morning, before temperatures rise, then ride to a cool, alpine lake in the afternoon, when the desert heats up. In general, biking is restricted to designated trails or roads. Off-trail biking is the surest way to bring even tighter restrictions on mountain biking in the future.

Information on road and mountain biking is available from **Bicycle Utah,** PO Box 738, Park City, UT 84060, ☎ 801/649-5806 or, for fat-tire aficionados, from **Utah Mountain Bike Association,** East South Temple, Suite 246, Salt Lake City, UT 84111.

Moab

Moab has clearly become one of the prime mountain biking areas in the country, and for good reason. The canyonlands in the vicinity of the town provide absolutely incredible biking terrain, ranging from 13,000-foot peaks to high mountain meadows, and from high desert flats to narrowing canyon-side descents. In fact, you may feel out of place in Moab without a mountain bike strapped to your vehicle.

There are hundreds of backcountry trails within easy reach of town, as well as jeep trails and driving routes (see above) that are fine for mountain bike riders. Paved roads through such places as Arches and Canyonlands national parks are certainly fair game for bike riders.

The **Moab Slickrock Bike Trail** is perhaps the best known bike route here, with a main loop covering 10½ miles. It is also the most crowded by far, and is something of a rite of passage for those who make the pilgrimage to this mountain bike Mecca. It starts east of town, out past the town dump, 2½ miles up Sand Flats Road. There is a 2½-mile practice loop at the start of the trail, which is especially recommended for those not accustomed to biking on rock. The trail is painted with broken white lines, and yellow caution lines – it's a good idea to stick to these markings as diversions from the main route can get you lost or in serious trouble. There are numerous sheer drops near the trail. Even those following the main loop will probably spend part of the time walking their bike up steep slopes. The route is filled with tight switchbacks and has earned a reputation of being more than challenging. Don't be fooled by the distance; this is a tough ride, noted for technical difficulty as well as beauty. Allow four to six hours to complete the loop, more if you digress on side trails leading to scenic spots overlooking Moab, the La Sals, the Colorado River, and Negro Bill Canyon.

Hurrah Pass Trail covers 30 miles from the junction of 5th West Street and Kane Creek Road at the south end of Moab. It's rated as easy to moderate, but it's no walk in the park. There are steep sections leading to the pass, but your sweat will be rewarded with a concentrated mini-version of the full variety of scenery to be found throughout the region.

Scenic Byway 279 (see above, under Moab Driving Routes) is a scenic 28-mile round-trip road ride alongside the Colorado River, framed by colorful cliffs containing petroglyphs and arches, including Jug Handle Arch, perched above the highway two miles before the end of the pavement.

Monitor and Merrimac Trail starts 15 miles north of Moab's visitor center on US 191. Turn left past the railroad tracks and go a half-mile to the trailhead. This is rated a moderate trail and it covers a 13-mile round-trip. Along the way you'll pass the Mill Canyon Dinosaur Site, Monitor and Merrimac Buttes, and Determination Tower.

Gemini Bridges Trail take a full day to travel. A vehicle shuttle needs to be arranged for your return from the 14-mile one-way ride. Your efforts are rewarded by views of the Arches, the La Sals, and the Gemini Bridge formation – two massive rock spans hundreds of feet long that arch gracefully from a sheer cliff to the ground. The trail starts 12½ miles north of Moab on UT 313, toward Deadhorse Point, and is rated as moderate, with much of the trail heading downhill. A number of side trails off the main route lead to stunning view sites.

Pritchett Canyon Road starts on Kane Creek Boulevard, a little before the road goes up into Kane Springs Canyon. It covers a nine-mile round-trip ride up the canyon to Pritchett Arch. This is also a tricky jeep road.

White Rim Trail in Island in the Sky is another rugged jeep road that is good for a multi-day mountain biking trip. It covers 100 miles, 75 of which are in the national park. The trail winds between the mesa top and the River District, descending 1,000 feet to the White Rim Sandstone Bench. On one side of the narrow trail, plunging sandstone cliffs drop 1,000 feet into maze-like canyons; on the other side, sheer rock walls, broken only by occasional hanging gardens watered by seeps, soar 1,500 feet above.

Kokopelli's Trail is the place to go for maximum mountain biking adventure. It is 128 miles long and connects Moab with Grand Junction, Colorado, encompassing dramatic canyon country and mountain scenery. It starts at the trailhead for the Slickrock Bike Trail and entails a 4,000-foot ascent.

The trip the other way, from Grand Junction, is suitable for active intermediate to advanced riders looking for rolling terrain, challenging climbs, and descents. It starts on a single-track trail hugging canyon walls along the Colorado River, and rises to expanses above the Colorado Plateau, with jagged snow peaks looming in the distance, in contrast to the horizontal red rock canyon terrain.

Climbing into the forested La Sals, the 12,000-foot snow caps are closer, while the canyons you've left behind drop abruptly below. The 4,000-foot descent into Moab begins amid high mountain pine and aspen, drops into sparser pinyon- and juniper-clad slopes, and ends on the sandstone domes of the Slickrock Trail.

Area bike shops can give you details about the Kokopelli Trail, which was named after the arched-back flute player whose image graces numerous ancient Indian petroglyphs and pictographs. The Hopi Indians consider Kokopelli a magical creature. Today you cannot avoid depictions of Kokopelli on souvenirs such as t-shirts and coffee mugs. Despite commercialization of the image, the trail is indeed a magical journey. Vehicle support is recommended.

For further biking information or guided tours, as well as bike sales, service and rentals around Moab, contact the following sources:

Western Spirit Cycling, 38 South 100 West, PO Box 411, Moab, UT 84532, ☎ 801/259-8732 or 800/845-BIKE, fax 801/259-2736, offers "civilized tours in uncivilized terrain," including guided and supported bike tours in Canyonlands Park, on the White Rim Trail, and in the Abajo Mountains. Bike rentals are available.

Poison Spider Bicycles/Nichols Expeditions, 497 North Main, Moab, UT 84532, ☎ 801/259-7882 or 800/635-1792, fax 801/259-2312, offers rentals, sales, and service.

Kaibab Mountain/Desert Bike Tours, 391 South Main Street, PO Box 339, Moab, UT 84532, ☎ 801/259-7423 or 800/451-1133, fax 801/259-6135, sells mountain bikes (these are available for rent, too), clothing, accessories, and camping equipment. Fully supported mountain bike tours, customized whitewater rafting/biking combination tours, and daily mountain biking descents are offered. Tours accommodate between four and 12 riders and follow hidden roads in deep, red-rock canyons and across towering mesas, including Canyonlands' White Rim Trail and routes in the rarely visited Maze District. Tours are planned to accommodate all levels of ability and include a fully equipped support vehicle along with friendly, knowledgeable guides who attend to all details, including gourmet trail-side meals. Combination trips are also offered, mixing all outdoor activities in five- or seven-day trips. These include biking, rafting, and scenic flights.

Rim Tours, 1233 South US 191, 94 West 1st North, Moab, UT 84532, ☎ 801/259-5223 or 800/626-7335, fax 801/259-7217, offers bike rentals, sales and service, as well as camping and climbing equipment sales.

Descent River Expeditions & Mountain Bike Tours, 321 North Main, PO Box 1267, Moab, UT 84532, ☎ 801/259-7983 or 800/833-1278, fax 801/259-5823, runs guided, vehicle-supported bike trips on the White Rim, and in the Needles and Maze districts of Canyonlands National Park. Mountain bike combination tours, meeting with watersport boats in Cataract Canyon, are available.

Slickrock Adventures, PO Box 1400, Moab, UT 84532, ☎ 801/259 6996, offers guided mountain biking excursions.

Scenic Byways Bicycle Touring, 942 East 7145 South, Suite 105, Midvale, UT 84047, ☎ 801/566-2662, offers guided, vehicle-supported mountain bike excursions of two to six days, with Dutch-oven meals included, for all levels of ability, in Utah's canyon country and mountains. Custom trips, equipment rentals, and combination biking/river trips are available.

Backroads Bicycle Touring, 1516 5th Street, Berkeley, CA 94710, ☎ 510/527-1555 or 800/245-3874, fax 510/527-1444, offers six-day trips on off-road bike trails, jeep trails, and paved roads through Arches and Canyonlands national parks. These are sometimes large trips with up to 20 participants, but they are carefully planned and well run.

Four Corners Center for Experiential Learning, 1760 Broadway, Grand Junction, CO 81503, ☎ 970/858-3607, fax 970/858-7861, offers customized bike trips of one to 12 days for two to eight riders in the Moab area. The excursions include descents to the Colorado River and all-day or overnight trips on the Kokopelli Trail between Moab and Grand Junction, Colorado.

Roads Less Traveled, PO Box 8187, Longmont, CO 80501, ☎ 303/678-8750 or 800/488-8483, offers guided, vehicle-supported bike trips for a maximum of 13 riders on quiet backroads and trails. Meals and accommodations are in century-old inns, secluded guest ranches, mountain huts, or tents. A five-day, five-night biking and camping tour, offered in late May or late September, covers the Kokopelli Trail between Grand Junction, Colorado, and Moab. A five-day, four-night trip offered weekly in April, May, September, and October, along the White Rim in Canyonlands National Park, moves at a relaxed pace, with time for hikes to hidden canyons, Indian ruins, and afternoon swims. Special interest tours for singles, families with children over 12, or adults over 50 are available.

Holiday River & Bike Expeditions, 544 East 3900 South, Salt Lake City, UT 84107, ☎ 801/266-2087 or 800/624-6323, fax 801/266-1448, runs guided, vehicle-supported, four-day mountain bike trips on the White Rim Trail or through the Maze District. Trips combining three days of biking on the White Rim or in the Maze, followed by four days of rafting in Cataract Canyon, are available.

Needles District

The **Colorado River Overlook** mostly follows a jeep trail over 15 miles of moderate riding varying only 250 feet in elevation. The ride can usually be accomplished in three or four hours. Along the way there are magnificent views of deep river canyons, the Needles, Junction Butte, Island in the Sky, Deadhorse Point, the La Sals and the Abajos.

The ride starts at the Needles District Visitor Center, 36 miles west of US 191 on UT 211, and essentially follows Salt Creek to its confluence with the Colorado River.

Beyond the visitor center, head north on the gravel road marked Colorado Overlook and follow it for 7½ miles to a spectacular, multi-colored, layer-cake overlook of Salt Creek Canyon and the Colorado River extending for miles to the north and south.

There are many other good bike riding trails in the Needles District, including the challenging, steep **Elephant Hill Road**, beginning at the Elephant Hill picnic area. For information see above under Needles District Jeeping.

For additional information, including maps and other rides in this area, contact local bike shops or the BLM Grand Resource Area office in Moab.

Monticello

Hot desert biking gives way to cooler climes on the **Gold Queen Basin Trail**, a nine-mile route through the Abajo Mountains, west of town. The trail starts on a paved road and leads to the inoperable Blue Mountain Ski Area. From there it winds through aspen and spruce forest along the way to views of 11,360-foot Abajo Peak, and finishes close to Loyd's Lake, near Monticello.

Bicycle rentals are available from **Monticello Cyclery**, 248 South Main, Monticello, UT 84535, ☎ 801/587-2138.

Mexican Hat

Valley of the Gods is a 27-mile loop rated as moderate. If you complete the entire loop without a vehicle shuttle, half of the ride is on paved highways; the other half on winding, dirt and gravel roads leading through remote territory sporting massive stone monoliths that rise from the valley floor. The ride can start at either end of the loop near small signs posted for the Valley of the Gods. One end of the loop is nine miles northeast of Mexican Hat on US 163; the other is nine miles northwest of Mexican Hat on UT 261.

Muley Point Overlook is a short, easy, four-mile one-way road that starts a mile north of the western terminus of the Valley of the Gods on UT 261 and leads west. The overlook offers outstanding views of Monument Valley, the Goosenecks of the San Juan River, Navajo Mountain, as well as the Abajos and Henrys.

Backcountry mountain biking is prohibited on the Navajo reservation, but there are still some pretty good bike routes.

The **Monument Valley Loop Road** covers 17 miles one way over dusty terrain mostly in the valley bottom, but with some short, steep climbs.

Tribal Route 16 north from AZ 98 in western Navajoland to Rainbow Lodge, covers 40 miles to Navajo Mountain and Lake Powell. A camping permit is needed from Navajo Parks & Recreation Department (PO Box 663, Window Rock, AZ 86515, ☎ 520/871-4941, extension 6647) for overnight travel in this area.

Glen Canyon, The Maze District & Goblin Valley

Panorama Point is a 17-mile ride that is considered moderate. No off-trail riding is permitted to Panorama Point, which affords staggering views of Utah's canyonlands and as far away as Colorado's San Juan Mountains. It's a long way to the start, though. Go 20 miles north of Hanksville on UT 24, then drive east for 25 miles at a sign for Hans Flat Ranger Station. At the ranger station you must pick up a free backcountry permit, then continue south for 2½ miles to the sign for Panorama Point and the start of the bike trail. The road actually drops 500 feet in 8½ miles on the way to the point. In several spots you hug narrow cliffside rims and there are a few steep downhill sections. You can camp at the point or turn around and ride back.

For information about other bike trails within this area, contact the Hans Flat Ranger Station (☎ 801/259-6513) or the Moab office of the National Park Service.

Goblin Valley State Park is named for the incredibly shaped hoodoos that look like sculptured incarnations of a disturbing dream. Gravel park roads here are good for bike riding and several routes lead from the park into the San Rafael Reef area.

A few mountain biking possibilities follow, or contact the BLM's Hanksville office (Box 99, Hanksville, Utah 84734, ☎ 801/542-3461) for further information.

Little Wild Horse Trail covers around 22 miles from the campground at Goblin Valley, first heading north and out of the park, then west across Wild Horse Creek. It passes close to the steepwalled narrows of Little Wild Horse Canyon and Bell Canyon, then through the bottom of Little Horse Creek. It's a moderate ride along the lower edge of the reef, with some sandy stretches, but only a 300-foot elevation change.

Temple Mountain Loop is a shorter but steeper ride, covering loops of eight or 19 miles, with a 1,500-foot change in elevation. Temple Mountain, which from certain angles resembles Mormon temple architecture, is the tallest point on the San Rafael Reef. The ride starts seven miles north of Goblin Valley State Park and turns west on a paved road past abandoned uranium mines and primitive Indian rock art sites. A half-mile after the pavement stops you can go straight for the longer loop, or turn right for the shorter one.

The short loop passes through a heavily mined area, sticking close to the slopes of Temple Mountain. In another mile the long loop starts climbing and continues to do so for seven miles, passing through layers of rock and onto the top of a forested mesa. The route then turns back toward Temple Mountain, starting a rugged and rocky descent, followed by sandy downhill areas.

Henry Mountains Bison Herd (see above under Jeeping), in the Henry Mountains south of Hanksville, can be seen on a 94-mile mountain bike ride. This is one of the largest free roaming bison herds in the United States.

Capitol Reef, Scenic Byway 12 & Escalante

Some people, including the author of the best reference book on mountain biking in Utah (see below), think the **Cathedral Valley Loop**, east of Capitol Reef National Park, is one of the premier multi-day mountain bike rides anywhere. It covers 65 miles, best accomplished in three days, with elevations varying by as much as 2,140 feet. Don't try this during rainy weather; you'll probably be slipping and sliding on foot, pushing your bike. Four-wheel-drive vehicle support is a wise idea, as is alerting the Capitol Reef National Park Rangers about your plans in this remote and isolated area.

The route starts 12 miles east of the Capitol Reef Visitor Center on UT 24, then north on Cathedral Valley Road, across the Fremont River. After going up and down short, steep slopes, it climbs into scenic terrain overlooking the Waterpocket Fold and briefly crosses the boundary of Capitol Reef National Park. You might want to camp in this area the first night. The route then climbs back through the national park for another 12 miles before swinging back on a park road 26 miles from UT 24, and heading over varied, difficult terrain in Upper Cathedral Valley. It then heads down into Lower Cathedral Valley, and up again over step-like stretches to a ridge-top approximately 55 miles from the start – another good place for camping. The third stretch covers more strenuous rugged terrain, along with more great views, that finally leads to UT 24, north of the starting point.

This is a serious outing, requiring a strategy and the logistical support to make your plan work. For more specific details, contact park rangers at Capitol Reef National Park and consult the book, *Mountain Biking in the Four Corners Region* by Michael McCoy (The Mountaineers 1990).

Notom-Bullfrog Road, a 60-mile dirt road along the east side of Waterpocket Fold, is good for biking. It starts nine miles east of the Capitol Reef Visitor Center on UT 24. About 30 miles south of UT 24 it intersects with the Burr Trail Road, which traverses the Waterpocket Fold across the southern portion of Capitol Reef National Park. In another 30 miles it reaches Bullfrog Marina.

Burr Trail Road is also good for biking – either west from the Notom-Bullfrog Road, or from Boulder in the east. From Boulder, the 40-mile-long, partly paved route starts in red hills, passes views of Lake Powell and the Circle Cliffs, and finishes at UT 276 north of Bullfrog Marina.

UT Scenic Byway 12, running south from UT 24 in Torrey, provides a good biking route and access through Boulder to the

Burr Trail Road. Between Torrey and Boulder, it offers a sinuous ride over 45 miles of mountainous terrain, topping out at 9,200 feet on Summit Mountain Pass. From Boulder, the road drops down through canyon country for 30 miles into the town of Escalante. Just about any of the dirt roads heading off from UT 12 are generally worthy of further exploration by bike, too.

Numerous bike routes branch off into the mountainous area north of Escalante, off Hell's Backbone Road, or south of Escalante, off Hole-in-the-Rock Road. For additional information contact BLM Teasdale or Escalante district offices.

Pedal Pusher Bike Tours, 151 West Main Street, PO Box 79, Torrey, UT 84775, ☎ 801/425-3378, fax 801/425-3378, can provide bike rentals or tours, as well as information about area biking.

Buffalo Jack's Trading Post, Jct. UT 12 and UT 24, Torrey, UT 84775, ☎ 800/999-2000, rents bikes by the hour or the day and provides shuttle service to and from trailheads. Maps, information, biking supplies and accessories are available.

Escalante Outfitters & Bunkhouse, 310 West Main Street, PO Box 158, Escalante, UT 84726, ☎ 801/826-4266, offers mountain bike tours and shuttles, specializing in the Escalante River canyons.

Dirt and gravel roads suitable for mountain biking wind through **Kodachrome Basin State Park** – named by the National Geographic Society for its range of colorful sandstone formations – and farther south to connect with US 89 between Kanab and Page, Arizona. For details see above, under Kodachrome Basin State Park Jeeping.

The best riding in the vicinity of Bryce Canyon National Park is probably in **Red Canyon**, west of the park. Try jeep roads off the **East Fork of the Sevier River Road** (see above), or **Dave's Hollow Trail**, an easy eight-mile round-trip. The trail starts a mile north of the visitor center and heads west into the forests of Red Canyon.

You can ride a bike on **Bryce Park's Scenic Drive**, but it's a narrow road that fills with traffic during the summer months. Try it in fall when the leaves are changing.

Eleven miles north of the Bryce Canyon junction on UT 22 is a turnoff for **Pine Lake/Powell Point**. The lake is six miles east of there on Forest Service Road 132, and has good fishing and a campground. A challenging bike ride begins at the parking area for the lake, continuing for four steep miles on FSR 132. It is also possible to drive to this point and bike four more miles on an easier hiking/biking trail south, at a marked turnoff atop the 10,188-foot Table Cliffs Plateau to Powell Point. At the end of the trail is Powell Point, named for the Colorado River runner, John Wesley Powell.

The views from 2,000 feet exceed 100 miles and are worthy of your sweat and his heroic stature.

Bike rentals at Bryce are available from **Ruby's Inn**. For details see below, under Accommodations. Another source for bicycle rentals and tours is **Bryce Canyon Mountain Bike Adventures**, PO Box 17, Bryce, UT 84764, ☎ 801/834-5341.

Once known to Indians as "The Circle of Painted Cliffs," **Cedar Breaks National Monument** contains a half-mile-deep amphitheater comprised of multi-colored rock carved into arches, columns, pinnacles, and terraces. A scenic, but difficult road ride into the area starts west of the park in Cedar City, climbing more than 4,000 feet on UT 14 and UT 148. Although the route can be ridden in reverse, the views are less appealing and the tight switchbacks are actually harder to negotiate under speed, going downhill.

Cedar Breaks overlooks abound on trails crossing lava fields and bristlecone pine forests atop the 10,000-foot-high plateaus surrounding Brian Head Ski Resort. There are more than a dozen specified bike trails in the vicinity of **Brian Head Peak**, all maintained and well marked by the Forest Service. You can ride one trail or combine several for an in-depth tour of the mountainous terrain of the Markagunt Plateau.

One of the easier routes is the 10-mile **Scout Camp Loop Trail**. It starts south of the Brian Head Hotel on UT 143, which leads to Bear Flat Road, and from there you should follow the signs to Henderson Lake. Alternatively, try the six-mile **Pioneer Cabin Trail**, also well signed from a turnoff on Bear Flat Road. A good road route comes down off the mountain from Brian Head onto the Cedar Breaks National Monument scenic drive. The round-trip from the resort area on UT 143 to the end of the scenic drive on UT 148 covers 16 miles.

Brian Head Cross Country, 223 West Hunter Ridge Drive, PO Box 190065, Brian Head, UT 84719, ☎ 801/677-2012 or 800/245-3754, is a bike sales, service, and rental operation in the lobby of the Brian Head Hotel. They can provide maps and information on local bike routes.

Another Brian Head area bike shop is **George's Ski Shop**, 612 South Brian Head Boulevard, Brian Head, UT 84719, ☎ 801/677-2013.

Two other places in the resort village offer mountain bike tours, rentals and shuttles.

Brian Head Bikes & Boards, 508 North UT 143, Brian Head, UT 84719, ☎ 801/677-3838.

Brian Head Sports, 329 South Brian Head Boulevard, Brian Head, UT 84719, ☎ 801/677-2014.

An advanced mountain biking trail (39 miles one-way) starts 25 miles southeast of Cedar City on UT 14 at Navajo Lake. From the lake, ride south on Forest Service Road 53 to the cliff tops overlooking the lake, then south on a mostly downhill route that crosses the Virgin River several times, connecting with UT 9 three miles west of the southeastern entrance to Zion National Park.

A similar 50-mile route, the **Kolob Terrace Road**, starts five miles east of Cedar City, and goes south through Zion National Park to the town of Virgin. For details, see above, under Cedar City, St. George & Zion National Park Jeeping.

Numerous bike routes are possible in the **Dixie National Forest** and **Pine Valley** areas. Contact the Pine Valley Ranger District office in St. George (196 East Tabernacle, St. George, UT 84770, ☎ 801/673-3431) for information, or inquire at area bike shops (see below).

A popular bike trip is the 24-mile **Snow Canyon Loop**, which begins on pavement in St. George at the northwest end of Bluff Street, follows UT 91 west through the village of Santa Clara, then heads north on UT 300 to Ivins. From there it becomes a dirt road eastbound to Snow Canyon State Park. The ride passes cacti-studded sand dunes, yucca and pinyon flats, red cliffs, and mesas that have served as backdrops for many movies.

The New Harmony Trail is a famed, four-mile single-track ride near the northwest corner of the Pine Valley Mountains Wilderness Area. It starts in the town of New Harmony, a mile north of Zion National Park's Kolob Canyons Road, and heads west.

The name of **Zion National Park's Scenic Drive** is an understatement. A seven-mile road starts at the park's south entrance, off UT 9, passes between purple cliffs and shining mesas, by Zion Lodge. It finishes at the Temple of Sinawava. In summer, try this route early in the morning before the tour buses and motorhomes come out to play.

Zion-Mt.Carmel Highway cuts across the southeastern corner of the park to the south entrance and is considered an engineering marvel. The ride from Mt. Carmel Junction to the south entrance covers 23 road miles. You first pass between Checkerboard Mesa and the White Cliffs, then the road drops sharply through two tunnels.

Check first with the ranger station before riding through this area. Bike riders must be escorted or transported through the tunnels, one of which is a mile long. Beyond the longer tunnel a series of switchbacks aid another sharp descent, with views of the

Great Arch, East Temple, and the Beehives. Upon reaching the visitor center, a number of other famous sights and rock formations can be seen.

Again, as beautiful as this ride can be, summer traffic congestion can detract from the experience. Try off-peak early morning hours for the most pristine experience.

Bike riders seeking to escape the congestion around Zion might try heading south of Springdale into the area of the **Vermillion Cliffs**. The scenery's less spectacular than in the park, but you won't be muscling for road space with motor homes, and the 360° views of the park and environs are unforgettable. For information, contact the BLM office in St. George.

INFORMATION SOURCES

Area bike shops that can provide information, service, and bike rentals include the following:

Bike Route, 70 West Center, Cedar City, UT 84720, ☎ 801/586-4242, offers sales, service, trail maps, information, rentals, and free minor repairs.

Red Rock Bicycle Company, 2180 West Arrowhead Trail, Santa Clara, UT 84765, ☎ 801/674-3185, specializes in daily cycling tours, map and trail information, bike rentals, repairs and service.

Bicycles Unlimited, 90 South 100 East, St. George, UT 84770, ☎ 801/673-4492, offers sales, service, and maps.

Sports Cyclery, 175 West 900 South, St. George, UT 84770, ☎ 801/628-1119.

St. George Cyclery, 420 West 145 North, St. George, UT 84770, ☎ 801/673-8876.

Swen's Cyclery, 1060 East Tabernacle, St. George, UT 84770, ☎ 801/673-0878.

Second Mile Pro Shop, 204 North Snow Canyon Road, St. George, UT 84770, ☎ 801/628-9558.

Just outside of the south entrance to Zion National Park is **Zion Canyon Cycling Company**, 868 ½ Zion Park Boulevard, PO Box 272, Springdale, UT 84767, ☎ 801/772-3396, fax 801/772-3814.

Bike Zion, 445 Zion Park Boulevard, Springdale, UT 84767, ☎ 801/772-3929, rents bikes, and offers guided tours, downhill cruises, repairs, parts and accessories.

Zion Excursions, PO Box 521436, Salt Lake City, UT 84152-1436, ☎ 801/581-9817 or 800/293-5444, fax 801/582-3308 (see above, under Hiking), operates from the 8,000-acre Zions Ponderosa Ranch, which shares seven miles with the eastern border of Zion National Park. There are hundreds of miles of bike trails that can be accessed from the private ranch and special packages, including a campsite and bike shuttles, are offered. Other excursions are offered for a half-day or full day.

The Road Less Traveled, PO Box 8187, Longmont, CO 80501, ☎ 303/678-8750 or 800/488-8483, offers combined biking and hiking trips in early June and early October around Bryce and Zion national parks, with accommodations nightly at inns offering a pool or hot tub. Trips begin in St. George; some itineraries include walking through Mammoth Cave, visiting an ice cave, cycling the plateau rim above Sunset Cliffs, and riding a bike or a horse through Bryce's rock spires, canyon mazes, and hoodoos. All trips include an exhilarating 4,000-foot switchback descent to Zion National Park and hiking in Zion.

Timberline Bicycle Tours, 7975 East Harvard, #J, Denver, CO 80231, ☎ 303/759-3804, runs five- to nine-day guided, vehicle-supported bike tours, with overnight reservations at inns and mountain lodges. Itineraries include a road bike tour of Cedar Breaks, Bryce Canyon, Zion, and the North Rim of the Grand Canyon. Bike tours of the Grand Canyon, Sedona, and Colorado's San Juan Mountains are also available.

Red Rock Cyclery, 819 North Navajo Drive, PO Box 486, Page, AZ 86040, ☎ 520/645-1479, offers rental bikes and guided tours on the single track and slickrock overlooking Lake Powell and the Grand Canyon. Also available are touring kayaks.

On Water

RIVER TRIPS

Moab, Canyonlands, Green, Colorado & San Juan Rivers

In Grand County (Moab) and San Juan County (Canyonlands National Park) the abundance of river recreation is staggering, ranging from the rugged wilderness areas of Cataract and Desolation/Gray canyons, to many more easily accessible areas of the Colorado, Green and San Juan rivers. There are whitewater rapids for white-knuckle thrills, and flat water stretches suited to canoes, jet boats and small power boats.

For the most part, there are no facilities on the rivers (the San Juan does flow through the small town of Mexican Hat), so planning is critical. Regulations are available from the National Parks Service office in Moab, or the BLM office in Monticello. Among the most popular areas for river recreation are the following:

Westwater Canyon is northeast of Moab and the Fisher Towers. It is the first canyon on the Colorado River within Utah, just west of the Colorado state line, and was the last stretch of the Colorado to be navigated. The brief, exciting Class IV run includes 11 rapids, passing through the oldest exposed rocks in Utah. These Precambrian black rock formations rise into 200-foot-tall inner canyon walls, above which rust-colored sandstone walls loom. Historic sites along the way include a miner's cabin and an outlaw cave. For those seeking fewer thrills, Ruby and Horsethief canyons, north of Westwater Canyon, offer 27 miles of mostly Class I & II waters, making for a popular two- to four-day trip in a canoe or kayak.

The **Colorado River Daily** is located below Westwater, closer to Moab, along UT 128, between Hittle Bottom and Sandy Beach. On a day trip you can raft six rapids and take in red rock views of named formations such as Fisher Towers, Castle Rock, the Priest and Nuns. **Cataract Canyon**, one of the best-known whitewater sections, is within Canyonlands National Park. It runs from the confluence of the Colorado and Green rivers to Lake Powell, at Hite. The route includes 26 rapids below mammoth red rock walls and spires that tower over the river. Side trip hikes lead to Indian ruins and rock art.

Commercial outfitters take care of everything relating to river travel, but independent travellers within park boundaries need to have a permit, life jackets, and fire pans for fires. Remember that all trash and solid human waste must be packed out. Contact the National Park Service office in Moab as far in advance as possible to insure you can meet all the permit requirements.

Desolation/Gray canyons are north of the town of Green River on the river itself, in Utah's deepest canyon. Sixty-seven rapids await whitewater enthusiasts 5,000 feet below the canyon rim at Rock Creek. Along the way there are hundreds of shaded campsites in cottonwood groves, numerous examples of Indian rock art, stunning red-rock topography, and outlaw hideouts.

The **San Juan River** forms the boundary between the Navajo Nation and San Juan County and is one of the fastest flowing major rivers in the United States. It flows from Colorado's San Juan Mountains through New Mexico and into an uncrowded wilderness of broad sandy beaches and chiseled, striated canyons in Utah. With only moderate whitewater, it is popular for family rafting trips lasting three to five days. These typically run for 30 miles from Bluff to Mexican Hat. Despite the modest whitewater, the river currents can be tricky on the San Juan, which is noted for deceptive sand waves. It is not recommended for novice rafters, canoeists, or kayakers travelling without an experienced companion, especially during high water. Several outfitters offer guided trips. Otherwise, a permit is required. Contact the **BLM** office in Monticello (435 North Main, PO Box 7, Monticello, UT 84535, ☎ 801/587-2141) far in advance of any independent San Juan River trip.

Sand Island Campground, three miles southeast of Bluff, is a popular put-in site. You can walk from the campground to see more than a mile of petroglyphs on the north side of the river. A number of the carvings feature Kokopelli, while more modern designs include river runners' graffiti.

River House Ruin is west of Bluff on the San Juan and six miles southwest of the Sand Island Bridge. It is a multi-room dwelling occupied by the Anasazi from 900 to 1300 A.D. It is constructed of sandstone and clay mortar and is situated in a cave. River runners or those alighting here by land via US 163 can stop to walk freely through the walled ruins which are still littered with fragments of pottery and stone tools.

Moab is the epicenter of the river outfitting business for all these routes, with daily raft trip departures of a half-day, one day or overnight down Cataract, Westwater, and Desolation canyons. Also available are jet boats, affording a quicker experience of the rivers and canyons, plus alternatives for rafters who do not want to paddle. Almost any sort of river travel you desire can be arranged in Moab, and a number of operators based outside the Moab area also offer trips in the region.

A good source of information sponsored by a marketing consortium of 19 Utah river outfitters and tour operators is **Raft Utah**, 153 East 7200 South, Salt Lake City, UT 84047, ☎ 801/566-2662. The service can provide information on individual operators, as well as a helpful, free, *Raft Utah Vacation Planner*, which explains many aspects of river travel.

Adrift Adventures, 378 North Main, PO Box 577, Moab, UT 84532, ☎ 801/259-8594 or 800/874-4483, fax 801/259-7628, offers three- or four-day motorized trips, or a five-day oar-powered excursion. The longer trip through Cataract Canyon is especially wild in May and June. A four-day trip through Desolation and Gray canyons on the Green River is great fun for families. Three-day Labyrinth Canyon trips on the Green River provide 45 miles of rafting and canoeing in waters without rapids. There are half- and full-day rafting trips on the Colorado River and combination adventures such as a morning of horseback riding in Arches National Park, followed by an afternoon of rafting the Colorado River. Two-day horseback trips in the La Sal Mountains can be combined with four days of rafting in Cataract Canyon. A three-day Cataract Canyon river trip can be mixed with two days of jeeping through Canyonlands back to Moab. Any river trip can be combined with two days at Pack Creek Ranch.

Sheri Griffith Expeditions, 2231 South US 191, PO Box 1324, Moab, UT 84532, ☎ 801/259-8229 or 800/332-2439, fax 801/259-2226, offers scheduled river trips on the Colorado and Green rivers from May to August. They are soft on risk but high in adventure and pampering.

Trips from two to five days use paddle- and oar-powered boats in Cataract, Westwater or Desolation canyons. For Colorado River trips minimum age is 10; on the Green River it is five.

A number of specialized excursions are offered. These include trips for women only, personal and professional development seminars for adults, family trips, and Cataract Canyon luxury trips featuring Canyonlands sunsets while a waiter flambées your dessert.

Combination trips are also available. These can include three days of mountain biking combined with four days of river rafting (April through September) or two days of horseback riding in the La Sal Mountains (in summer) or Canyonlands (in spring and fall) combined with a raft trip in Cataract Canyon.

Tag-A-Long Expeditions, 425 North Main Street, Moab, UT 84532, ☎ 801/259-8946 or 800/453-3292, fax 801/259-8990, offers a variety of river trips in Cataract, Westwater, and Desolation canyons. Major class whitewater trips of three or four days through Cataract Canyon are offered during high water season. A six-day trip combines Westwater and Cataract canyons river trips with a half-day of land exploration in Arches National Park. An overnight stay at a Moab motel is included.

A Westwater Canyon "Rapid Escape" trip is a two-day whitewater trip. "Wilderness Accent Expeditions" are led by experts who focus on geology, natural history, desert ecology, and ancient and modern Indian cultures. Half- and full-day rafting trips, and winter backcountry ski tours are available.

North American River Expeditions & Canyonlands Tours, 543 North Main, Moab UT 84532, ☎ 801/259-5865 or 800/342-5938, fax 801/259-2296, also offers river excursions, including full-day raft trips, half-day jet boat trips, full-day tours combining jet boating and jeep touring, and two- to four-day motorized raft trips through Cataract Canyon.

The **San Juan Touring Company**, PO Box 801, Moab, UT 84532, ☎ 801/259-RAFT, offers one- to five-day whitewater trips through the canyons of the San Juan River.

Downstream River Works, 401 North Main, Moab, UT 84532, ☎ 801/259-4121, fax 801/259-4122, offers half-and full-day Colorado River rafting trips plus a sunset dinner float that includes a cook-out on a beach. Inflatable kayaks, rafts, and all necessary river equipment rentals are available. Custom trips can be arranged.

Tex's Riverways, Box 67, Moab, UT 84532, ☎ 801/259-5101, offers full-day and overnight raft trips, jet boat trips into Canyonlands National Park, guided canoe trips, canoe rentals, and vehicle shuttles for Green River trips.

Canyon Voyages, 352 North Main, PO Box 416, Moab, UT 84532, ☎ 801/259-6007 or 800/488-5884, fax 801/259-4121, runs half- or full-day trips plus overnight Colorado River rafting excursions with inflatable kayaks. Free motel and campground pick-up is included.

World Wide River Expeditions, 625 North River Sands Road, Moab, UT 84532, ☎ 801/259-7515 or 800/231-2769, offers half- or full-day Colorado River rafting trips and evening float trips.

Wild Water: The Moab Rafting Company, PO Box 801, Moab, UT 84532, ☎ 801/259-RAFT or 800 RIO-MOAB.

Colorado River Tours, 1861 North US 191, PO Box 328, Moab, UT 84532, ☎ 801/259-5261, fax 801/259-2628.

Navtec Expeditions, 321 North Main, PO Box 1267, Moab, UT 84532, ☎ 801/259-7983 or 800/833-1278, fax 801/259-5823.

River Runner Sports, 1 North Main, PO Box 1361, Moab, UT 84532, ☎ 801/259-4121, fax 801/259-4121.

Ross River Ed-Ventures, Monticello, UT 84535, ☎ 801/587-2859 or 800/525-4456, offers Colorado and San Juan river trips.

Wild River Expeditions, 101 Main Street, PO Box 118, Bluff, UT 84512, ☎ 801/672-2244 or 800/422-7654, fax 801/672-2365, runs one- to eight-day educational adventures guided by archaeologists and geologists on the Colorado and San Juan rivers. Airport and river shuttle services plus supplies are available.

Charlie Purcell, Bluff, UT 84512, ☎ 801/672-2262, runs San Juan River trips.

Don and Meg Hatch River Expeditions, 53 East Main, Box 1150, Vernal, UT 84078, ☎ 801/789-4319 or 800/342-8243, fax 801/789-8513, runs four-and five-day trips through Cataract Canyon employing oar- and paddle-powered rafts as well as inflatable kayaks.

Hondoo Rivers & Trails (PO Box 98, Torrey, UT 84775, ☎ 801/425 3519 or 800/332-2696) runs seven-day kayak trips and six-day oar-powered raft trips, with inflatable kayaks and paddle boats for those who want them, through Desolation Canyon. Kayak trips progress from gentle water through turbulent areas and include instruction for novice and intermediate kayakers. Oar-powered trips are well suited to families.

Mind Body River Adventures, PO Box 863, Hotchkiss, CO 81419, ☎ 970/527-4466, runs four-day whitewater and flatwater trips on the Colorado and Green rivers. These are actually retreats focusing on ecology, yoga, tai-chi, massage, or drawing and painting. They include vegetarian meals unless otherwise requested.

Customized trips of one to six days through Westwater or Labyrinth canyons on the San Juan River are run from April through October.

Adventure Bound River Expeditions, Inc., 2392 H Road, Grand Junction, CO 81505, ☎ 970/241-5633 or 800/423-4668, fax 970/241 5633, offers scheduled one- to five-day trips in oar, paddle, or pontoon boats, as well as inflatable kayaks, from May to September, through Westwater, Desolation, Gray and Cataract canyons. Custom charter trips are available in April, October, and November.

Holiday River & Bike Expeditions, 544 East 3900 South, Salt Lake City, UT 84107, ☎ 801/266-2087 or 800/624-6323, fax 801/266-1448, offers two-to five-day, oar-powered river trips on the Green, Colorado, and San Juan rivers. Inflatable kayaks are available on request. Special instructional trips focus on kayaking or whitewater guiding. Canoe trips are available, as are biking trips, or combinations of the two.

Western River Expeditions, 7258 Racquet Club Drive, Salt Lake City, UT 84121, ☎ 801/942-6669 or 800/453-7450, fax 801/942-8514, offers three- to six-day oar-powered trips scheduled from May to September through Westwater Canyon and motorized river trips through Cataract Canyon.

Colorado River and Trail Expeditions, 5058 South 300 West, PO Box 57575, Salt Lake City, UT 84157-0575, ☎ 801/261-1789 or 800/253-7328, fax 801/268- 1193, offers river trips combined with off-river hiking in areas of the Colorado Plateau. These include a one-day rowing trip in the Fisher Towers area on the Colorado River, two- or three-day trips in Westwater Canyon, and five-day trips through Cataract Canyon. The longer trip through Cataract starts with a lazy float past slickrock canyons and is followed by 15 miles of rapids. Also scheduled are spring hiking trips on the Green and Colorado rivers, women's, youth, or senior camping trips on the Green River, and motorized raft trips in Cataract Canyon.

O.A.R.S., Inc., Box 67, Angels Camp, CA 95222, ☎ 209/736-4677, fax 209/736-2902, offers motorless Canyonlands river trips from one to 18 days, including options for oar-powered boats, paddle boats, inflatable kayaks, sea kayaks, and wooden dories.

Sunrise County Canoe Outfitters, Cathance Lake, Grove Post Office, ME 04638, ☎ 207/454-7708, offers nine-day springtime canoe trips on the Class I and II waters of the San Juan River.

Dvorak Expeditions, 17921 US Highway 285, Nathrop, CO 81236, ☎ 719/539-6851 or 800/824-3795, fax 719/539-3378, offers unusual whitewater canoeing skill seminars. They begin on flat water and progress to mastering fast-moving water. Six-day trips are offered on Utah's Green River through Desolation and Gray canyons. Also available are two- to five-day river rafting trips.

Lake Powell

You could spend a lifetime boating in the secluded coves and bays of Lake Powell and never see it all. Swimming is great at numerous Lake Powell beaches, with big rocks to leap from into the turquoise waters. Activities abound; jet skis, the ubiquitous houseboats, waterskiers, people having picnics along the shore, or floating in the shallows in an inner tube, dragging a fishing pole. Summer is by far the busiest season at Lake Powell, but it gets hot, with daytime temperatures routinely topping 100°. You can rent or buy virtually any equipment you might need out here at the marinas (see below), but be sure to make houseboat rental reservations far in advance. There are currently around 300 houseboats and 250 powerboats available for rent, as well as all kinds of personal watercraft, but these can go fast on the Fourth of July or any summer weekend. Fall is a much quieter time to visit. The water is still warm and great for swimming, but the air temperatures are much lower.

Year-round marinas at Hite Crossing, Bullfrog Basin, Halls Crossing, and Wahweap are operated by **ARA Leisure Services**, PO Box 56909, Phoenix, AZ 85079, ☎ 602/278-8888 or 800/528-6154, or fax 602/331-5258. All offer boat rentals for fishing, waterskiing, or houseboating on the enormous lake, as well as tours to Rainbow Bridge and other sites.

A floating marina at **Dangling Rope**, ☎ 520/645-2969, a quarter of the way up the 186-mile-long lake, can only be reached by boat. There is a ranger station, a store, and gas. Addresses and phone numbers for the ARA-operated marinas are listed above, under Touring. Additional information regarding marinas, boat tours and rentals, plus accommodations and restaurants, may be obtained from ARA Leisure Services. Below are a variety of "Explorer Packages" available through ARA.

- ❑ The *Rainbow Explorer* trip combines a full- or half-day 100-mile guided tour from Wahweap or Bullfrog to Rainbow Bridge, side trips to several major canyons, lunch, and two nights lodging.
- ❑ *Colorado Combo Explorer* includes a half-day Colorado River float trip from Glen Canyon Dam to Lee's Ferry, a day-tour to Rainbow Bridge and three nights accommodations at Wahweap Lodge.
- ❑ A *Famous Monuments Explorer* offers three nights accommodations at Wahweap Lodge, a full-day guided cruise to Rainbow Bridge, a half-day tour of Monument Valley, plus a scenic flight over both sites.
- ❑ *Houseboat-Lodging Explorer* packages combine a one-night houseboat rental with one night's lodging or two night's RV space at any of the ARA marinas.

ARA's houseboat rentals are particularly popular for navigating the scenic miles of Lake Powell. The lake offers astounding red rock side canyons, some displaying Indian rock art or ruins, others simply blissfully quiet spots to fish, calm waters beneath scenic buttes, spires and multi-colored striated cliffs that may be explored on foot. If you prefer, just kick back with a cocktail on the deck. Self-sufficient houseboats, which are similar to floating motor homes, range in size from 36 feet to 50 feet, and are available for rent year-round. The lowest rental prices are from November to March. Boating instructions are included with rentals. You can also rent an 18-foot powerboat to tow behind a slow-moving houseboat for daytime cruising and exploring, or other water equipment, such as waterskis and jet boats.

There are National Park Service-operated boat ramps and campgrounds at all the marinas, except Dangling Rope, and each also has a ranger station.

Sailboating is popular around **Wahweap Bay** and **Bullfrog Bay**, where the most reliable winds are found, although storms and high winds can, of course, make any sort of boating treacherous.

Scuba diving allows you to explore Indian ruins that were covered by water when the lake was created by flooding Glen Canyon.

Blue Water Adventures, 697 North Navajo, Page, AZ 86040, ☎ 520/645-3087, is a full-service dive shop and offers guided trips for snorkelers and scuba divers, including overnight camping trips to Lake Powell.

Probably the most popular trip on Lake Powell is to **Rainbow Bridge National Monument**, 50 miles up the lake from Wahweap, and the same distance down the lake from Bullfrog or Hall's Crossing. The colorful, 290-foot-tall, 275-foot-wide natural bridge is the largest in the world and is instantly recognizable to anyone who has browsed through the local postcard displays. The actual site is accessible only by water, or by rugged foot or horseback trails through Navajoland. No camping is permitted at Rainbow Bridge.

Other worthwhile sites on the lake include **Antelope Island,** south of Rainbow Bridge, which was a campsite for the first white explorers in the area, and **Cha Canyon,** 10 miles east of Rainbow Bridge on the San Juan River Arm, which is filled with ancient Indian rock art.

Wilderness River Adventures, 50 South Lake Powell Boulevard, Page, AZ 86040, ☎ 520/645-3279 or 800/528-6154, runs raft trips below Glen Canyon Dam and Lake Powell, on the Colorado River to Lee's Ferry. These excursions pass through the only land remnant of the original Glen Canyon.

The Jet Ski M.D., 136 Sixth Street, PO Box 3966, Page, AZ 86040, ☎ 520/645-3121, provides sales, service and repairs, along with a rental hotline for waverunners and jet skis.

High Image Marine Center, 920 Hemlock Avenue, PO Box 2004, Page, AZ 86040, ☎ 520/645-8845, provides sales and service for small and large boats plus all personal watercraft. They stock marine supplies and accessories as well as RV parts. A rental department offers boats, jet skis, waterskis, skurfers, kneeboards, tubes, hydrosleds, water worms, windsurfers, beach canopies, diving equipment, wet suits, and camping equipment.

Doo Powell, 130 6th Avenue,Page, AZ 86040, ☎ 520/645-1230 or 800/350-1230, rents personal watercraft.

Outdoor Sports Lake Powell, 861 Vista Avenue, Page, AZ 86040, ☎ 520/645-8141, provides sales and service along with rentals of boats, waverunners, water toys, kneeboards, waterskis, and rod and reel sets.

Lake Powell Tours, PO Box 40, St. George, UT 84771, ☎ 520/645-2263, operates two- to five-day boat-camping tours of Lake Powell, Rainbow Bridge, Stevens Arch, and Hole-in-the-Rock. Guests are provided with all transportation, meals and snacks, plus camping and sleeping gear. Departures from April to October.

FISHING

Many people come to southern Utah just for the fishing in streams, lakes and reservoirs. Non-resident fishing licenses are required for anyone over 12 and are sold on an annual basis, for five days, or for one day. A number of other rules and regulations apply, both in general and with specific requirements for fishing in certain areas. For complete information, contact **Utah Natural Resources**, Division of Wildlife Resources, 1596 West North Temple, Salt Lake City, UT 84116, ☎ 801/538-4700.

As for fishing in Lake Powell, which spreads across two states (Utah and Arizona), residents of either state who hold a valid fishing license at home can get a stamp to fish the waters of the neighboring state, but visitors are required to purchase the appropriate licenses from each state. Numerous businesses sell fishing licenses throughout Utah, and Arizona licenses are readily available in Page.

Moab, Canyonlands & San Juan County

In the La Sal Mountains you can fish for native cutthroat trout in streams at higher elevations or for rainbow trout in Mill Creek and area reservoirs.

Ken's Lake, south of Moab on the La Sal Mountains Loop Road, is good for bass and rainbow trout. The lake is also excellent for swimming.

In the Monticello area fishing and non-motorized boating are available in **Loyd's**, **Monticello**, and **Foy lakes**.

Recapture Reservoir, four miles northeast of Blanding, is an excellent location for boating, waterskiing and trout fishing. There are no visitor services here.

UT 12, Boulder Mountain, Escalante & Bryce

With nearly 100 backcountry lakes and streams, the Aquarius Plateau (west of Boulder and north of Escalante), also known as **Boulder Mountain**, offers some of the state's best fishing, including world-class trout fishing, and ice fishing in winter. Best access is from the Hell's Backbone Road, but roads or trails you may have to follow to reach certain prime fishing spots can be difficult to negotiate in bad weather. Always inquire locally about road and trail conditions. The forest service roads that criss-cross Boulder Mountain are closed in winter, although many ambitious anglers employ snowmobiles for winter passage.

For complete fishing information in the Boulder Mountain and Bryce Canyon areas, contact **Garfield County Travel Council** (PO Box 200, Panguitch, UT 84759, ☎ 801/676-2311 or 800/444-6689).

Among the more accessible fishing sites are the following:

Situated between Boulder and Escalante, **Boulder Creek** and **Deer Creek Lake**, on the east side of the highway, and **Calf Creek** on the west side, offer fishing for German brown, cutthroat, brook and rainbow trout. You can drive to Boulder and Calf creeks, but you have to hike two miles to reach Deer Creek Lake. There are several other smaller lakes nearby that you would need to hike to reach, including **Chriss Lake** (brook and rainbow trout) and **West Deer Lake** (brook trout).

Barker Reservoir is accessible by passenger car. It is five miles west of Escalante on UT 12, then 17 miles north on North Creek Canyon Road. The 12-acre lake is stocked with brook and rainbow trout and there are several other stocked lakes within a mile or so of here. Ice fishing is best from mid-November to January.

Posey Lake, 15 miles north of Escalante off the Hell's Backbone Road, contains rainbow and brook trout. A few miles farther north is Blue Spruce Campground and a stream nearby contains trout.

Wide Hollow Reservoir in the Escalante Petrified Forest State Park, 1½ miles northwest of Escalante, is stocked with rainbow trout, bluegill, and bass. There is a cement boat ramp. Open year-round, with ice fishing in winter, the best trout fishing is from March through June. The rest of the year is good for bluegill.

Eleven miles due north of the Bryce Canyon junction on UT 22 lies the **Pine Lake**/Powell Point turnoff. The lake is six miles east of there on Forest Service Road 132, and has good fishing and a campground. It's a great area for hiking and biking, too, particularly to Powell Point (10,188 feet). Named for explorer John Wesley Powell of Colorado River running fame, it lies at the tip of the Table Cliffs Plateau, 2,000 feet above the valley floor. On clear days, the views exceed 100 miles. For information on reaching Powell Point, see above, under On Wheels.

Tropic Reservoir contains rainbow, cutthroat, and brook trout. It's at the King's Creek Campground, three miles west of the UT 63-UT 12 (Bryce Canyon) junction, then seven miles south on East Fork of the Sevier Road. The lake is situated in a popular recreation area, with access to numerous hiking, biking and jeep trails. There's ice fishing here in winter, but you need a snowmobile to reach the reservoir.

Fishing information, gear, tackle, and licenses are available from **The Outfitter**, 310 West Main, Escalante, UT 84726, ☎ 801/826-4207.

Cedar Breaks

Duck Lake, 12 miles west of Long Valley Junction and north of UT 14, has trout fishing and a campground.

Duck Creek Village, two miles east of Duck Lake, is a year-round resort community. It comprises several resorts, restaurants, and equipment rental facilities for mountain biking, boating, cross-country skiing, and snowmobiling.

Navajo Lake, 16 miles west of Long Valley Junction, is a 3½-mile lake offering trout fishing, a marina, boat ramps, boat rentals, several campgrounds, and a lodge. Ice fishing is popular in winter. Nearby is the Cascade Falls Recreation Trail, a one-mile round-trip hike to a waterfall that drains out of the Pink Cliffs from the lake.

Panguitch Lake is a 1,200-acre reservoir good for trout fishing. It is situated midway between Panguitch and Cedar Breaks National Monument on UT 143. There are three national forest campgrounds at the lake and another just a few miles north of the lake. There are also three fishing lodges featuring cabin accommodations, RV parks, restaurants, groceries, fishing supplies, and boat rentals. The campgrounds and most services are open mid-May to mid-September, though some of the facilities are open in winter for ice fishing, which is quite popular here.

For information about Panguitch, Duck or Navajo lakes contact the **Forest Service** office in Panguitch (225 East Center Street, PO Box 80, Panguitch, UT 84759, ☎ 801/676-8815); Teasdale (PO Box 99, Teasdale, UT 84773, ☎ 801/425-3435); or the **Garfield County Travel Council**, also in Panguitch (PO Box 200, Panguitch, UT 84759, ☎ 801/676-2311 or 800/444-6689).

Fishing is permitted in **Alpine Pond**, off Alpine Pond Trail in Cedar Breaks National Monument.

Eagle Basin Outfitters & Guide Service, PO Box 947, Parowan, UT 84761, ☎ 801/477-8837, runs guided fishing trips in the area north of Cedar Breaks National Monument.

Cedar City & St. George

Enterprise Reservoirs are two lakes for rainbow trout fishing. You can reach them by heading 30 miles west of Cedar City on UT 56, 12 miles south on UT 18 to the town of Enterprise, and 11 miles west to a signed turnoff. Facilities, including boat ramps and a campground, are a few miles farther south.

Pine Valley Reservoir, five miles southeast of Pine Valley in the Pine Valley Recreation Area, offers trout fishing.

Baker Dam Recreation Site is two miles south of Central, off UT 18. It has rainbow and brown trout in a 50-acre lake administered by the BLM office in St. George. There is a campground and a boat ramp.

Gunlock Reservoir, four miles southwest of Veyo on UT 91 at Gunlock State Park, offers 266 acres of lake great for bass, catfish and bluegill fishing. It has boat ramps and docks, making it a fine place for waterskiing.

Quail Creek State Park, PO Box 1943, St. George, UT 84770, ☎ 801/635-9412, contains a 600-acre lake stocked with trout, bass, catfish and bluegill. It has a boat ramp and campground. Waterskiing, jet-skiing and windsurfing are popular here. The park is three miles east of I-15 on UT 9, then two miles north.

There's fishing for trout and a boat ramp just north of Zion National Park at **Kolob Reservoir,** three miles north of Lava Point on the Kolob Terrace Road.

OUTFITTERS & INFORMATION SOURCES

Ron's Sporting Goods, 138 South Main, Cedar City, UT 84720, ☎ 801/586-9901.

McKnight's Sporting Goods, 968 East St. George Street, St. George, UT 84770, ☎ 801/673-4919.

Allen's Outfitters & Guide Service, 584 East 300 South, PO Box 77, Kanab, UT 84741, ☎ 801/644-8150.

Last Frontier Guide & Expedition, 263 South 100 East, Kanab, UT 84741, ☎ 801/644-5914.

Lake Powell

Lake Powell is 186 miles long, with 1,960 miles of shoreline. The many species of fish found here include largemouth, smallmouth, and striped bass (up to 30 pounds), carp, catfish, walleye, northern pike, perch, bluegill, and sunfish. March to November is the most popular fishing season, but the lake is open year-round and doesn't freeze, so fishing is possible any time.

Inquire at the marinas for the best places to fish. Experienced anglers head to the most remote waters up the various canyon arms, such as the extensive **Escalante River Arm**, past Hole-in-the-Rock, or the **West Canyon Arm**, 10 miles south of Dangling Rope. The ubiquitous houseboats seen on the lake are usually equipped with a fishing boat trailing behind on a tow line.

Since most of Lake Powell is in Utah, a Utah fishing license is required for those waters. To fish the Arizona portion of the lake, approximately the lower five miles, you need an Arizona fishing license. Appropriate licenses are available at the marinas.

Arizona Reel Time, PO Box 169, Marble Canyon, AZ 86036, ☎ 520/355-2222, runs guided fishing trips for largemouth, smallmouth or striped bass on the lake plus trophy trout fishing trips below the Glen Canyon Dam at Lees Ferry.

On Snow

The big, famous ski areas in northern Utah, including Park City and Alta, are known throughout the world for the quality of their product. Their presence in the pantheon of ski nirvanas overshadows southern Utah; hardly anyone thinks about this area for skiing, which is great for those who want to get away from crowds. The cross-country skiing and snowmobiling options in southern Utah are extensive, and the large downhill complex at Brian Head is considered by many to be on a par with its better known northerly neighbors, but without the big crowds.

MOAB & THE LA SAL MOUNTAINS

There are no developed ski areas in the La Sals, so you need to be careful. Good maps probably won't be much help in a sudden blizzard. A certain level of winter backcountry experience, including route finding, avalanche awareness skills and the appropriate equipment (avalanche beacons and shovel), may come in handy. This in mind, snow-packed mountain roads are open for cross-country skiing and snowmobiling. Cross-country skiing is good in **Beaver Basin**, **La Sal Pass**, and **Dark Canyon** among many other sites.

Cross-country skiing facilities in these parts include the backcountry huts in the **La Sal Mountain Hut System**. These provide accommodations with heat, light, cooking and sanitary facilities, plus kitchen supplies, mattresses and pillows. Large huts at Mount Tomasaki, Dark Canyon, or Beaver Lake sleep 10 to 12 skiers. Smaller cabins on the shore of Dark Canyon Lake sleep up to four skiers.

Huts may be reserved exclusively for your group. Information about backcountry skiing and the hut system is available from the following sources:

La Sal Mountain Adventures, 2200 Munsey Drive, Moab, UT 84532, ☎ 801/587-2859, runs guided backcountry ski tours.

Pack Creek Ranch (see below, under Moab Accommodations) offers guided cross-country tours in the La Sals and winter ski-accommodation packages.

Tag-A-Long Tours (425 North Main Street, Moab, UT, 84532, ☎ 801/259-8946 or 800/453-3292, fax 801/259-8990) runs customized backcountry ski tours in the La Sals and also offers car shuttles, trailhead transportation, overnight accommodations, and guide services.

SAN JUAN COUNTY

There are many trails and jeep roads for cross-country skiing and snowmobiling in the Abajos, west of Monticello and north of Blanding. Check with information sources listed under Touring for information and maps.

Ruby's Inn (see below under Accommodations), just north of Bryce Canyon National Park's Visitor Center on UT 63, offers ski rentals, lessons, and backcountry cross-country ski tours on 30 km of groomed trails in Dixie National Forest or into Bryce Canyon.

Bryce can feel remarkably close to magical during winter. Under a clear blue sky, clean white snow tops the radiant red and multi-colored rock scenery. The chances are that you can have the park pretty much to yourself. Skiers and snowshoers need to pick up a free permit from the visitor center; they also lend snowshoes at no cost.

You can ski from Ruby's along the rim of Bryce Amphitheatre on the **Paria Ski Trail**, a groomed five-mile loop, or the **Fairyland Ski Trail**, a 2½-mile loop.

Bryce Canyon Snowmobile Service, PO Box 17, Bryce, UT 84764, ☎ 801/834-5341, rents snowmobiles at Ruby's Inn (where else?) and runs guided tours.

East Fork Trail, which begins at Ruby's Inn and covers 20 miles, leads to many additional miles of trails near Tropic Reservoir and the East Fork of the Sevier River. It encompasses wondrous rim top views of Bryce Canyon in winter.

North of Ruby's Inn, in the **Aquarius Plateau/Griffin Top** area, 40 miles of marked and signed snowmobile trails ascend the highest plateau in North America.

Panguitch Lake offers cross-country skiing and snowmobile trails plus ice fishing.

Brian Head Ski Resort, Box F, Cedar City, UT 84720, ☎ 801/677 2035 or 801/586-7101 (snow report, ☎ 800/782-6752), offers seven chairlifts leading to 53 downhill skiing runs on two mountains. This full-service ski area provides 20% beginner terrain, 40% intermediate terrain and 40% advanced terrain. Brian Head Peak tops out at 11,307 feet and the longest vertical run on the mountain is 1,150 feet.

This is a great family ski area, far removed from the glitz of trendier Deer Valley or Park City, Utah's world renowned resorts. Brian Head would probably be better known, too, were it not for these other places, but the world's loss is the Brian Head skiers' gain.

This is a fine resort, offering varying terrain, and a host of services, including relatively low-cost lift tickets, special lodging/ski packages, ski school, kid's ski school and day care, adult learn-to-ski packages (including a special learn-to-ski powder area), ski rentals, and groomed cross-country skiing and snowmobiling trails. Contact the resort for details.

Brian Head Cross-Country Ski Center has 25 kilometers of groomed cross-country trails and provides backcountry maps to routes through Cedar Breaks National Monument and other local areas.

For information on resorts operating in **Duck Creek Village** see below, under Cedar City/St. George Accommodations. The village offers groomed trails for cross-country skiing and snowmobiling. Equipment rentals are available.

Also in the area is **Navajo Lake** with groomed cross-country ski and snowmobile trails plus ice fishing.

Cedar Mountain Complex, 30 miles east of Cedar City, is a large winter sports area with an extensive groomed snowmobile trail system connecting Panguitch Lake, Brian Head/Cedar Breaks, and Duck Creek Village.

Majestic Mountain Tours, 151 South Main, Cedar City, UT 84720, ☎ 801/865-0001 or 800/223-8264, fax 801/865-0011, or 61 Movie Ranch Road, Duck Creek Village, UT 84762, ☎ 801/682-2567 or 800/223-8264, fax 801/682-2564, operates winter snowmobile, cross-country skiing, and sleigh riding tours based out of Duck Creek Village, east of Cedar Breaks off UT 14.

Pine Valley Recreation Area has an extensive network of trails for cross-country skiing and snowmobiling.

In Air

Redtail Aviation, US 191, PO Box 515, Moab, UT 84532, ☎ 801/259-7421 or 800/842-9251, fax 801/259-4032, offers scenic flights year-round from Moab's airport, 18 miles north of town on US 191. Options include flights over Arches, Canyonlands, Capitol Reef national parks or Dead Horse Point State Park.

Mountain Flying Service, 21 North Main Street, PO Box 33, Moab, UT 84532, ☎ 801/259-8050, offers charter and scenic flights.

Needles Outpost (see above, under Touring Canyonlands National Park/Island in the Sky) offers scenic flights.

Midway Aviation, PO Box 113, Monticello, UT 84535, ☎ 801/587-2774 or 800/684-2419, offers charters and scenic flights.

Scenic Aviation, PO Box 67, Blanding, UT 84511, ☎ 801/678-3222 or 800/888-6166, offers a number of scenic tours, including a one-hour flight over Canyonlands National Park or Monument Valley, the Goosenecks of the San Juan and Valley of the Gods. Charters and rentals are available.

Two Jays Helicopters, ☎ 801/727-3200, is based in an enviable position for a flightseeing operator, on UT 163, in between Gouldings and Monument Valley. It runs tours of Monument Valley, Goosenecks of the San Juan, Lake Powell, Natural Bridges, Grand Gulch, Navajo Mountain and Rainbow Bridge.

Bryce Canyon Helicopters, PO Box 4, Ruby's Inn, Bryce Canyon, UT 84764, ☎ 801/834-5341, offers aerial tours.

Cedar City Air Service, PO Box 458, Cedar City, UT 84720, ☎ 801/586-3881, fax 801/586-8021, operates scenic flights and charters.

Scenic Airlines has numerous flightseeing itineraries. Options include half-hour trips over Lake Powell and Rainbow Bridge or longer flights to the Grand Canyon, Monument Valley, or Bryce Canyon. Customized charters are also available. For information contact one of three offices: 2281 West Kitty Hawk Drive, Cedar City, UT 84720, ☎ 801/586-3881, fax 801/586-3882; 475 South Donlee Drive, St. George, UT 84770, ☎ 801/628-0481, fax 801/628-1568; 901 Sage, PO Box 1385, Page, AZ 86040, ☎ 520/645-2494 or 800/245-8668, fax 520/645-9318.

Kanab Air Service, 2378 South 175 East, #125, Kanab, UT 84741, ☎ 801/644-2904 or 801/644-2299, offers scenic fixed-wing flights over the Kanab area and the Grand Canyon. Based out of the Kanab Airport (☎ 801/644-2299), you can take a tour of the North Rim of the Grand Canyon (40 minutes), or much of the entire canyon, from Kanab and the North Rim to Havasu Falls (85 minutes).

Eco-Travel & Cultural Excursions

Canyonlands By Night, 1861 North US 191, Moab, UT 84532, ☎ 801/259-5261, has been a popular tourist attraction for more than 25 years. The nightly trip combines a motorized sunset ride on a jet boat along the Colorado River with a slide and light show projected onto canyon walls. Accompanying narration describes local geology, Indian legends, pioneers and outlaws. The show is complete with synchronized music.

Canyonlands Field Institute, Box 68, Moab, UT 84532, ☎ 801/259-7750, is a non-profit organization promoting understanding and appreciation of the Colorado Plateau. They run a variety of educa tional tours year-round in settings throughout canyon country. Among the extensive offerings are: hiking with packstock and studying either Grand Gulch archaeology or Navajo culture; backpacking in Salt Creek Canyon; hiking across the Maze and Needles districts of Canyonlands National Park; a nature trip, river rafting and canoeing on the Colorado River for women only; naturalist tours focusing on animal ecology, red rock geology, or ethnobotany; and seminars on avalanche awareness and safety. A variety of specialized photo workshops add to your choices. Most trips are university accredited. Also offered are river safety and rescue seminars, half- and full-day naturalist walks, private photography sessions, backpacking trips, and summer morning outings for children aged six to 10. Elderhostel trips are offered for participants over 60 years old.

The Canyon's Edge is a 40-minute, multi-media slide show produced by CFI. It explores human relationships on the Colorado Plateau through Native American stories, photographs, and music. It is shown nightly at the Hollywood Stuntman's Hall of Fame in Moab (see above, under Touring Moab).

Cloud Ridge Naturalists, 8297 Overland Road, Ward, CO 80481, ☎ 303/459-3248, offers a range of field seminars for exploring Canyonlands National Park. Groups of 12 to 20 participants are led by knowledgeable instructors who have conducted first-hand research or have working experience in subjects such as dinosaur tracks, butterfly ecology, wildflowers, and desert rivers. Accommodations on these two- to 10-day trips vary from lodges to camping. They are scheduled May to October and you do not need a scientific background to enjoy them, only an interest in learning.

Four Corners School of Outdoor Education, East Route, Monticello, UT 84535, ☎ 801/587-2859 or 801/587-2156, a non-profit organization, runs a variety of outdoor and environmental education programs on archaeology, geology, and wildlife. The school also teaches outdoor skills, natural sciences and land stewardship by creating a community of individuals who share interests through informal, relaxed, hands-on experiences.

Some of the programs include excavating archaeological sites, while others offer hiking with pack stock to remote areas near Lake Powell, where you help record, map, photograph and analyze Anasazi sites. There are also trips rafting the San Juan combined with hiking in Grand Gulch. Itineraries run throughout the Four Corners and workshops for wilderness first aid, photography and writing are given.

White Mesa Institute, 639 West 100 South, Blanding, UT 84511, is associated with the College of Eastern Utah and offers educational programs focusing on archaeology, geology, pioneer life, wildlife, and modern Indians.

Hondoo Rivers & Trails, PO Box 98, Torrey, UT 84775, ☎ 801/425-3519 or 800/332-2696, offers naturalist-led trips in various areas of the Colorado Plateau from June to September. Participants are accommodated for five days in base camps and have the option of riding a horse or travelling by jeep to prime habitats of elk, buffalo, bighorn sheep, antelope, and wild horses.

In addition, a five-day field seminar and canyon-country vehicle tour is scheduled in May, August, and September. A seven-day trip combines an Indian rock art seminar with rafting the Green River, camping and staying several nights at a Ute Indian-run lodge. Trips depart from Torrey.

Colorado River & Trail Expeditions (PO Box 57575, Salt Lake City, UT 84157-0575, ☎ 801/261-1789 or 800/253-7328, fax 801/268-1193) offers a series of "Earthway Education Expeditions," which explore Desolation and Gray canyons from an ecological, historical, or recreational perspective. These guided tours for up to 15 participants expand the length, focus and participatory elements of river trips by teaching ecology through information collected in the field. They also focus on the specific interests and demographics of each group. Special itineraries include a seven-day ecology and conservation youth camp for high school students in June. This combines off-river hiking, paddling, field work, camp chores, fireside discussions, star-gazing, orienteering, knot-tying, and low-impact camping. A senior citizen's camp on outdoor skills and ethical views is run in August and a woman's camp called "The River as Metaphor" is offered in early June.

Ruby's Outlaw Trail Rides (PO Box 1, Bryce, UT 84764, ☎ 801/834-5341 or 800/679-5859, puts on a rodeo Monday through Saturday nights at 7:30 PM, Memorial Day (late May) through September at the Ruby's Inn Rodeo Grounds, just outside the entrance to the national park, at Ruby's Inn.

Utah Shakespearean Festival, 351 West Center Street, Cedar City, UT 84720, ☎ 801/586-7878 or 800/PLAYTIX, includes six plays on a rotating basis, with two performances daily from late June to early September. There are other Shakespearean-related activities, such as costumed jugglers and puppet shows, backstage tours, production, costume, and literary seminars and a Renaissance Feaste that you eat without utensils. It all takes place at Southern Utah University, 351 West Center, Cedar City, UT 84720, ☎ 801/586-7700. There's a recreation of Shakespeare's Globe Theater at the school, said to be the most accurate one anywhere, as well as other special Shakespeare-related events throughout the summer season. The scene, encompassing actors in period costumes speaking careful Olde English, with the Globe Theatre in the background, all right in the middle of a Western town filled with pickup trucks driven by men in cowboy hats, is so improbable that it's worthwhile even if you don't like Shakespeare. And if you're curious, but just don't get what all the fuss is about, play orientations explaining the sometimes difficult language of Shakespeare are offered frequently throughout the season.

The hand of nature has generously endowed this region with enormous red rocks, labyrinthine canyons and snow-capped mountains. It's easy to understand that most people come to this part of the world to experience wild and primitive beauty found in the truly monumental geological wonders of Bryce Canyon and Zion national parks, or perhaps to boat or swim in the Colorado River waters enclosed by Lake Powell. But Utah's never been an easy place to live. Extremes of weather, geographical isolation and challenging topography rebuffed most explorers and settlers until the Mormons came along in the mid-19th century. No one else wanted Utah, and no one really wanted the self-assured Mormons around, either, so this was a perfect match. At that time, in the late 1840s, the hand of man, guided by the will of God, stepped in. Today, reflections on those activities, both curious and interesting, are still going on around here, deep in the heart of Utah's Dixie, named to commemorate the early Mormon settlers who grew cotton in the hot climate of Utah's southernmost city.

Utah is perhaps the only one of the United States to so proudly preserve its earliest religious affiliation. Mormonism remains a big thing in these parts, and it would probably be impossible to completely separate theology from local culture. Large Mormon temples are situated smack dab in the center of Utah's cities. Towns, big or small, all have wide streets broad enough to turn a team of oxen pulling a wagon in one swoop. No, oxen and wagons are not very common these days, but this was part of the master plan for the state drawn up by church and state leader Brigham Young, and that is simply the way thing are done around here. He was also the gent who directed male followers to consummate multiple marriages, to more quickly populate Utah with other good Mormons. All this and more is revealed in a newly opened outdoor drama production entitled, *Utah!*

The setting for the play combines man-made and natural attributes in stunning Snow Canyon, situated just outside of St. George. There, at a spanking new performing arts center called Tuacahn, on an outdoor stage built into the side of a 1,500-foot sandstone cliff, a troupe of seasoned pros sing and dance their way through a three-hour production detailing the life of one Jacob Hamblin, who was sent south from Salt Lake City to settle this part of the state by Mr. Young. Along the way, while making peace with the local Indians, building a fort, farming, and establishing the city of St. George, Mr. Hamblin also found the time to father 24 children by four wives.

Only two of these wives are included in the stage play, but nevertheless, a viewer gets the idea he was a busy guy, and the energetic production reflects these activities. You probably won't walk out humming the tunes, such as you might after viewing another play named after a state called Oklahoma, but the faith and certitude of Mormon beliefs does come through loud and clear. This is refreshing in a complex world where questions are usually much easier to find than answers. The dancing is fine, and the clever way that the natural cliffs are incorporated as part of the set design is unique. Add riders on horseback, gun fights, Indian raids, horse-drawn wagons, colorful costumes and special effects, including lightning storms and a flood, and you get the picture that this is one elaborate show. It's a little heavy on Mormon theology, but then again, the religion was the unifying force that settled this rugged state and a few hours spent here will probably add to your insight about what makes this state tick.

The production of *Utah!* at Tuacahn is being offered in the summer months only, from Memorial Day to Labor Day. At other times of the year, the performing arts complex will host symphony orchestras, ballet performances, the Vienna Boys Choir and comedian Victor Borge, among other special events. For schedules, ticket prices and information, contact **Tuacahn Amphitheater and**

Center for the Performing Arts, PO Box 1996, St. George, UT 84771, ☎ 800/746-9882, fax 801/674-0013.

The Grand Circle, a multi-projector slide show with music, is presented nightly from late May to early September, at the **O.C. Tanner Amphitheater**, UT 9, Springdale, UT 84767, ☎ 801/673-4811. The outdoor theater is just outside the south entrance to Zion National Park and the movie, shown on a 24-by-40-foot screen, depicts highlights of Zion and many other scenic areas of the Southwest.

Audubon Ecology Camps and Workshops, 613 Riversville Road, Greenwich, CT 06831, ☎ 203/869-2017, are operated by the National Audubon Society and include a southwest Canyonlands itinerary in early October. The trip covers Bryce, Zion and the North Rim of the Grand Canyon national parks. Participants travel with a naturalist guide and explore the ecology of the area, learning how the landscape of pinnacles, spires, and shaded canyons was carved by rain, wind, ice, and snow. Also included are explorations of waterfalls, springs, unique plant life and weeping rocks. They also teach how to search for tracks left by ring-tailed cats and cougars. Listen for the calls of canyon wrens, golden eagles and pinyon jays.

The Outdoor Source, ☎ 801/836-2372, offers "stress management at 11,000 feet." Flyfish southern Utah's pristine lakes, and hike Capitol Reef's Navajo Sandstone canyons. Tours can be customized for families, small groups, or corporate stress/flyfishing seminars. They also offer wilderness camera workshops and flyfishing instruction.

Where To Stay & Eat

Accommodations are getting better in southern Utah, or at least more plentiful. With new construction of motels throughout the region, your chances of finding a bed are better than ever before, although these are generally not the fanciest places, mainly just standard motels. Expect prices to be inexpensive to moderate, with some upward pressure around Moab and close to the national parks, particularly Zion, and around Lake Powell in high summer season.

INFORMATION SOURCES

Bed & Breakfast Inns of Utah, PO Box 3066, Park City, UT 84060, ☎ 801/645-8068.
Hotel/Motel Association, 9 Exchange Place, Suite 812, Salt Lake City, UT 84111, ☎ 801/359-0104.

Accommodations

MOAB, CANYONLANDS & SAN JUAN COUNTY

There are plenty of motels lining Main in Moab. Many of these have small pools. A lot of them are marginal properties charging premium prices during the busy summer season. Safe bets for unexceptional accommodations are several **Best Western** motels (☎ 800/528-1234), a 146-room **Super 8 Motel** (☎ 800/800-8000), or an 84-room **Ramada Inn** (☎ 800/2-RAMADA). There are also other more interesting choices, as well as a number of new guest houses, condos and B&Bs opening all the time and catering to the mountain biking masses. Some of the rates being charged are as steep as the local slickrock trails. Consult with the **Grand County Travel Council** (PO Box 550, Moab, UT 84532, ☎ 801/259-8825 or 800/635-MOAB) for complete listings.

Castle Valley Inn, 424 Amber Lane, Moab, UT 84532, ☎ 801/259 6012, is 15 miles northeast of town on Utah 128, then south a couple of miles on La Sal Mountain Road.

The site provides views of red rocks and mountains and the 11-acre property has an orchard, five lodge rooms, three bungalows with kitchens, and an outdoor hot tub. Breakfast is included. Box lunches and a fixed-price dinner are available.

Pack Creek Ranch, PO Box 1270, Moab, UT 84532, ☎ 801/259-5505, fax 801/259-8879, is off the south end of La Sal Mountain Road, 16 miles southeast of Moab. The picturesque 300-acre ranch is set amid mountains and red rock scenery at 6,000 feet and offers one- to four-bedroom cabins with kitchens, a heated pool, and a hot tub. During high season all meals are included. The dining room is one of the area's best, serving a sort of gourmet cowboy-style cuisine. It's open to the public by reservation only.

The ranch runs a variety of tours that are covered in the Adventures section. If you stay here, you can come back after your travels and have a massage, a dip in a jacuzzi, and a satisfying meal.

Cottonwood Condos, 338 East 1st South, Moab, UT 84532, ☎ 801/259-8897 or 800/447-4106, have full kitchens and cable.

Sunflower Hill Bed & Breakfast, 185 North 300 East, Moab, UT 84532, ☎ 801/259-2974, is a six-room B&B, with all private baths, in an old, remodeled adobe house. Close to downtown.

Cedar Breaks Condos, Center Street and 4th Street East (10 South 400 East), Moab, UT 84532, ☎ 801/259-7830, fax 801/259-4278, features two-bedroom condos with full kitchens. Breakfast foods are supplied. You prepare it yourself.

Kokopelli Lodge, 72 South 100 East, Moab, UT 84532, ☎ 801/259 7615, caters to bike riders with eight small rooms. Prices include a continental breakfast.

Slick Rock Inn, 286 South 400 East, Moab, UT 84532, ☎ 801/259 2266, is a cozy five-bedroom house with shared baths. It can accommodate up to 10 people.

Red Valle Homes, 200 East 100 North, Moab, UT 84532, ☎ 801/259-4508, consists of 11 houses available for overnight accommodations.

Canyon Country Bed & Breakfast, 590 North Main, Moab, UT 84532, ☎ 801/259-5262 or 800/635-1792, offers five rooms, some of which share a bath. It also has bike rentals and runs guided tours.

Westwood Guest House, 81 East 100 South, Moab, UT 84532, ☎ 801/259-7283 or 800/526-5690, has seven one-bedroom apartments with full kitchens.

Moab/Canyonlands Central Reservations Service, PO Box 366, Moab, UT 84532, ☎ 801/259-5125 or 800/232-7247, is a complete reservation service for accommodations, tours, and transportation in the Moab area.

Home Ranch, PO Box 247, UT 46, La Sal, UT 84530, ☎ 801/686-2223 or 800/982-1540, is a working cattle ranch that accommodates guests in the mountains between Moab and Monticello.

The Grist Mill Inn Bed & Breakfast, 64 South 300 East, Monticello, UT 84535, ☎ 801/587-2597 or 800/645-3762, has nine rooms with private baths in a remodeled flour mill, and a private guest room in a renovated 1924 caboose. Some rooms have a kitchen. A full breakfast is included and there's a jacuzzi.

The Cottage, 649 Circle Drive, Monticello, UT 84511, ☎ 801/587-2597 or 800/645-3762, is a private cottage with a kitchen.

Day's Inn Monticello, 549 North Main, Monticello, UT 84511, ☎ 801/587-2458, is the largest motel in town. The 43 rooms are a cut above average for these parts. Continental breakfast is included and there's a pool and jacuzzi.

Cliff Palace Motel, 132 South Main, Blanding, UT 84511, ☎ 801/678-2264, is a comfortable, basic 16-room motel.

Best Western Gateway Motel, 88 East Center, Blanding, UT 84511, ☎ 801/678-2278, is a clean, standard motel with 56 rooms and a pool.

The Old Hotel Bed & Breakfast, 118 East 300 South Street, Blanding, UT 84511, ☎ 801/678-2388, has been in the same family for generations. It has seven rooms with private baths and a private two-bedroom cottage. Open April to November.

Recapture Lodge and Pioneer House, PO Box 309, Bluff, UT 84512, ☎ 801/672-2281, is a basic motel with 32 rooms, some with kitchenettes. Also offered are geologist-guided tours, llama treks, slide shows, vehicle shuttles, bike rentals, and topo maps.

San Juan Inn & Trading Post, US 163 and the San Juan River, PO Box 535, Mexican Hat, UT 84531, ☎ 801/683-2220, is a river runners' favorite that offers 24 rooms, some with kitchenettes. They also sell camping supplies, Indian rugs, pottery, jewelry and baskets. There is a restaurant on the premises – **The Olde Bridge Bar & Grille**.

MONUMENT VALLEY

Goulding's Lodge, PO Box 1, Monument Valley, UT, 84536, ☎ 801/727-3231, is just north of the Arizona-Utah border on the west side of US 163, three miles west of Monument Valley Tribal Park. Established in 1924 by Harry Goulding and his wife, Goulding's has grown from a small trading post housed in a tent into the only full-service, year-round motel in Monument Valley. The hillside property includes 62 rooms with balconies, an indoor heated pool, a gift shop open March through October, and a campground with RV hook-ups a grocery store and laundry. A free slide show several times daily, called *Earth Spirit*, depicts Monument Valley in all seasons. It's a good introduction to the park by the pioneers in tourism for the area. You can visit the park on your own, but you can't see much than way. Monument Valley and Mystery Valley tours, escorted by Navajo guides, are available. They are highly recommended and necessary for more than a superficial glance at the valley.

Goulding's Museum & Trading Post, adjacent to the motel complex, is housed in the original trading post. It includes exhibits of Anasazi artifacts and historical photos. And it contains motion picture memorabilia from the Gouldings' long-time association with director John Ford, actor John Wayne and others who trekked out here to work among the sage and monumental stone backdrops on such classic films as *Stagecoach* and *Fort Apache*. A set from *She Wore A Yellow Ribbon* is on display. The museum is open April through October.

Additional motel rooms close to Monument Valley are available in Mexican Hat, 25 miles north of the park. These include the following:

Burch's Valley of the Gods Inn & Indian Trading Company, PO Box 310-337, Mexican Hat, UT 84531, ☎ 801/683-2221.

Canyonlands Motel, Mexican Hat, UT 84531, ☎ 801/683-2230.

Mexican Hat Lodge, Mexican Hat, UT 84531, ☎ 801/683-2222.

San Juan Inn & Trading Post, PO Box 535, Mexican Hat, UT, 84531, ☎ 801/683-2220.

Valley of the Gods Bed & Breakfast, PO Box 307, Mexican Hat, UT 84531, ☎ 303/749-1164.

NORTH LAKE POWELL AREA

The following offer modest individual trailer/housekeeping units with kitchens:

Hite Resort & Marina/ARA Leisure Services, Lake Powell, UT 84533, ☎ 801/684-2278 or 800/528-6154; **Halls Crossing Resort & Marina/ARA Leisure Services**, Lake Powell, UT 84533, ☎ 801/6842261 or 800/528-6154, fax 801/684-2326; **Bullfrog Resort & Marina/ARA Leisure Services**, PO Box 4055, Bullfrog, Lake Powell, UT 84533, ☎ 801/684-2233 or 800/528-6154, fax 801/684-2312. Fully equipped houseboat rentals are also available at the marinas.

Defiance House Lodge at Bullfrog Resort offers 48 better-than-average rooms done in Southwestern decor overlooking Lake Powell or a garden area.

Ticaboo Lodge, Restaurant & RV Park, UT 276, Ticaboo, UT 84533, ☎ 801/788-2110, is 11 miles north of Bullfrog, Lake Powell, with 66 guest rooms, a restaurant, pool, hot tub, and some kitchenettes. The RV park has 35 hook-ups.

HANKSVILLE, TORREY & ESCALANTE

Pickings are really slim in Hanksville; the best idea is to keep going or camp out. If you really need a place to stay, there are two marginal B&Bs and the funky **Whispering Sands Motel**, UT 95, Hanksville, UT 84734, ☎ 801/542-3238.

Rim Rock Resort Ranch, 2523 East UT 24, Torrey, UT 84775, ☎ 801/425-3843, is not very fancy but does provide good views of Capitol Reef National Park, for which it is the closest accommodation. There is a restaurant (see below) and the ranch also offers horseback trips.

Capitol Reef Inn & Café, 360 West Main Street, Torrey, UT 84775, ☎ 801/425-3271, is right in downtown Torrey. It has large, inexpensive rooms and the best restaurant in the area (see below).

Wonderland Inn, UT 12 & 24, PO Box 67, Torrey, UT 84775, ☎ 801/425-3775 or 800/458-0216, fax 801/425-3212, offers 50 rooms, a grocery store, gift shop, tour services, pool, spa, sauna, and a restaurant.

Road Creek Inn, 90 Main Street, PO Box 310, Loa, UT 84747, ☎ 801/836-2485 or 800/38-TROUT, fax 801/836-2489, is a surprisingly nice 13-room hotel in a 1912 building, with a jacuzzi, exercise room, and restaurant.

Austin's Chuck Wagon General Store and Motel, 12 West Main, Torrey, UT 84775, ☎ 801/425-3344 or 800/863-3288, fax 801/425-3434, is a recently built motel, with a pool and spa, facilities for RVs and campers, a general store (with camping supplies), bakery, and laundromat.

There are several small places to stay in Boulder, including a new guest ranch. There are rooms in modest motels (including several new ones) in Escalante, or rustic log cabins with a separate bath-house.

Boulder Mountain Lodge, Jct 12 and Burr Trail, PO Box 1397, Boulder, UT 84716, ☎ 801/335-7460 or 800/556-3446, fax 801/335-7461, was opened in 1994 with 20 luxury guest rooms representing the plushest accommodations for many, many miles. Llama pack trips and backcountry pack trips are available through Red Rock 'n Llamas, or Escalante Canyon Outfitters (see above, under Adventures), and the lodge will provide gourmet trail foods and equipment for roughing it in luxury. Also available are guided jeep tours, as well as shuttle services for hikers, mountain bikers and cross-country skiers.

Boulder Mountain Ranch, Salt Gulch/Hell's Backbone Road, Box 1373, Boulder, UT 84716, ☎ 801/335-7480, is a working cattle ranch with two guest rooms and three cabins. Cattle drives, trails rides, and fishing trips are available, and there is a gym. Continental breakfast is included.

Boulder Pines Bed & Breakfast, 330 East Boulder Avenue, Boulder, UT 84716, ☎ 801/335-7375, has four guest rooms on a working horse ranch.

Circle Cliffs Motel, 48 Main Street, PO Box 1399, Boulder, UT 84716, ☎ 801/335-7353, is a classic in its own right, a do-it-yourself motel without a desk clerk. You drive up, see if one of the three guest room doors is open, and it's yours for the taking. The place runs on the honor system and you leave your money behind for a maid who comes in once a day to clean and collect the fees. The facilities and rates are modest, and one of the rooms has a kitchenette.

Escalante Outfitters & Bunkhouse, 310 West Main Street, Escalante, UT 84726, ☎ 801/826-4266, is an outdoor store and tour guide service offering seven small, modest log cabins for guests. The showers and toilets are in a separate building.

Prospector Inn, 380 West Main Street, Escalante, UT 84726, ☎ 801/826-4653, is the newest motel in town, with 51 rooms. Continental breakfast is included.

BRYCE CANYON NATIONAL PARK AREA

Accommodations can be scarce during the summer in the immediate vicinity of Bryce Canyon. Even the mammoth Ruby's Inn, which seems to add more rooms every year and now offers a total of 368, sells out frequently. Consider nearby Panguitch, about a 30-minute drive from the park. It's a quiet little town with a number of modest and moderately priced motels. The town of Hatch, south on US 89 from Panguitch, is another possibility, with several motels, but a much smaller selection than Panguitch.

World Host Bryce Valley Inn, 200 North & Main Street, PO Box A, Tropic, UT 84776, ☎ 801/679-8811 or 800/442-1890, fax 801/679-8846, is a better than standard motel, offering perks including Tropic's best restaurant (Tropic has three restaurants), a hot tub, pool, and an ice cream shop.

Bryce Point Bed & Breakfast, 61 North 400 West, PO Box 96, Tropic, UT 84776, ☎ 801/679-8629, fax 801/679-8629, is a cozy six-room B&B with private baths. There is also a separate "honeymoon" cabin. Originally from Bryce Canyon, the cabin was moved here and renovated. Expert area touring advice is available from your hosts here, the LeFevre's.

Francisco's Bed & Breakfast, 51 Francisco Lane, PO Box 3, Tropic, UT 84776, ☎ 801/679-8721 or 800/642-4136, offers three rooms with private baths in a log home on a 10-acre working ranch owned by Evadean and Charlie Francisco. She runs the B&B, and he's a lifelong resident and good-humored gentleman who knows the Bryce Canyon area and backcountry as well as anyone.

Bryce Pioneer Village, 80 South Main Street, PO Box 119, Tropic, UT 84776, ☎ 801/679-8546 or 800/222-0381, fax 801/679-8607, offers 29 guest rooms, 19 cabins, a campground, and a snack bar.

Bryce Canyon Pines Motel & Restaurant, UT 12, PO Box 43, Bryce Canyon, UT 84764, ☎ 801/834-5330, has 50 rooms, a heated pool, and an above average coffee shop. People rave about the pies.

Best Western Ruby's Inn, PO Box 17, Bryce Canyon, UT 84764, ☎ 801/834-5341 or 800/528-1234, fax 801/834-5265, is the closest motel outside Bryce. It has 328 rooms, an indoor pool, restaurant, bookstore, and the largest gift shop in the state. Vehicle tours, helicopter tours, car or bike rentals, horseback rides, cook-outs, and winter ski rentals are available. Open year-round, Ruby's completed a $7 million addition in 1995. Although it does get quite busy in the summer, the whole operation is professionally run. Ruby's is an institution in these parts and the incredible gift shop and bookstore alone are worth a stop.

Bryce Canyon National Park Lodge, TW Recreation Services, 451 North Main Street, PO Box 400, Cedar City, UT 84720, ☎ 801/586-7686, fax 801/586-3157, is a classy, 1930s vintage log and stone lodge offering duplex cabins or motel rooms. The lodge is within walking distance of Bryce Canyon Amphitheater. The restaurant serves three meals a day, but you need to make reservations for dinner. There's also a general store, gift shop, laundromat, horseback rides and tours in a 1938 limousine. Make reservations far in advance. Open mid-April to November.

Rockin 'R Ranch, mailing address 1021 North University Avenue, Suite 205, Provo, UT 84601, ☎ 801/344-8588 or 800/767-4386, fax 801/344-8586, is a working cattle ranch 37 miles south of Bryce Canyon, in Antimony, Utah. It accommodates 41 guests, offering family vacations, cattle drives or mountain trail rides. Rates include three meals a day, riding lessons, entertainment, history lessons, team penning, horse relay, barrel racing, pole bending, calf roping, roping clinic, hayrides, herd riding, fence riding, rounding-up strays, Western dancing and relaxing. You can stay for just a day, but you'll probably need several more to recover from all these activities.

The best motel in Panguitch is no great shakes. It's a **Best Western** (☎ 801/676-8876 or 800/528-1234) with 55 rooms.

A newer hotel in a noisy spot near a convenient road junction is **Bryce Junction Inn,** US 89 and UT 12, Panguitch, UT 84759, ☎ 801/676-2221 or 800/437-4361, fax 801/676-2291. It has 32 rooms.

Mae Mae's Bed & Breakfast, 501 East Center Street, PO Box 387, Panguitch, UT 84759, ☎ 801/676-2388, offers three bedrooms in an 1890s brick home.
The Old Rock House Bed & Breakfast, 506 North Main, Panguitch, UT 84759, ☎ 801/676-8514, has only three rooms.
Lake View Resort, 905 South UT 143, PO Box 397, Panguitch Lake, UT 84759, ☎ 801 676-2650 (summer), 602/628-2719 (winter), is a rustic fishing lodge featuring 10 housekeeping cabins with kitchens, and an RV park, boat rentals, and fishing.
Beaver Dam Lodge, 225 North Shore Road, PO Box 278, Panguitch Lake, UT 84759, ☎ 801/676-8339, has 10 rooms and a restaurant (with a liquor license) on the lake, boat rentals, bait, fishing licenses, snowmobiling, and ice fishing.
Rustic Lodge, 186 West Shore Road, Panguitch Lake, UT 84759, ☎ 801/676-2627, has nine cabins, a restaurant with a liquor license, campground, boat rentals, and ice fishing.
Meadeau View Lodge, PO Box 356, Duck Creek Village, UT 84762, ☎ 801/682-2495, is on UT 14, 10 miles west of US 89, 30 miles east of Cedar City. It offers nine rooms in a rustic lodge with breakfast included. Caters to bikers, hikers, fisher-folk and cross-country skiers in winter.
Pinewoods Resort, PO Box 1148, Duck Creek Village, UT 84762, ☎ 801/682-2512 or 800/848-2525, fax 801/682-2543, features two-bedroom suites with full kitchens, a restaurant, and numerous tours, including mountain biking trips, boating and fishing on Navajo Lake, and excursions to Bryce Canyon, Cedar Breaks, and Zion.
Navajo Lake Lodge, PO Box 1239, Duck Creek Village, UT 84762, ☎ 702/646-4197, offers 11 rustic housekeeping cabins on Navajo Lake. They offer activities such as trout fishing, boating (motor boat, canoe or row boat rentals), and hiking. There is no phone service at the lodge, and electricity is available only from 6 PM to 11 PM. Cabins are equipped with gas stoves, heaters and bathrooms, but it is recommended that you bring an ice chest and a lantern to best enjoy your stay here.
Brian Head Hotel, 223 Hunter Ridge Road/UT 143, Brian Head, UT 84719, ☎ 801/677-3000 or 800/27-BRIAN (800/272-7426), fax 801/677-2211, has 200 rooms (some with kitchens), jacuzzis, a pool, sauna, and a very good restaurant. After the standard road food available throughout much of southern Utah, the strawberry wholewheat pancakes with real maple syrup here were a breakfast delight. And they serve liquor, which might not be so strange to think about at breakfast-time if you've been in Utah awhile.

The **Lodge at Brian Head**, 314 Hunter Ridge Road, Brian Head, UT 84719, ☎ 801/677-3222 or 800/386-5634, fax 801/677-3202, offers 72 rooms and suites in the heart of the ski village. There is a restaurant with a liquor license, also a pool and hot tub. Some rooms have kitchens.

Karen's Cabins, ☎ 801/278-4885, is a recently built, private log cabin in Brian Head. The cabin, called the "Eagle's Nest," sleeps eight and comes with a fully equipped kitchen.

There are 3,000 rooms in Brian Head, ranging from inexpensive lodges to fairly deluxe and expensive condos. **Brian Head Reservations Center**, PO Box 190055, Brian Head, UT 84719, ☎ 801/677-2042 or 800/845-9781, fax 801/677-2827, represents 30 centrally located condos, all one- to three-bedrooms, with two baths, fully furnished, with a kitchen and a fireplace. **Brian Head Condo Reservations**, PO Box 190217, Brian Head, UT 84719, ☎ 801/677-2045 or 800/722-4724, fax 801/677-3881, represents more than 100 rooms. **Inner Harmony Retreats**, ☎ 800/214-0174, offers mountain biking, hiking, yoga, cross-country skiing, and sightseeing based in a secluded lodge near Brian Head, including a jacuzzi, sauna, and vegetarian food.

Additional rooms may be available in Parowan, a little farther north of Brian Head and a possibility if everything else is full.

Eagle's Nest Bed & Breakfast, PO Box 160, 500 West Lydia Canyon Road, Glendale, UT 84729, ☎ 801/648-2200 or 800/293-6378, is a four-room B&B south of UT 14 and about a half-mile off US 89 in the tiny village of Glendale. Each of the rooms is decorated in a theme, including Country Garden, Oriental Odyssey, Anasazi Suite, and the Loft.

The **Historic Smith Hotel Bed & Breakfast**, US 89, PO Box 106, Glendale, UT 85729, ☎ 801/648-2156, was built in 1927 as a boarding house, and now has seven inexpensive redecorated guest rooms with private baths.

CEDAR CITY & ST. GEORGE

Grand Circle Reservations, PO Box 1369, St. George, UT 84771, ☎ 801/673-7650 or 800/233-4383, fax 801/628-7359, is a booking reservation service for all areas of southern Utah.

Cedar City has many chain motels run by **Best Western**, ☎ 800/528-1234, **Holiday Inn/Quality Inn**, ☎ 800/228-5151, and **Rodeway Inn**, ☎ 800/228-2000. One of the better ones is **Holiday Inn Cedar City**, 1575 West 200 North, Cedar City, UT 84720,

☎ 801/586-8888 or 800/432-8828. It has 100 rooms, a pool, jacuzzi, exercise room, and a restaurant.

The Abbey Inn, 940 West 200 North, Cedar City, UT 84720, ☎ 801/586-9966, offers rooms and suites with a refrigerator and microwave, and a free continental breakfast. There is an indoor pool and spa, and some suites have hot tubs.

Paxman Summer House Bed & Breakfast, 170 North 400 West, Cedar City, UT 84720, ☎ 801/586-3755, is a four-room B&B in a 100-year-old farmhouse. Rooms have private baths.

Pine Valley Lodge, 960 East Main, Pine Valley, UT 84722, ☎ 801/574-2544, is the only place to stay in the valley and features cabins. Horseback trips and backcountry guide services are available.

St. George has many of the same chain motels as Cedar City, except more of them, and some more unusual properties.

Greene Gate Village Bed & Breakfast, 76 West Tabernacle Street, St. George, UT 84740, ☎ 801/628-6999 or 800/350-6999, has 16 rooms in nine restored houses, a cozy garden setting, a pool, hot tub, and a restaurant.

Seven Wives Inn, 217 North 100 West, St. George, UT 84740, ☎ 801/628-3737, has 13 rooms with private baths. They are all furnished in antiques, and many have wood stoves or fireplaces. There's a pool.

Bluffs Motel, 1140 South Bluff, St. George, UT 84740, ☎ 801/628-6699, has 33 large rooms with microwaves and refrigerators, outdoor pool, and jacuzzi. A continental breakfast is included. Two king suites with private jacuzzis are available.

One of the newer motels in town is a **Ramada Inn**, 1440 East St. George Boulevard, St. George, UT 84770, ☎ 801/628-2828 or 800/228-2828, fax 801/628-0505. It has 136 rooms, a pool and a hot tub, but its most noteworthy feature is probably its immediate proximity to the Zion Factory Outlet Mall. The motel sits at one end of the strip of name brand discount stores, where you can stock up on clothing, furniture, housewares, toys, and all manner of good stuff at bargain prices.

Holiday Inn Resort Hotel, 850 South Bluff, St. George, UT 84740, ☎ 801/628-4235, has decent rooms, indoor and outdoor pools, jacuzzi, tennis, an exercise room, and a restaurant.

Pah Tempe Hot Springs, 825 North 800 East, Hurricane, UT 84737, ☎ 801/635-4010 or 800/682-6336, fax 801/635-4025, is a wonderfully funky hot springs resort with six rooms. For years the natural springs were a draw here, but a few years ago a rare earthquake apparently jolted the underground source out of the way. The place, however, is open and is laden with character, hot springs or not.

Harvest House Bed & Breakfast, 29 Canyon View Drive, Springdale, UT 84767, ☎ 801/772-3880, has four rooms with private baths, great views, full breakfasts, and mountain bikes for guests.

Under the Eaves Guest House Bed & Breakfast Inn, 980 Zion Park Boulevard, PO Box 29, Springdale, UT 84767, has five rooms, some with shared baths, an outdoor jacuzzi and big breakfasts.

Cliffrose Lodge & Gardens, 281 Zion Park Boulevard, Springdale, UT 84767, ☎ 801/772-3234 or 800/243-UTAH, has 44 rooms with good views and a pool. It is set on five acres of lawns and gardens.

Flanigan's Inn, 428 Zion Park Boulevard, Springdale, UT 84767, ☎ 801/772-3244, has large and small rooms, a pool, and a restaurant.

Zion National Park Lodge, TW Recreational Services, 451 North Main Street, PO Box 400, Cedar City, UT 84720, ☎ 801/586-7686, fax 801/586-3157, was built in 1925, burned down in 1960 and was then rebuilt. It's open year-round and offers rooms, suites, or cabins in a stunning setting surrounded by lush greenery and looming cliffs. A restaurant offers dinner by reservation only and there is a gift shop. Tram and bus tours in a convertible 1936 bus are available.

Zions Ponderosa Resort, PO Box 521436, Salt Lake City, UT 84152-1436, ☎ 801/581-9817 or 800/293-5444, fax 801/582-3308, is an 8,000-acre private ranch, which shares seven miles with the eastern border of Zion National Park. There are log cabins and private campsites at the ranch, and packages providing accommodations, meals, hiking (see above, under Hiking), biking (see above, under Biking), or horseback excursions. They also offer rentals of all-terrain vehicles, mountain bikes, tents and sleeping bags.

Kolob Mountain Ranch, 1025 Indian Hills Drive, Suite 229, St. George, UT 84770, ☎ 800/365-3035, fax 801/628-9544, is an exclusive private ranch on the west rim of Zion National Park, offering guest accommodations including meals, horseback riding, heated pool, hot tub, hiking, dancing, and fishing. Horseback lunch rides can be arranged, or overnight pack trips, guided trout fishing, photography and drawing classes. Mountain biking is offered on 718 private acres, or in the national park.

KANAB TO PAGE, ARIZONA

Thunderbird Best Western Motel, UT 9 & 89, PO Box 36, Mount Carmel Junction, UT 84755, ☎ 801/648-2203 or 800/528-1234, fax 801/648-2239, is a 66-room motel with a pool and restaurant. Consider this as an alternative to staying or dining in Kanab.

Shilo Inn, 296 West 100 North, Kanab, UT 84741, ☎ 801/644-2562, or 800/222-2244, fax 801/644-5333, is among the best places to stay in Kanab. It offers 118 spacious rooms, continental breakfast, and a pool.

Parry Lodge, 89 East Center Street, Kanab, UT 84741, ☎ 801/644-2601 or 800/748-4104, fax 801/644-2605, has 89 rooms, a pool and a restaurant.

A recently built Holiday Inn Express, 815 East US 89, Kanab, UT 84741, ☎ 801/644-8888, fax 801/644-8880, has 67 rooms.

Best Western Red Hills, 125 West Center, Kanab, UT 84741, ☎ 801/644-2675 or 800/528-1234, fax 801/644-5919, has 72 rooms.

International Hostel, 143 East 100 South, Kanab, UT 84741, ☎ 801/644-5554, is the cheapest place to stay in a town its ads refer to as "the greatest earth on show." A free breakfast buffet is included, and extensive maps and references to all of southern Utah and northern Arizona are available.

Deer Springs Ranch, Kanab, UT 84741, ☎ 800/651-8838, is a 40,000-acre cattle ranch nestled at the foot of Bryce Canyon. There are over 100 miles of roads and trails on the property, several private trout ponds and horse stables. Guests are accommodated in rustic cabins with private or shared bath (electricity is available only three hours daily). Everything is run on gas, and there are no TVs or phones (except for emergencies). Guests stay for a week, with all meals, accommodations, transportation, guides, horses and state park fees included. The standard itinerary includes several days of horseback riding, visits to Bryce Canyon, Zion, and Grand Canyon national parks, fishing and hiking. A "hot tip" for guests is offered: Practice riding prior to your ranch vacation. Bring a hat and boots (a must!). For camcorders, bring at least two hours of battery due to limited electricity.

Inn at Lake Powell, 716 Rim View Drive, PO Box C, Page, AZ 86040, ☎ 520/645-2466 or 800/826-2718, is an above average motel.

Page Lake Powell Holiday Inn, 287 North Lake Powell Boulevard, PO Box 1867, Page, AZ 86040, ☎ 520/645-8851 or 800/232-0011, fax 520/645-5175, offers no surprises, but decent accommodations in 130 rooms. It has an outdoor pool and the

Family Tree Restaurant that serves three meals daily and features Southwestern and American cuisine.

Lake Powell Suites, ☎ 520/645-3222 or 800/525-3189, six miles north of the Glen Canyon Dam, offers nightly or weekly rates for studio suites with full kitchens and laundry facilities in each.

Weston Inn, 207 North Lake Powell Boulevard, Page, AZ 86040, ☎ 520/645-2451 or 800/528-1234, is a standard 91-room motel. It has a pool and courtesy car service to the airport and Wahweap Marina.

Courtyard by Marriott, Page, AZ 86040, ☎ 800/321-2211, is a recently built property overlooking Glen Canyon Dam and the Colorado River. Facilities include a pool, exercise room, gift shop, dining room and lounge.

Wahweap Lodge & Marina, PO Box 1597, Page, AZ 86040, ☎ 520/645-2433 or 800/528-6154, fax 520/645-5175, has a large pool. Most of the motel rooms are probably a hair above standard, and the newest rooms are pretty nice, with a fantastic view of the lake. The lodge offers food in the Rainbow Room and the marina serves a buffet (see below).

Restaurants

MOAB, CANYONLANDS & SAN JUAN COUNTY

There are plenty of places to eat in booming Moab, some of them good. Farther south the pickings get slimmer.

Golden Stake Restaurant, 550 South Main, Moab, ☎ 801/259-7000, serves big and tender steaks.

Pack Creek Ranch (see above, under Accommodations) has an imaginative restaurant. Reservations are required for non-guests.

Mi Vida Restaurant, 900 North US 191, Moab, ☎ 801/259-7146, serves steaks and seafood north of town in a remodeled home. The house was once owned by a gentleman who went from being a down-on-his-luck prospector to a millionaire overnight, starting the uranium boom at the same time.

Grand Old Ranch House, North US 191, Moab, ☎ 801/259-5753, was built in 1896 and serves steaks and seafood. Open for lunch and dinner. Reservations suggested.

Slickrock Café, Main and Center streets (across the street from the visitors center in Moab), ☎ 801/259-8004, serves three meals daily to a crowd consisting of many mountain bikers.

Jailhouse Café, 101 North Main, Moab, ☎ 801/259-3900, serves homegrown organic vegetables, burgers, and chicken salad. Open daily for breakfast and brunch.

Westerner Grill, 331 North Main, Moab, ☎ 801/259-9918, serves breakfasts, burgers, and other diner fare 24 hours a day.

Center Café, 92 East Center, Moab, ☎ 801/259-4295, is as close to chi-chi as you'll find around here. It serves grilled lamb sausage, spinach pesto and goat cheddar, espresso and much more.

Eddie McStiff's, 57 South Main, Moab, ☎ 801/259-2337, serves six types of home-brewed beer, home-made root beer, pizza, and burgers.

Sundowner Restaurant, North US 191, Moab, ☎ 801/259-5201, serves steaks, German and Southwestern dishes.

Elk Ridge Restaurant, North US 191, Blanding, ☎ 801/678-9982. As for eating out in Blanding, this is the best of a thin selection. Burgers, sandwiches, and other ordinary dishes are available and there is a modest salad bar.

Cow Canyon Trading Post & Restaurant, US 191 and 163, Bluff, ☎ 801/672-2208, serves much better than average Navajo dishes, plus Mexican and vegetarian fare. This place is a real find and is unquestionably the best restaurant in San Juan County. There's a real Indian trading post attached. It is set in an evocative log and adobe structure with a glassed-in patio where you can watch the San Juan River flow by. Open April to November.

The Olde Bridge Bar & Grille (see above, under San Juan Inn & Trading Post), serves breakfast, lunch, and dinner, featuring mainly Navajo-inspired dishes.

El Sombrero Restaurant, US 163, Mexican Hat, ☎ 801/683-2222. If you want Mexican food in Mexican Hat, here it is.

MONUMENT VALLEY

Goulding's Stagecoach Dining Room (in Goulding's Lodge, above) serves three meals daily, including traditional Navajo and American food, Mexican food made with blue corn meal, *huevos rancheros*, roast leg of lamb and salads.

NORTHERN LAKE POWELL AREA

Anasazi Restaurant at Defiance House Lodge (see above), the only restaurant for many miles, serves three meals a day. The steaks and Mexican dishes are average.

HANKSVILLE, TORREY & ESCALANTE

Tropical Jeem's, north of Hanksville on UT 24, looks frightening but actually serves good Mexican food and American standards.

Stage Coach Inn, the restaurant at Rim Rock Rustic Inn (see above), serves steaks, sandwiches, and typical Western grub.

Capitol Reef Café, at Capitol Reef Inn (see above), actually serves vegetables, a rarity in these parts. You'll also find fresh trout, espresso and imported beers.

La Buena Vida Mexican Café, 599 West Main, Torrey, ☎ 801/425 3759, serves good Mexican food; open May to November.

Bicknell might be worth a side trip if you favor Western kitsch.

The Aquarius Café, 240 West Main Street, Bicknell, ☎ 801/425-3835 or 800/833-5379, has a dining room that looks like a garage sale of spurs, barbed wire, and animal skulls, among many other things. Try the pickle pie at the Sunglow Café, 63 East Main Street, Bicknell, ☎ 801/425-3821. Each of these establishments has a motel attached.

Road Creek Inn (see above) serves fresh trout many different ways.

Boulder and Escalante have a few Western American eating establishments, some of which do not seem able to distinguish between food and feed. You might want to stuff yourself on pickle pie in Bicknell and keep driving. If you're really hungry, try the Circle 'D' Restaurant, 475 West Main Street, Escalante, ☎ 801/826-4282, or Cowboy Blues Diner & Bakery, 530 West Main, Escalante, ☎ 801/826-4251.

BRYCE CANYON NATIONAL PARK AREA

El Hungry Coyote, 200 North Main, Tropic, ☎ 801/679-65811, is a restaurant attached to the World Host Bryce Valley Inn. There is actually a stuffed coyote employed as a permanent greeter at the door to this place, where choices range from burgers and fries to a salad bar and several Mexican plates.

Pizza Place, North Main Street, Tropic, ☎ 801/679-8888, serves a very edible pizza.

Bryce Canyon Pines (see above) serves soups and sandwiches.

Best Western Ruby's Inn (see above) has a large restaurant serving tolerable but unexceptional steaks and chicken.

Bryce Canyon Lodge (see above) serves above-average fare in a nice log and stone restaurant.

Buffalo Java, 47 North Main, Panguitch, ☎ 801/676-8900, is an unlikely gourmet coffee house in a small Mormon town (Mormons don't drink coffee – no stimulants allowed), serving espresso and bagels. Breakfast, lunch and dinner are served in the cozy Western art gallery and bookstore about 30 minutes from Bryce Canyon.

Cowboy's Smokehouse Bar-B-Q, 95 North Main, Panguitch, ☎ 801/876-8030, offers Western barbecue (mesquite smoked meats) in an old brick building in the heart of Panguitch's commercial district, which is all of about five blocks long. There are antlers and animal heads mounted on the wall, a singing cowboy, and immense servings of smoked beef, turkey, pork and chicken, pinto beans, and peach cobbler that will leave no question in your mind (or your stomach) about the real Western spirit imbued in this place.

Summit Dining Room, at the Brian Head Hotel (see above), has seafood and pasta. Open for dinner only.

CEDAR CITY & ST. GEORGE

All the chains are represented along with a few stand-outs offering better than average selections.

Black Swan, 164 South 100 West, Cedar City, ☎ 801/586-7673, serves lunch and seven-course dinners (reservations only) featuring steaks, seafood, chicken, lamb, and pork dishes.

Market Grill, 2290 West 400 North, Cedar City, ☎ 801/586-9325, is a funky place serving solid Western breakfast fare and steaks.

Yogurt Junction, 911 South Main, Cedar City, ☎ 801/586-2345, is one of the best spots in town for soups and sandwiches.

Milt's Stage Stop is five miles east of Cedar City on UT 14, ☎ 801/586-9344, but worth the drive for steaks and seafood. Dinner reservations are suggested.

Dis I'L Dew Steak House is 10 miles north of St. George on UT 18, in Dammeron, ☎ 801/574-2757. You can cook your own steak for dinner. Closed Mondays and Tuesdays.

Libby Lorraine's, 2 West St. George Boulevard, St. George, ☎ 801/673-0750, serves imaginative breakfasts and lunches.

Andelin's Gable House, 290 East St. George Street, St. George, ☎ 801/673-6796, is the most upscale restaurant in St. George and offers five-course dinners of beef, seafood, chicken, and other lighter fare. It's all served in a classy old house in a residential neighborhood.

Flanigan's Inn Restaurant (see above, under Accommodations) serves family fare.

Bit & Spur Saloon and Mexican Restaurant, 1212 Zion Park Boulevard, Springdale, ☎ 801/772-3498, looks funky but it's in the running for best Mexican restaurant in the state.

Driftwood Restaurant, 1515 Zion Park Boulevard, Springdale, ☎ 801/772-3224, serves family fare. Standard breakfasts and lunches, beef, chicken and seafood, including local trout, for dinner. It also has a motel, the **Driftwood Lodge**.

Zion Lodge Restaurant (see Zion Lodge above), ☎ 801/772-3213, serves three fairly ordinary meals a day, but the setting is terrific. Dinner by reservation only.

KANAB TO PAGE, ARIZONA

Wahweap Lodge's (see above, under Accommodations) large Rainbow Room restaurant overlooks Lake Powell and serves a large amount of beef and poultry to a lot of people. It's not great, but then, neither are most of the other numerous family-style or chain restaurants in the Page area. Count on bacon-and-egg breakfasts, burgers, steaks, and other standard fare. You might do better whipping something up in the kitchen of your houseboat with provisions from the 24-hour Safeway at 650 Elm Street. **Wahweap Marina** also offers a dinner buffet nightly from 6 PM to 9 PM in the Cathedral Room, ☎ 520/645-2433, extension 6303.

The Cookie Jar, 520/645-1023, a café at the top of the ramp overlooking Wahweap Marina, provides three meals daily from 6 AM to 8 PM.

The Pizza Deck at Wahweap, is open 6 AM to 10 PM for breakfast, pizza, subs and salads. In-room and dockside delivery is available 5 PM to 10 PM.

Stromboli's Italian Restaurant and Pizzeria, 711 North Navajo, Page, ☎ 520/645-2605, serves lunch and dinner. The menu includes New York-style pizza, seafood, pasta, chicken, and salads. There's a children's menu, and they offer free delivery.

Zapata's Mexican Restaurant, one block south of the Circle K on Lake Powell Boulevard, ☎ 520/645-9006, serves Mexican food, Mexican and domestic beers, and a popular "Margarita Ultima," made with Patron Tequila, a 100% Blue Agave tequila that is considered one of Mexico's finest.

Camping

The extensive list of public camping areas that follows is offered because of Utah's splendor and the scarcity of decent accommodations in certain areas. Camping may be the preferred alternative in some cases or the only possibility for many miles in remote stretches. During the busy summer season, limited accommodations, even not very good ones, may be filled.

Camping in national forests, national parks, recreation areas, and on BLM land is generally first-come, first-served. For state parks, reservations can be made by calling ☎ 801/322-3770 or 800/332-3770. Mail in applications can be sent to **Utah Division of Parks and Recreation**, 1636 W. North Temple, Salt Lake City, UT 84116. If you pay for a camping reservation with a major credit card, you receive an instant confirmation. Most of Utah's state park campgrounds are well kept, and some, like the one in Snow Canyon, are exceptional.

For national forest reservations, ☎ 800/283-2267.

Overnight camping or day-use fees are charged at most public campgrounds. Primitive sites are generally free, but backcountry permits are usually required. These are available free from the administering agency. Backcountry restrictions regarding fires and off-road vehicles apply in certain areas. Check first with the administering agency.

There's usually room to pull in an RV at public campgrounds, but hook-ups are not often available. Numerous private campgrounds on the outskirts of public lands can generally provide full service to RVs.

Camper-van rentals are available from the following source: **Adventure Werks Utah VW Camper Rentals**, mailing address, 3713 Seeley Street, Bellingham, WA 98226, ☎ 206/738-1159 or 800/736-8897, fax 206/738-1062.

MOAB, CANYONLANDS & SAN JUAN COUNTY

Arches National Park's **Devil's Garden Campground** is close to the end of the paved park road. It is open year-round but water is only available March to October.

Deadhorse Point State Park's **Kayenta Campground** offers year-round campsites with water and electrical hook-ups in summer; water only in winter. Reservations are recommended.

Among seasonal La Sal National Forest campgrounds are **Oowah Lake**, 22 miles east of Moab off US 191, and **Warner**, 26 miles east of Moab off US 191, both open June to October. **Dalton Springs**, five miles west of Monticello off US 191, and **Buck Board**, 6½ miles west of Monticello of US 191, are open late May to late October.

Devil's Canyon, nine miles northeast of Blanding on US 191, is open mid-May though October.

All the national forest campgrounds have drinking water in season and may be open in off-season without water.

Canyonlands National Park allows year-round camping in designated campgrounds at **Willow Flat**, 23 miles southwest of US 191 on UT 313, north of Moab in the Island in the Sky District; or at **Squaw Flat**, 35 miles west of US 191 on UT 211 in the Needles District. Backcountry camping is allowed, but a permit is required.

Newspaper Rock State Park, 12 miles west of US 191 on UT 211, has a year-round campground with 10 sites but no drinking water.

BLM's Canyon Rims Recreation Area offers year-round camping at **Wind Whistle** and **Hatch Point** campgrounds. Water is available only April to November.

BLM's **Sand Island Recreation Area**, three miles south of Bluff, offers primitive camping year-round, without water. It is set under cottonwood shade on the shore of the San Juan River.

Natural Bridges National Monument, 50 miles west of Blanding, has a 13-site campground open year-round. The only water available is from a tap at the visitor center, a quarter-mile away.

THE NAVAJO RESERVATION

❑ Fires are permitted only in grills, fireplaces or similar control devices. No open ground fires are allowed. Campers must provide their own firewood or charcoal.

❏ Please observe quiet hours from 11 PM to 6 AM at all camping areas.

❏ Bring water and everything else you'll need. Most of the camping areas provide few facilities, although many do offer picnic tables and shaded sites.

Mitten View Campground, Monument Valley Tribal Park, PO Box 93, Monument Valley, UT 84536-0289, ☎ 801/727-3287. Located a half-mile from the visitor center, the 100-site campground generally fills up by late afternoon in the summer and reservations are accepted only for groups of 10 or more. Plan to check in early for a choice campsite.

The camping area offers little privacy. It is on a sloping promontory overlooking the spacious valley, Sentinel Mesa, West Mitten Butte, Merrick Butte, and East Mitten Butte. The panorama from the campground ranks high among choice vistas to see from your tent in the morning desert light. Showers and RV hook-ups available.

NORTHERN LAKE POWELL AREA

There are public campgrounds at **Halls Crossing** (65 spaces, cold water showers), **Bullfrog Basin** (87 spaces), and **Hite Crossing** (12 spaces). There are also primitive campgrounds close to these areas. Contact local ranger stations for directions.

The BLM operates several campgrounds in the **Henry Mountains**. The sites may or may not have water and the rough dirt roads leading to them may not be in be very good shape; at the best of times they are probably only suited to four-wheel-drive vehicles. Contact the BLM office in Hanksville (see above, under Touring) for road conditions and details on the following sites:

Starr Springs Campground, 23 miles north of Bullfrog Basin and 43 miles south of Hanksville, off UT 276, is open year-round with water available May to October.

Lonesome Beaver Campground, 27 miles south of Hanksville on 100 East, is open May to October, but there is no water.

HANKSVILLE, TORREY & ESCALANTE

Goblin Valley State Park has a year-round campground with water and showers, 21 miles north of Hanksville and 12 miles southwest of UT 24.

The 71-space, year-round **Fruita Campground** at Capitol Reef National Park, just south of the visitor center, is set amid fruit orchards watered by the nearby Fremont River.

The primitive, five-site **Cedar Mesa Campground** is 25 miles south of the east entrance to Capitol Reef Park, on the dirt Notom Bullfrog Road. It's open year-round but has no water. Five other primitive campsites without water are 25 miles north on Hartnet Road, at **Cathedral Valley Campground**.

The National Forest Service operates several campgrounds between Torrey and Boulder, on UT 12. Three are open, with water available, only in the summer: **Singletree Campground** is 15 miles south of Torrey; **Pleasant Creek** is 20 miles south of Torrey; **Oak Creek** is 21 miles south of Torrey.

Five miles east of Pleasant Creek on a rough dirt road is the primitive **Lower Brown's Reservoir Campground**. It is open year-round, has no water, but does offer trout fishing in the reservoir.

Calf Creek Recreation Area, 15 miles east of Escalante on UT 12, has a seasonal campground, open May to October, with 11 sites, restrooms, and drinking water.

Dixie National Forest seasonal campgrounds near Escalante include **Posey Lake** and **Blue Spruce**, 15 and 20 miles north of town respectively, on the Hell's Backbone Road. Both are open June to October with water available.

Escalante Petrified Forest State Park has a shaded 22-site year-round campground with restrooms and drinking water, around Wide Hollow Reservoir. The reservoir is used for trout fishing and boating. Short trails from the campground lead to areas filled with petrified wood. The park is a mile west of Escalante on UT 12, then a half-mile north.

BRYCE CANYON NATIONAL PARK AREA

Kodachrome Basin State Park has a 26-site campground with restrooms, hot showers, and drinking water.

Bryce Canyon National Park is home to **North Campground** and **Sunset Campground**. North is next to the visitor center and open year-round, with restrooms and drinking water. Sunset is three miles farther south, across from Sunset Point on the park's scenic drive. The campgrounds are quite popular in summer months so you may need to look outside the park for alternatives.

Three campgrounds are fairly close to Bryce Canyon. Ask Bryce park rangers for information on **Kings Creek Campground**, seven miles southwest of the visitor center at Tropic Reservoir; **Red Canyon Campground**, 14 miles west of the visitor center, off UT 12; and **Pine Lake Campground**, eight miles northeast of the center off UT 63. These Dixie National Forest campgrounds only supply drinking water from May to October but remain open year-round if weather permits. For additional information, contact the Escalante Ranger District office in Escalante, or the Powell Ranger District office in Panguitch (see both above, under Touring Torrey to Bryce Canyon).

Also administered by the Powell Ranger District is a campground at **Duck Lake**, eight miles west of Long Valley Junction; three campgrounds at **Navajo Lake**, 16 miles west of Long Valley Junction; a campground at **Cedar Canyon**, midway between Cedar Breaks National Monument and Cedar City on UT 14; and four campgrounds at **Panguitch Lake**, midway between Cedar Breaks National Monument and Panguitch on UT 143.

CEDAR CITY & ST. GEORGE

Point **Supreme Campground** in Cedar Breaks National Monument is open mid-May to mid-October (depending on snowfall) with flush toilets and drinking water. It has 30 spaces.

There are campgrounds all over the Dixie National Forest southwest of Cedar City and north of St. George. These include ones at **Pine Valley Recreation Area, Enterprise Reservoir**, and **Baker Dam Recreation Site**.

The campground at **Snow Canyon State Park** has restrooms with showers plus some trailer hook-ups.

Quail Creek State Park, 14 miles north of St. George off I-15, has a campground on the shore of a 600-acre reservoir. For information see above, under Fishing.

Red Cliffs State Recreation Site is three miles north of Quail Creek on I-15 to the Leeds exit, then three miles south on a frontage road and two miles west. For information about this small, scenically situated campground, contact the BLM office in St. George, ☎ 801/628-4491.

Zion National Park campgrounds include **Watchman** and **South**, with a combined total of 373 sites. Both campgrounds are near the south entrance to the park, off UT 9 north of Springdale. Both have drinking water, flush toilets and dump stations, and are situated near the Virgin River, which provides excellent swimming.

Some sites are open in winter. **Lava Point Campground** is a primitive site on the Kolob Terrace Road with no drinking water.

KANAB TO PAGE, ARIZONA

Coral Pink Sand Dunes State Park, south of Mt. Carmel junction, off US 89, has a year-round campground. Drinking water and showers may only be available from March to November. The BLM also maintains a primitive campground north of the park.

There's the 189-site, Park Service-operated **Wahweap Campground**, north of Page, Arizona, and several primitive campgrounds nearby on the shore of Lake Powell.

Camping is permitted almost anywhere on the shoreline of **Lake Powell**, but not within one mile of developed areas (the marinas and Lees Ferry), and no camping is permitted at Rainbow Bridge National Monument. There is a 14-day consecutive limit for interior sites; the limit is 30 days for camping along the Lake Powell shoreline. You can't camp in roadside pull-outs, picnic areas or on posted beaches.

For information, contact the park ranger station west of Wahweap Lodge or the Carl Hayden Visitor Center at Glen Canyon Dam.

The Forest Service also operates a 54-space campground at **Lees Ferry** (below the Glen Canyon Dam) on a first-come, first-served basis. Sites include tables, grills, water and flush toilets. Primitive campgrounds are located at **Lone Rock**, near Wahweap, **Warm Creek**, **Bullfrog Bay**, **Farley**, and **Stanton canyons**, as well as at **Hite Marina**.

Concessionaire-operated campgrounds may be found at **Wahweap**, **Bullfrog** and **Hall's Crossing**. For information contact ARA Leisure Services, ☎ 800/528-6154.

Index